Library of
Davidson College

MISGUIDED EXPENDITURE:
An Analysis of the Proposed MX Missile System

David Gold
Christopher Paine
Gail Shields

With: David Brooks
Robert DeGrasse Jr.
Nick Jordan

Preface by John Marshall Lee
Vice Admiral, USN (Ret.)

Council on Economic Priorities
New York City

Editors: Alice Tepper Marlin
James J. Storrow, Jr.
Susan Young
Managing Editor: Neal Karrer
Cover: Jerry Fargo
Production: Adeline Olmer

355.03
G6181m

International Standard Book Number: 0 87871 014 0
© 1981 by the Council on Economic Priorities
All rights reserved.

Council on Economic Priorities
84 Fifth Avenue, New York, NY 10011
212/691-8550

83-4841

Printed in the United States of America

Table of Contents

Preface	1
Acknowledgements	5
Summary of Findings	7

PART I:
Does the U.S. Need the MX Missile?

Introduction	19
History of Strategic Doctrine	21
Origins and Early History of the MX	39
The Pentagon's Case for the MX – An Evaluation	49
Hedging the Triad	57
Essential Equivalence	67
Extended Deterrence	77
Multiple Aimpoint Basing: A Pointless Idea	91
Conclusion: Is the MX Needed?	107

PART II:
Economic Impacts of MX Spending

Introduction	115
What Will the MX Cost?	117
The Air Force's Analysis	131
Economic Impact of Military Spending	137
Input-Output Analysis of Guided Missile Production	143
Shifting MX Expenditures to Energy Conservation	165
The MX Contracting Network	173

Preface

The military arguments in favor of the proposed MX system are numerous. Further, they are in general internally inconsistent, mutually contradicting, and/or based on strategic concepts and definitions so amorphous as to be virtually meaningless. In this remarkably timely analysis, the Council on Economic Priorities first equips the reader with all necessary background to evaluate these arguments by covering both strategic theory and the MX project itself. CEP then punctures—indeed devastates—each of the principle rationales used to justify the system.

Whether lay citizen or defense professional, anyone who takes the trouble to absorb the discussion herein ought to be convinced that the current project, with its shell-game deployment in the Great Basin of Utah and Nevada, should be promptly and unequivocally cancelled.

In addition, the reader will gain a number of invaluable insights into the operations of the Defense establishment; two of these merit special attention.

The first is an understanding of the enormous momentum that an ongoing major project acquires. What is now the MX project started some twenty years ago as a theoretical examination of possible follow-on systems to the Minuteman missile even before the Minuteman itself was in place. The development was not in response to any specific foreseen need but rather to the ingrained notion that new systems should be kept coming along, analogous to the practice in the U.S. automobile industry of producing a new model every year. During the two decades of its life the program has ground along with more and more people devoting more and more of their professional lives to working on it, more and more money going into it, and more and more defense contractors, strategic theorists and legislators becoming involved in it. A variety of rationales for the program and its various elements have been generated, altered, discarded and regenerated. Now, in spite of its defects, the doubtful need, the existence of a preferable alternative, and the multi-billion dollar costs in this time of deep budget cutting, the program has the locked-in advocacy of large and influential elements in Defense, in the Administration, in the Congress, in the media and in industry. It will take a major effort and substantial investment of Presidential political capital to stop it. Even if normally cancelled it can be expected to come to the surface again and again, much as the B-1 bomber, supposedly killed during the Carter administration, is now rising like a Phoenix from its ashes.

A second insight, one which is essential for the public to absorb, is the progressive strengthening of a profoundly dangerous strategic concept in American military planning. It is the concept of nuclear "war-fighting": the creation of a collection of plans—and preparing of forces to carry them out—for the limited use of strategic nuclear forces in specific areas or against specific systems. This concept has been publicly defended both on the grounds that it enhances deterrence by making nuclear retaliation a more realistic response to a less than all-out, central attack, and that if deterrence were to fail, nuclear "war-fighting" capabilities would provide partial measures—using or threatening escalation— which might make it possible to stop the exchange short of an ultimate nuclear catastrophe. These purposes are not intrinsically irrational, although the counter-arguments are much more powerful—specifically that the availability of "limited" options dangerously increases the probability of crossing the fateful line into nuclear warfare, and that the chances of stopping nuclear exchange short of destruction are low indeed once started.

But as this book shows, nuclear "war-fighting" ideas are developing far beyond the stated deterrent or limiting purposes. Concepts are under study for initiating nuclear operations—first use of American forces—not only in the case, long part of our declaratory policy, of an overwhelming Soviet conventional attack in NATO Europe beyond the capacity of NATO conventional forces to resist, but also in a variety of other contingencies (the Persian Gulf, for example). These scenarios, in brief, contemplate our resorting to nuclear weapons not when we ourselves are under nuclear attack nor when NATO (including U.S. forces) is under overpowering conventional attack, but whenever, in conflict with the Soviet Union, we cannot achieve our objectives with conventional forces. They are based on the hope that the use of nuclear weapons could be kept one-sided and used only by us, or that a limited two-sided nuclear operation could be conducted so as to be, on balance, to the operational advantage of the U.S. Both of these hopes are probably illusory, but the critically dangerous illusion is that nuclear operations once started can be controlled. For such control to work, it must be remembered, the U.S. and U.S.S.R., while engaged in combat including nuclear weapons, would have to function in parallel. They would have to recognize and abide by approximately the same limitations and accept the same outcome, functioning under appalling pressures of time and stress, with different information, different weapons, different concepts, and diametrically opposed objectives. The probability of stopping short of mutual devastation is far too low to justify the risk.

This book, then, equips the reader with the information he needs to formulate his own judgement on the MX project, a critical current concern, and in addition to evaluate other aspects of our prospective military buildup and strategic concepts. It should be widely read.

John Marshall Lee
Vice Admiral, USN (Ret.)

Acknowledgements

A book is written by its authors, but no group of authors can function without substantial support from others. In this instance a large number of people gave generously of their time and energy, shared data and opinions, performed needed tasks with good cheer, and helped in numerous additional important ways.

We have been supported by the entire research and administrative staffs of CEP as well as by others connected to the Council. In particular, we would like to thank Lee B. Thomas Jr., Gordon Adams, Bill Hartung, Paul Murphy, and especially Alice Tepper Marlin, all of whom read, commented upon, and helped shape our work at various stages. Ellen Goldbaum helped with research on contractors. Neal Karrer took over as Managing Editor, literally at the last minute, and performed this task with speed, efficiency and good cheer. Claude Barrileux and Geoff Quinn gave advice and helped with numerous production tasks. Alice Tepper Marlin, James Storrow and Susan Young edited the manuscript. Camille Tibaldeo proofread the text, and Adeline Olmer created real pages out of the galleys. Jerry Fargo designed the cover, and LIllian Bogeinsky helped with the charts. Jennifer Blood and Michelle Raymond typed the manuscript.

Requests for research and information on the MX system from the Coalition for a New Foreign and Military Policy, the Federation of American Scientists, and SANE were instrumental in organizing CEP's work.

Numerous organizations, both private and governmental, helped us with data. NARMIC generously shared their information on contractors and subcontractors. The Air Force's Ballistic Missile Office at Norton Air Force Base answered many questions and provided crucial pieces of data. We were also helped by individuals within many other federal government agencies including the Department of Defense, the Department of Commerce, and the Department of Labor. We would like to acknowledge the assistance of a number of persons who, in deference to their professional responsibilities, must remain anonymous.

We would also like to thank the MX Great Basin Alliance who originated the phrase *Misguided Expenditure*. The cartoon in Chapter 8 is the work of Mike Keefe, editorial cartoonist of the Denver Post, and is reprinted with his permission.

Portions of the manuscript were read by friends and colleagues, and we received advice and support from many individuals. We would like to thank Charles Bowman, Antonio Costa, Ronald Drake, Faye Duchin, Michael Edelstein, Daniel Ellsberg, Randall Forsburg, Richard Garwin, Albert S. Hirch, Thomas Karas, Frank Lysey, Michael Mann, Michael Mawby, Marilyn McNabb, Philip Morrison, Sylvia Nasar O'Brien, Mark Penzel, Craig Peterson, Bob Pollin, Eli Romanoff, Herbert Scoville Jr., Anwar Shaikh, Mark Shapiro, Jeremy Stone, George Wallerstein, Steve Wheeler, and Joel Wit.

Amy Glasmeier, Erika Schoenberger, and Mark Beyeler provided substantial data on the environmental impact process and the socioeconomic impacts of the basing mode in Nevada and Utah. While we were unable to include this material in the present study, its importance to us cannot be overstated.

We would like to offer a special acknowledgment to the Women's Caucus, Department of Economics, New School for Social Research, and especially to Sandy Schilen and Jane Dean, for continued support and critical assistance during the research and writing phases of this project. phases of this project.

We are also grateful for the financial support of George Wallerstein, another donor who prefers to remain anonymous, and the many individuals and institutions that donate to the Council for its general support. Without their generosity, this study could never have been undertaken.

Summary of Findings

In undertaking an extensive study of the proposed MX mobile missile system, the Council on Economic Priorities analyzed the arguments made by various administrations in support of the MX system, traced the development of U.S. policy governing the use of strategic nuclear weapons since the early 1950s, and investigated the development of the MX since its origins in a 1959 Air Force proposal for a land-based mobile missile. The Council concludes that the MX will not perform as advertised in preserving the security of land-based mssiles, and that the missile, no matter how it is based, will not contribute to the deterrence of either nuclear or conventional war.

CEP also analyzed the economic impacts of spending tens of billions of dollars, and perhaps even hundreds of billions of dollars, on a new ICBM and its basing mode. The Council determined that the cost of the system will be far higher than has been claimed by the Air Force. Furthermore, CEP found that the economic analysis employed by the Air Force in assessing impacts was used improperly and biased toward overemphasizing benefits and underemphasizing possible costs.

To remedy such defects, CEP performed its own economic analysis using readily available input-output data. In comparing the effects of expenditures on a new missile (not including the basing system) with five alternatives, we found that guided missile expenditures had the weakest positive impacts on desirable factors such as output and employment, and the strongest negative impacts on undesirable factors such as inflation.

Continuing the analysis of MX economic impacts, CEP analyzed the effects of diverting MX expenditures to a ten-year program of conservation of fuel oil and found that such a program could reduce oil imports by between 44 and 75 per cent.

Finally, CEP identified the prime contractors and many of the subcontractors who would construct the MX system. This portrait of the MX contracting network, the most complete available, is presented in tabular format.

Does the U.S. Need the MX Missile?

The Air Force, civilian leaders of the Department of Defense, and representatives of various Administrations have four basic arguments to support building a new, land-based, mobile intercontinental ballistic missile: the vulnerability of existing ICBMs, hedging possible vulnerabilities in the air and sea legs of the Triad, maintaining equivalence with Soviet nuclear forces, and expanding the range of nuclear options for deterrence. CEP analyzed their reasoning and found each argument fundamentally flawed.

Minuteman Vulnerability

According to the first argument, increases in the number and improvements in the accuracy of Soviet warheads have raised the possibility that the Soviet Union could launch a first strike that would destroy more than 90% of U.S. land-based ICBMs (the Minuteman and Titan forces). U.S. land-based missiles are now said to be vulnerable to a Soviet attack and need to be made more secure. The Pentagon's solution to the problem is to build a new mobile missile, and to create many more shelters than there are missiles, so that the Soviet Union would have to expend a huge portion of its strategic force hitting not just missiles but also empty shelters in order to destroy the U.S. force. With so many targets to be hit, the Soviets would be deterred from attempting a first strike.

The vulnerability of U.S. land-based forces depends on the ability of the Soviet Union to mount a successful surprise attack. There are, however, numerous technical and operational uncertainties inherent in such an endeavor. They include:

- *Accuracy*—There is no way to ensure that the accuracies of missiles obtained from test firings could be duplicated with totally new targets and flight paths. The problem of "bias," i.e. missiles drifting from their flight paths because of unforeseen atmospheric and other physical conditions, is considered by many scientists to be insurmountable without substantial testing, which of course is impossible in a surprise attack.

- *Reliability*—Some missiles would fail to launch or fail in flight, and some warheads would fail to detonate. Moreover, the degree of unreliability would not be known in advance.
- *Timing and Fratricide Effects*—The effects of nuclear explosions would in some instances destroy or deflect other warheads before the latter reach their targets, a phenomenon known as fratricide. Launching hundreds of missiles from diverse locations within the Soviet Union so that they arrive in precise sequence at widely scattered targets in the U.S. poses severe problems of timing, problems that are beyond either side's ability to surmount with a high degree of confidence.
- *Launch on Warning*—The Soviet Union could never be sure that U.S. missiles would not be launched upon confirmation of an approaching Soviet attack. Although U.S. officials have downplayed launch on warning as a strategy, it remains one of the options available to the President.
- *U.S. Retaliation*—The most powerful deterrent to a Soviet first strike is the size of the U.S. nuclear force that would survive such a strike and be available for retaliation against the Soviet Union. This force includes submarine based missiles, bombers, air launched cruise missiles (ALCMs) which are soon to enter the strategic force, and land-and carrier-based aircraft. It also includes some 105 land-based missiles carrying 215 warheads, the 10% that would probably survive even the worst Russian first strike posited by the Pentagon. Moreover, other planned improvements in U.S. nuclear forces would increase during the 1980s both the number and accuracy of U.S. warheads that would be expected to survive a Russian attack.

On the basis of this analysis, CEP concludes that Minuteman is not nearly as vulnerable as claimed by the Pentagon and that even a vulnerable Minuteman would leave the Soviet Union faced with a massive retaliatory capability. Thus, the rationale for MX must lie elsewhere.

In an analysis of the multiple shelter system of basing *(Multiple Aimpoint Basing: A Pointless Idea)*, CEP concludes that the elaborate scheme proposed for making the MX secure is unlikely to work. If the Soviet Union, in response to the MX, adds large numbers of warheads to their land-based missile force, then the MX would eventually be no more secure than Minuteman is today. Indeed, many Pentagon officials have spoken of the need to append a ballistic missile defense system to the MX in order to protect against Russian warhead growth. Thus, the multiple shelter system may well be the beginning of a major leap in the arms race, stimulating not only greater offensive forces on both sides but also the abrogation of the limit on anti-ballistic missile systems, the major arms control achievement of the 1970s.

In addition, a Russian attack on the MX shelter system would leave the U.S. with about as large a force of land-based missiles as is assumed to presently be the case with Minuteman since, while there are many shelters, each shelter is less protected than a silo; such an attack would do greater damage to the civilian population than an attack on Minuteman, thereby incurring greater loss of life and productive capacity for no military gain; the shelter system would force this imposition of tight security on the civilian population; and the system would be subject to many of the same operational uncertainties that currently surround the survival of existing land basing systems. In short, the tremendous cost of the basing system will yield virtually no measurable military benefit.

Hedging the Triad

The second main argument used to justify the MX is that a new survivable ICBM is needed to hege against pending vulnerabilities in the remaining two legs of the strategic Triad. The Triad includes land-based missiles, submarine launched missiles, and long-range penetrating aircraft carrying nuclear bombs. The Triad exists, according to military planners, in order to diversify the technical risks and military vulnerabilities of our nuclear deterrent. Actual or potential weaknesses in one leg can be offset by assuring the vitality of the remaining legs. Countering possible weaknesses in bombers and submarines is one of the arguments put forward in support of MX.

In investigating this argument, CEP concludes that already planned improvements in the air- and sea-based legs of the Triad, specifically the introduction of ALCMs to penetrate improved Soviet air defenses and deploying the Trident I missile on existing submarines, are more than sufficient hedges against possible weaknesses in these areas. Moreover, the Soviet Union has consistently lagged far behind the United States in anti-submarine warfare, indicating that U.S. missile carrying submarines will remain secure for some time to come.

CEP suggests that there are less expensive ways of hedging against vulnerabilities than building a massively expensive new ICBM. Thus, for example, continuing the current research and development program for countering possible Soviet advances in anti-submarine warfare would ensure the security of missile carrying submarines.

Essential Equivalence

The third main argument in support of MX is that a new ICBM is needed to maintain a U.S. strategic nuclear force that is equivalent in all essential aspects to that of the Soviet Union. CEP found that defense officials do not have a clear definition of what constitutes essential equivalence. Since U.S. and U.S.S.R. forces are structured differently, there are large subjective and indeed psychological elements in any definition of essential equivalence.

CEP found that at the root of the notion of essential equivalence is the belief that a new ICBM is needed not so much to maintain real strength but rather perceptions of American strength. If we do not build MX while the Russians expand their missile force the rest of the world will perceive us as a declining military power. CEP concludes that the existence of 900 strategic nuclear warheads, some 17,000 additional tactical nuclear warheads, planned expansions and improvements in submarine launched missiles and ALCMs, new warheads for Minuteman, and continued improvements in missile accuracy, are more than sufficient to preserve the perception of the United States as a strong military power, equivalent to the Soviet Union. The MX is not needed to preserve essential equivalence.

Extended Deterrence

The fourth argument is that the MX, being secure from Soviet attack and having highly accurate warheads, is needed to increase the military options available to the United States in the event of a severe Soviet challenge to Allied security interests in Europe or elsewhere. Increased accuracy, in theory, increases the probability that a warhead can destroy smaller and better protected targets such as missile silos and command posts. The U.S. would purportedly have greater flexibility in planning for the use of nuclear weapons in situations short of all out nuclear war. According to CEP's investigation, this expanded flexibility is designed to deter the Soviets and their allies from launching conventional military actions against United States allies and interests.

CEP found *(The Evolution of Strategic Doctrine)* that while strategic doctrine has in the public eye emphasized that nuclear weapons exist to deter the Soviet Union from thinking it could succeed in attacking the United States, U.S. policy has also emphasized that nuclear weapons should deter other types of military activity.

The development of the MX *(Origins and Early History of the MX)* has been dominated by two considerations, one being the search for a basing system that could provide substantial protection from a Soviet nuclear attack, and the other the quest for a highly accurate missile, a missile that can threaten a wide range of targets in the U.S.S.R. including those considered "counterforce" or military, as well as those labelled "countervalue" or largely urban and industrial. With the MX the U.S. could in principle threaten those military targets with greater effectiveness.

CEP concludes that the search for a counterforce missile is the main rationale behind MX. Because the required levels of reliability, accuracy, and split second command and control cannot be assured in advance nor even approximated for any duration in peacetime, this search will not be successful. However, the more explicit shift to a doctrine of using nuclear weapons in a limited nuclear war, apparently codified in the widely discussed but unreleased Presidential Directive 59, suggests that U.S. policy now assumes that limited use of nuclear weapons is possible. Any attempt to employ the MX for such objectives would more likely lead to nuclear escalation, the exact scope and consequence of which cannot be known in advance. The lethal effects of such escalation would nevertheless be unprecedented given the potential damage arising from the detonation of just a few weapons.

CEP concludes:

- The MX multiple aimpoint basing system is not capable of providing the degree of protection required and is likely to lead to the expansion of the nuclear arsenals of both the U.S. and the U.S.S.R.
- The four basic arguments used to support the MX are fundamentally flawed:
  —Minuteman vulnerability has been overstated; but even a vulnerable Minuteman would leave the Soviet Union facing a massive U.S. retaliatory capability.
  —The possible future vulnerability of sea and air legs of the Triad can be hedged far less expensively than by building the MX.
  —The U.S. nuclear deterrent is equivalent to that of the U.S.S.R. without MX.
  —Using MX to extend deterrence increases the instances in which a nuclear weapon might be employed in a crisis.
- The United States strategic nuclear force is capable of deterring a possible attack by Soviet nuclear forces. The MX is not needed for deterrence.
- The United States does not need the MX missile.

Analysis of Economic Impacts of MX System

CEP analyzed Air Force estimates of the cost of building the MX system and Air Force research on the system's economic impacts. CEP performed its own economic analysis and compared the impact of spending on a new guided missile with five alternatives. We assessed the effect of shifting the money earmarked for the MX to a long-term program of oil conservation. CEP also gathered data on the extensive contracting and subcontracting network being assembled for production of the MX.

What Will the MX Cost?

The Air Force has consistently claimed that the MX system will cost $34 billion measured in 1980 prices. CEP concludes that the cost will be substantially greater. In real terms without including future inflation, the MX will cost at least $52 billion and perhaps as much as $116 billion.

When inflation is included, the MX will cost between $104 billion and $232 billion. The reasons for this cost growth include the following:

- Air force estimates earlier included but now exclude operations and maintenance costs.
- Air Force estimates assume there will be no cost growth from schedule slippages, contractor problems, or changes in system requirements, despite the fact that the General Accounting Office has already identified areas of cost growth.
- Air Force estimates assume that the system is large enough to withstand the threat from Russian missiles, but the Congressional Budget Office and other observers have concluded that even if the U.S.S.R. stays within SALT II limits on warheads, the MX would have to be expanded. If the Russians exceed SALT II limits, the expansion of MX would be large. The wide range in CEP's cost estimate is derived from likely U.S. responses to different levels of U.S.S.R. nuclear forces.
- Air Force estimates do not include the cost of warheads, which are built by the Department of Energy, and where cost figures are classified.
- Air Force estimates do not include the costs of adding a ballistic missile defense system, even though this is increasingly seen as an eventual addition to the system. Neither of the last two items were included in CEP's estimate. Thus, CEP's estimates may prove to be too low.

The Air Force's Analysis of the Economic Impact of MX Spending

The Air Force, as part of its analysis for the Milestone II Environmental Impact Statement, assessed the economic impact of spending $5 to $7 billion on Full Scale Engineering Development of MX. CEP analyzed the Air Force's work and found it seriously deficient.

- Although admitting that their results are biased upwards, the Air Force released to the press high estimates of employment and income gains resulting from the expenditure.
- The Air Force refused to analyze inflation as a possible outcome of MX expenditures.
- The Air Force used economic models inappropriately and relied on previously derived results for the effect of increasng government expenditures as a whole rather than investigating MX expenditures specifically. They also assumed MX expenditures would be financed by tax increases, a possibility hardly consistent with the Reagan Administration's policies.
- The Air Force did not compare the economic impacts of MX with any alternative uses of the same money. A brief survey of the literature on economic effects of military expenditures *(Economic Impact of Military Spending)* leads CEP to conclude this is a serious omission. Weak-

nesses of military outlays, such as their employment and investment effects, are often apparent only when compared with alternatives.

Input-Output Analysis of Guided Missile Production

CEP used existing input-output data to analyze the impact on the national economy of expenditures on a new guided missile. (We analyzed the missile alone, not including the basing system.) We also used input-output data to compare the effects of guided missile expenditures with five alternative patterns of domestic spending. The five alternatives are residential construction, urban rail transit, inter-city rail transit, public utilities construction, and solar energy equipment. We compared guided missile expenditures with the five alternatives in terms of effects on output, capital formation, employment, and inflation.

- *Output*—Of the six spending patterns analyzed, guided missiles would generate the smallest increase in gross output. The secondary output multiplier, which measures the increase in the quantity of inputs needed for a change in final output, is twice as high for solar energy equipment as it is for guided missiles.
- *Impact on manufacturing and capital goods*—The reason guided missile production has a low impact on output is that it has a high impact on service production. Surprisingly, the production of guided missiles requires a higher proportion of inputs from service industries and a lower proportion from manufacturing industries than any of the five civilian alternatives tested. The second and third largest inputs into guided missile production are Business Services and Gifts, Entertainment and Travel. The surprisingly low manufacturing content of guided missiles also has implications for capital formation for guided missiles has the lowest stimulative impact on key capital goods producing industries of the six spending patterns tested.
- *Employment*—Of the six alternatives tested, guided missile production would create the fewest jobs per billion dollars of expenditures by the government.
- *Inflation*—Of the six alternatives tested, guided missile production would likely generate the highest rate of inflation because the industries providing inputs into guided missiles are operating at higher levels of capacity utilization than is the case for the other five spending patterns. This result is consistent with other research indicating that military production industries in general are experiencing shortages of capacity, labor, and key inputs, and are already exhibiting cost increases far above national inflation rates. The huge increase in military procurement planned for the 1980s, including the MX, can only make this situation worse.

Shifting MX Expenditures to Energy Conservation

Responding initially to a query from Representative John Sieberling (D-OH), CEP also analyzed the effect of transferring the money currently being planned for the MX to a long-term program of fuel oil conservation. If the money is spent over a ten year period in equal annual installments on existing technologies in residential and commercial locations, CEP concludes that oil imports can be reduced by between 44% and 75% per year. The 1980 balance of trade deficit ($24.4 billion) could be completely eliminated and converted into a substantial surplus.

The MX Contracting Network

Building the MX will require the services of a large number of companies. The MX operates under an associate prime contractor system with many companies receiving prime contracts from the Department of Defense with the Air Force's Ballistic Missile Office at Norton Air Force Base in California acting as program coordinator. The prime contractors then employ numerous additional companies as subcontractors. Drawing on data obtained from a variety of sources, CEP has compiled information on the companies, the type and location of work being performed, the dollar amounts involved, the period of performance, and on the government agencies involved in MX work. This data is presented in a series of tables.

CEP has identified 37 companies that have received 47 contracts from the Department of Defense for MX work, totalling $3.5 billion. The companies that have received the largest dollar amount of contract awards are Rockwell ($723.7 million), Martin Marietta ($708.2 million), GTE Sylvania ($333.7 million), Northrop ($274.2 million), Boeing ($253.6), and General Tire and Rubber's Aerojet Strategic Propulsion Subsidiary ($242.5 million).

CEP identified 88 subcontractors with $124 million in MX business, although both the number of companies and the amount of business is seriously understated. An additional 12 companies have received contracts totalling $126 million for work closely linked to the MX program. CEP also identified federal government agencies that have been involved in the MX project.

PART I:
Does the U.S. Need the MX Missile?

1.
Introduction

The MX (for Missile Experimental) is a new land-based intercontinental ballistic missile (ICBM) designed to replace the existing U.S. force of 550 Minuteman III, 450 Minuteman II, and 52 Titan ICBMs. The most widely discussed feature of the MX is its basing system. Present plans call for the MX to be housed in underground, horizontal shelters, like huge garages, rather than in vertical silos that contain the Minuteman and Titan forces. In addition, the MX will be mobile, carried on huge transporter vehicles—resembling giant earth movers used in open pit mining operations—from shelter to shelter. Existing ICBMs are difficult to move and are considered to be fixed in location. Also, the MX will be deceptively housed—a single missile will be shuttled among 23 shelters in a manner designed to confuse the Soviet Union as to its precise location.

The MX will be larger than Minuteman and carry more warheads—ten on the MX as opposed to three on the Minuteman III and one each on the Minuteman II and Titan. Although initially designed to carry the same warhead as the Minuteman III, MX is expected to be more accurate due to improvements in guidance systems. Thus, deployment of MX is designed to give the Air Force a better capability to attack Russian military targets.

The MX project will be massive. It will require vast amounts of space and resources for the basing system, currently projected for the Great Basin region of Nevada and Utah. It will cost tens of billions of dollars, and perhaps even hundreds of billions of dollars, and take a decade to complete. A project of this scope will have substantial economic impacts. CEP reports on its investigation of some of these in Part II.

CEP's analysis in Part I is concerned with the weapon itself. While most of the public attention and debate has focused on the basing system, especially its complexity and the environmental and socioeconomic effects in Nevada and Utah, our research suggests that the missile dominates official thinking and that the missile, no matter how it is based, has serious implications for U.S. national security. The material we present in Part I is primarily, but by no means totally, concerned with evaluating the history of and rationale for the missile.

Chapters 2 and 3 trace the history of national security doctrine and of the MX exploring the arguments that lie behind public statements and widely held public beliefs. Chapter 4 through 7 examine the four main arguments used by the Pentagon in support of the MX. The first two, that Minuteman is vulnerable to a Soviet surprise attack and that MX will preserve deterrence in the sea and air legs of the Triad, are inconsistent with the facts. The third, that MX is needed to retain essential equivalence with Soviet forces, is based upon highly subjective, political considerations and not military ones. The U.S. has more than enough strength in its strategic nuclear forces to maintain essential equivalence without building the MX. The fourth argument, that MX will extend the range of deterrence vis-a-vis Soviet conventional and nuclear forces, is consistent with recent arguments that a more accurate missile will allow the U.S. to actually fight a limited nuclear war. This rationale for the MX is far from the notion of strategic forces deterring Soviet attacks on the United States. Instead it would increase the instances where nuclear weapons might be used and increase the chances of actually engaging in a nuclear conflict.

Chapter 8 analyzes the multiple shelter basing system and concludes that the system will not work and will most likely lead to further escalation in the arms race between the U.S. and the U.S.S.R. Chapter 9 summarizes our conclusions regarding the military arguments for building the MX system.

2.
History of Strategic Doctrine

What function do our strategic nuclear forces serve? Strategic forces, in military jargon, are those that can reach beyond a battlefield and strike an enemy's home territory.* On a question of such fundamental importance to the security of the United States and the world, one might expect to find either general agreement among strategists and policy makers, based on a coherent body of doctrine and analysis, or alternatively an informed, sustained public debate. Unfortunately, this is not so. A widespread and sometimes bitter divergence of views persists among well-informed persons in government, academia, industry, and the military, while rational public discussion is virtually precluded by severe misconceptions about the nature of American strategic policies and capabilities.

The Chairman of the Joint Chiefs of Staff, General David C. Jones, has observed, "there has been too much concentration in our national debates

---

* In World War II, the German bombing raids on London, General James H. Doolittle's attack on Tokyo, and the Allies' saturation bombing of Hamburg, are examples of strategic bombing. Tactical forces are those that are confined to the battlefield. With nuclear weapons, the line is frequently blurred. Land-based and sea-based intercontinental ballistic missiles and long-range penetrating bombers are clearly strategic weapons. Shorter-range weapons, such as the Pershing II missile and the F-111 fighter-bomber, both with nuclear capability, can reach the Soviet Union from certain bases but could not if they were based in or near the United States. A Soviet missile that can reach Western Europe may be part of the strategic balance between NATO and Warsaw Pact nations, but not between the United States and the U.S.S.R.

on specific characteristics of individual weapons systems, such as yield*
and accuracy, and not enough on fundamental strategic issues."¹ The
Joint Chiefs Chairman wants to forge a new national consensus to settle
the question of whether nuclear forces, confined to an "assured destruction" role, can provide adequate deterrence, or whether a sustained and
more flexible "warfighting" capability is required.

The popular conception is that the purpose of our vast nuclear arsenal is
to deter a massive Soviet nuclear attack on the United States or our
Western European allies, especially an attack that totally destroys our
nuclear forces, a scenario termed a "disarming first strike" by the military.
Deterrence of a first strike is achieved when our arsenal is large enough
and secure enough that large numbers of weapons could survive a first
strike, hit back at an aggressor, and inflict severe damage. It is the threat of
retaliation that deters.

But, said General Jones, public opinion is a prisoner of the "assured
destruction" doctrine, which holds that "as long as the U.S. can wreak
substantial damage on Soviet society—that is, destroy a given number of
cities with some certainty—that's all we need in terms of strategic
equilibrium. Under this view, anything beyond that point is regarded as
overkill and unimportant." One consequence of this doctrine, according
to General Jones, is a belief that the Soviets "can continue to enlarge their
strategic forces and 'waste their resources' without ill effect on our national
security." He maintains, however, that the concept of exclusive reliance on
assured destruction is "flawed because the mission of our strategic forces is
broader than merely deterring an attack on our cities."²

Although the ability to inflict what the Pentagon calls "unacceptable"
damage on an attacker is undoubtedly one mission assigned to our nuclear
forces, it is not the only mission, and may not even be the primary one.
The forces required to inflict severe damage on Soviet society make up less
than 10 per cent of the missiles and bombers available for the delivery of
nuclear weapons and of the weapons themselves.³

What then are the objectives served by the remaining 90 per cent of the
U.S. nuclear arsenal? Are these objectives necessary or desirable, and
what role, if any, is the MX designed to play in achieving them? To answer
these questions requires a brief review of the evolution of United States
strategic doctrine and strategic capabilities.

Over the years, declared American policy governing the use of nuclear
weapons has undergone a significant evolution, one that has been summarized under the following descriptive headings:

"Massive Retaliation" (1954-1961)
"Flexible Response" (1961-1965)
"Assured Destruction" (1965-1967)
"Mutual Assured Destruction" (1967-1971)

---
*The force of a nuclear explosion expressed as the equivalent of the energy produced by tons of TNT.

"Strategic Sufficiency" (1971-1974)
"Essential Equivalence" (1974-?)

In spite of these six nominal changes in policy, the official Executive branch guidance to the military services for the employment of nuclear weapons has been revised just twice since the formulation in 1960 of the first single integrated operational plan for use of nuclear weapons against the Soviet Union, China, and their allies. The first time was in 1961, when a modicum of flexibility and the concept of a strategic reserve force were introduced; the second in 1974, when Secretary of Defense James Schlesinger emphasized the need for a wider range of strategic options. What accounts for this split between declared doctrine and military practice?

"Massive Retaliation" (1954-1961)

In the 1950s, strategic targeting policy was primarily the responsibility of the Strategic Air Command (SAC), and the Air Force "covered" Soviet military and industrial targets in a manner similar to the procedures used for conventional bombing during World War II. Most American nuclear weapons were carried by a bomber force that totaled, by the end of the decade, some 2,000 jets. These included 600 B-52s and 1,400 medium-range B-47s, the latter stationed at overseas bases encircling the U.S.S.R.[5]

During the second half of the decade, the United States also deployed several thousand so-called "tactical" (that is, short range) nuclear weapons in Europe, in Korea, and on surface vessels and submarines: nuclear artillery shells and atomic demolition mines, short range battlefield missiles, air defense missiles, surface-launched anti-submarine rockets, submarine-launched anti-submarine rockets, torpedoes and depth charges. One hundred and fifty Thor and Jupiter missiles based in the United Kingdom, Italy, and Turkey and carrier-based aircraft capable of carrying nuclear weapons stationed in the Mediterranean and the Pacific added to U.S. tactical forces. By the end of the decade, the United States had also test-launched its first Polaris ballistic missile submarine, had begun deployment of 200 Atlas and Titan I ICBMs, and had constructed an air-defense system with 1,500 surface-to-air missiles and several thousand interceptor aircraft.

In 1960, rivalry between the Air Force and the Navy over which should control the budgets and targets of U.S. strategic forces was alleviated somewhat by the appearance of the Gates Report,* which recommended an integrated approach to strategic targeting and led to the formation of the Joint Strategic Target Planning Saff (JSTPS) at SAC Headquarters in Omaha, Nebraska. The Director of JSTPS is the SAC Commander, and

---

*Eisenhower's last Secretary of Defense, Thomas Gates, headed a DoD study committee aimed at reducing competition among the services on nuclear weapons policy.

the Vice-Director, a Navy admiral. Since 1960, the JSTPS has prepared and continually updated the Single Integrated Operational Plan (SIOP) that decides which of the thousands of nuclear weapons in our arsenal are aimed at which targets in the U.S.S.R., China, North Korea, and Eastern Europe. Land-based ICBMs, submarines, bombers, carrier-aircraft and land-based NATO aircraft and missiles were all included in the plan, and remain so today. Contrary to popular notions of the U.S. strategic policy, the SIOP has always included a number of counterforce* options, including the option of a massive counterforce first strike.

By 1960, the U.S.S.R. had deployed a force of 150 intermediate-range bombers which could, with aerial refueling, strike targets in the United States with nuclear weapons; significant numbers of medium-range aircraft; and a smaller number of SS-4 intermediate-range ballistic missiles capable of reaching Western Europe from launch points in the western U.S.S.R. The Soviet bomber force, none of whose planes were kept on airborne alert, was vulnerable to a surprise attack at its bases, as was the SS-4 IRBM, a surface-launched missile whose non-storable liquid fuel had to be fed in over a ten-hour period prior to launch.[6] The Russians had no ICBM force.

By 1960 the United States had a strategic arsenal of some 4,000 deliverable nuclear warheads; the Soviet Union, about 200. The doctrine which accompanied this huge imbalance in strategic power was called "massive retaliation." Secretary of State John Foster Dulles announced the policy in a speech to the Council on Foreign Relations on January 12, 1954:

> Local defense will always be important. But there is no local defense which alone will contain the mighty landpower of the Communist world. Local defenses must be reinforced by the further deterrent of massive retaliatory power. . . .
>
> The basic decision was to depend primarily upon a great capacity to retaliate instantly, by means and at place of our choosing. Now the DOD and Joint Chiefs of Staff can shape *our* policy, instead of having to try to be ready to meet the enemy's many choices.[7]

Under the massive retaliation doctrine, the threat to employ nuclear weapons was intended to deter not only nuclear attacks upon the United States and its allies, but also conventional attacks anywhere in the world which impinged on U.S. interests. The policy did not pledge to meet every local conflict by nuclear means. It left open the question of what the United States response would be, saying only that it would be "instantly by means and at place of our choosing." The threat that the United States would not refrain from again being the first to use nuclear weapons was implicit in the doctrine, and was reinforced by the acquisition of thousands of tactical

---

*Counterforce means directed at the enemy's military forces and military industry.

nuclear weapons for use in local and regional conflicts.*

Ironically, it was during this era of unquestioned U.S. nuclear supremacy that the Pentagon first proposed a Soviet surprise nuclear attack scenario. The attack was predicated on an alleged "missile gap" identified by the secret Gaither Committee report to President Eisenhower in the fall of 1957.[8] The Gaither panel warned that SAC was already vulnerable "to a Russian surprise bomber attack in a period of low tension," and would soon become vulnerable "to an attack by Russian ICBMs" that the Committee characterized as "a late 1959 threat."

The Gaither Committee recommended drastic acceleration of U.S. IRBM, ICBM, and SLBM programs, hardened** silos for ICBM's, a crash development program for ABMs, and a nationwide fallout-shelter program. The last two recommendations, the Committee noted, were related not to deterrence of a surprise attack but rather to preservation of the option to use nuclear weapons in lesser contingencies. "As long as the U.S. population is wide open to Soviet attack," the panel observed, "both Russians and our allies may believe that we shall feel increasing reluctance to employ SAC in any circumstance other than when the United States is directly attacked." Along the same lines, the panel also suggested that "a study be undertaken at the national rather than at a service level, to develop current doctrine on when and how nuclear weapons can contribute to limited operations."[9]

The credibility of the Committee's surprise-attack scenario was strained, even at the time, by the fact that the American bomber bases to be attacked by Soviet forces were all over the world; to strike them simultaneously would have required launching the attacking missiles at different times, providing some warning.*** Furthermore, the United States, both then and now, has thousands of nuclear weapons stationed in Europe, South Korea, and Japan, and aboard aircraft carriers. Of possibly greater consequence, however, was the fact that the Russians *did not even possess the missiles on which the attack was premised nor could they possibly have built them by 1959, the year the threat was supposed to begin.*

Eisenhower largely ignored the recommendations of the Gaither report, but many of them were taken up in a modified form by the Kennedy Administration. By 1965, eight years later, the U.S.S.R. still had only 200 vulnerable, non-storable, liquid-fueled SS-7 and SS-8 ICBMs, while the comparable U.S. force of 200 Atlas and Titan I missiles had already been retired and replaced by a force of close to 1,000 Titan II and solid-fueled

---

*In 1954 the Soviets had no counter-European missiles and were only starting production of the Badger medium-range bomber.

**Hardened targets are protected against the blast heat and radiation effects of nuclear weapons of specific yields. Hardening is usually accomplished with earth and reinforced concrete and is measured by the number of pounds per square inch of blast overpressure which a target can withstand.

***If the missiles had been launched simultaneously, then they would have arrived at their targets at different times, likewise providing some warning. Such problems of timing continue to confound the Pentagon's current scenarios for a Soviet surprise attack.

Minuteman missiles in hardened underground silos.* The Soviet arsenal of deliverable strategic nuclear weapons stood at about 450 warheads; deliverable U.S. warheads numbered around 3,500.[10]

From "Flexible Response" to "Assured Destruction" (1961-1967)

In 1962, after it became clear that the Minuteman program would guarantee the U.S. many more missiles than the Soviet Union for several years, Secretary of Defense Robert S. McNamara went public with the Pentagon's counterforce strategy in a speech at Ann Arbor:

The U.S. has come to the conclusion that, to the extent feasible, basic military strategy in a possible general nuclear war should be approached in much the same way that the more conventional military operations have been regarded in the past. That is to say, principal military objectives, in the event of nuclear war stemming from a major attack on the [NATO] Alliance, should be the destruction of the enemy's military forces, not his civilian population.[11]

But as the Soviet Union actually began a serious effort to match U.S. strategic nuclear capabilities, which resulted in the construction of 1,400 ICBMs and 70 SLBMs between 1965 and 1972, McNamara ceased his public advocacy of counterforce and began to talk instead about deterrence and assured destruction. The latter policy was announced to the House Armed Services Committee on February 19, 1965:

The strategic objectives of our general nuclear war forces are:
1. To deter a deliberate nuclear attack upon the U.S. and its allies by maintaining a clear and convincing capability to inflict unacceptable damage on an attacker, even if that attacker were to strike first;
2. In the event such a war should nevertheless occur, to limit damage to our population and industrial capacities.[12]

McNamara's announced policy was limited to deterrence of an attack with nuclear weapons. It did not address the issue of a conventional weapons attack on American allies, thereby fostering the impression that the United States was drawing back from the threat to use nuclear weapons in a conventional conflict. The classified version of Defense Secretary McNamara's FY1966 posture statement, quoted by Defense Secretary Schlesinger in 1974, told a somewhat different story. "General nuclear war" was defined simply as ' a war in which nuclear weapons are launched against the homelands of the United States and the Soviet Union. '

Such attacks might be directed against military targets only, against cities only, or against both types of targets, either simultaneously or

---

*The U.S. ICBM force reached its programmed deployment of 1,054 missiles in 1967. Solid-fueled missiles can be launched quickly. Liquid fuel must be fed into the missile over a number of hours.

with a delay, They might be selective in terms of specific targets attacked or they might be general.

NATO should not only have an improved capability to meet major non-nuclear assaults with non-nuclear means but it should also achieve a true tactical nuclear capability which should include a broad, flexible range of nuclear options, short of general nuclear war, and the means to implement them.[13]

It is important to note that McNamara did not limit American use of nuclear weapons in a "general nuclear war" to retaliation after absorbing a nuclear strike, nor would such retaliation always be designed to inflict "unacceptable damage" or "assured destruction." On the contrary, as McNamara had noted three years before: "We should plan for the 1965-67 time period a force which could, one, strike back decisively at the entire Soviet target system simultaneously; or, two, strike back, first, at the Soviet bomber bases, missile sites, and other military installations associated with their long-range nuclear forces to reduce the power of any follow-on attack—and then, if necessary, strike back at the Soviet urban and industrial complex in a controlled and deliberate way. Such a force would give us the needed flexibility to meet a wide range of possible general war situations."[14]

Contrary to the general impression created by the newly declared policy, assured destruction doctrine did not abandon counterforce targeting, but rather confined it (publicly) to second-strike retaliation and renamed it "damage limitation." The idea was that the United States would employ its offensive as well as defensive (ABM)* forces in an attempt to limit damage to the United States if the Russians should launch a nuclear attack. Since limiting damage means destroying the remainder of the Soviet nuclear force, the strategy requires a counterforce capability. Although this strategy seemed farfetched in 1965—the United States had no effective ABM defense and the Russians were developing supposedly invulnerable submarines[15]—the Soviet force was still very small by comparison, and the United States had just committed itself to the development of Multiple Independently Targetable Reentry Vehicles (MIRVs), which held out the prospect of enough warheads to target at least Soviet land-based forces in a retaliatory attack.

During the mid-and late-sixties, the Pentagon's Soviet surprise attack scenario became even more unbelievable. This time our military planners proposed a "bolt-out-of-the-blue" attack not only on bomber bases but on 1,000 U.S. missile silos and submarines in port as well. The retaliatory strike by hundreds of missiles from our Polaris submarines at sea would be blunted, we were told, by the Russians' anti-ballistic missile system. Aside from the fact that no sane military strategist could rely,

---

*A system of missiles and radars capable of defending against a ballistic-missile attack by destroying incoming offensive missiles. The defensive missile may be armed with either nuclear or non-nuclear warheads.

then or now, on a ballistic missile defense to shoot down hundreds of incoming reentry vehicles (RVs) — (the Polaris force has 1,968 RVs, 1,100 at sea) the Soviet Union did not even possess a ballistic missile defense, nor sufficient missiles to destroy more than a small fraction of U.S. land-based military targets.

"Mutual Assured Destruction" (1967-1971)

The "assured destruction" doctrine remained in favor for only two and a half years. As the Russians continued to build up their numbers of ICBMs and SLBMs, it became clear, according to one former Pentagon research official, that "There were just too many [Soviet] aim-points for us to have an effective damage-limiting attack."[16] Thus in September 1967, McNamara announced the concept of "mutual assured destruction" (MAD):

> The fact is, then, that neither the Soviet Union nor the U.S. can attack the other without being destroyed in retaliation; nor can either of us attain a first strike capability in the foreseeable future. Further, both the Soviet Union and the U.S. now possess an actual and credible second-strike capability against one another, and it is precisely this mutual capability that provides us both with the strongest possible motive to avoid a nuclear war.[17]

McNamara's systems analysis staff calculated that the delivery of 400 "equivalent megatons"* on urban-industrial targets would kill some 30 per cent of the Soviet population and destroy 75 per cent of the industrial capacity through blast and thermal effects alone. Such a level of destruction was judged to be adequate to deter even the most desperate Soviet leader, and in any case, not worth exceeding, because higher levels yield sharply diminishing returns per warhead. Radiation, firestorms, fallout and delayed socio-economic effects such as interruption of essential services (e.g., food distribution, medical care) would kill millions more.[18]

Since we already possess substantially more than the capacity needed for assured destruction, that criterion does not justify further expansion of the strategic forces. For example, by June 1979, the United States had 820 equivalent megatons in its submarine forces alone, and this number is scheduled to rise to 1,053 EMT by 1982 as the Trident missile enters the force.

McNamara's doctrines, however, appear to have had little effect on the actual make-up of the SIOP. From an arms-control perspective, their one restraining effect — confining the size of the Minuteman force to

---

*As a measure of blast damage or "area destruction" potential, strategic planners use equivalent megatons in place of the unadjusted yield in megatons. EMT is defined as the explosive yield raised to the 2/3 power, in recognition of the fact that an increase in yield produces a less than proportional increase in blast effects.

1,000 missiles — was more than offset by the introduction of MIRVs in 1970.

In fact, the Joint Strategic Target Planning Staff's choice of targets has never been limited to those included in the assured-destruction calculation. Since this level of destruction was already exceeded in the first SIOP in 1960, it is apparent that the "assured destruction" figure of 400 EMT has never played an important role in determining the size of the U.S. nuclear arsenal — except for establishing the number of submarines that would have to be at sea at any given time and therefore, indirectly, the size of the SLBM force. On the contrary, as new warheads and delivery vehicles become available, they are routinely incorporated in the SIOP, either through allocation to new targets or as a back-up to targets already covered.

Despite the twists and turns of publicly stated policy, the Executive guidance governing the SIOP remained basically unchanged for 14 years. As one high-ranking participant in the first SIOP recalls, "When I returned to the staff in the early seventies and pulled out the top-secret folder to look at the Presidential guidance, it was the same damn stuff — still had my handwritten notes all over it."

In short, U.S. nuclear forces have never been structured solely as a deterrent to nuclear attack upon the United States and its allies, nor has deterrence inevitably taken the form of threatening an "assured destruction" attack against Soviet cities. From the beginning, U.S. nuclear forces were designed to deter conventional, and then limited nuclear, attacks by providing "credible" options for escalation to the nuclear level. Some of these options include the use of tactical nuclear weapons on the battlefield, regional attacks with forward-based systems, and a massive counterforce first strike.

As the Soviet Union expanded and diversified its nuclear arsenal in the late 1960s, however, the range of possibilities available to U.S. strategic forces began to appear limited. Since the Soviets were gaining the ability to absorb a nuclear attack, even an all-out counterforce attack, and retain enough weapons to assault the United States, a nuclear response to a conventional attack in Europe or some other corner of the globe no longer seemed to be a rational, and therefore credible, policy. The emergence of a Soviet-American nuclear standoff prompted a desire on the part of U.S. military planners to restore the previously held American superiority, especially in counterforce capacities. As the Nixon Administration discovered, the new weapons and programs that would be needed to achieve this superiority were at odds with the policy of "mutual assured destruction." It decided to win Congressional, media and public support for what it perceived were U.S. strategic objectives by the public airing of a shift in doctrine.

"Strategic Sufficiency" and "Essential Equivalence" (1971– ?)

The change in doctrine was not formally announced until January 1974, but its broad outlines could be detected as early as 1970 in the President's State of the World message for that year. "Should a President," Nixon asked rhetorically, "in the event of a nuclear attack, be left with the single option of ordering the mass destruction of enemy civilians in the face of the certainty that it would be followed by the mass slaughter of Americans? Should the concept of assured destruction be narrowly defined and should it be the only measure of our ability to deter the variety of threats we may face?"[20]

As should be obvious from the previous discussion, Nixon's characterization of a President's options under the assured-destruction doctrine was a gross distortion of actual U.S. military planning. "I don't think the professional planners are dimmer than us," remarked Pentagon consultant Herman Kahn during a Congressional hearing in 1976. He continued:

> They will often invent controlled response even if there are sharp gaps occasionally between the Department of Defense's current public verbal policies and its real, in the event, action policies. The Department of Defense is a very large organization and the right hand doesn't know what the left hand is doing. Further, it is very difficult to discuss these bizarre possibilities in public . . . I would argue that the biggest single problem we have is that the Department of Defense is not clear. It itself doesn't understand its own plan. These issues go back to 1960, and they still don't understand them.[21]

Clearly, President Nixon and Secretary of Defense Schlesinger, the chief architect of the renewed counterforce emphasis, did understand their own plan and knew very well how they were misrepresenting the assured-destruction strategy. "In fact," Schlesinger admitted during a hearing in 1974, "this is not the way the forces were targeted, but the overt public doctrine stressed only going against cities."[22] The exact nature of this deception was outlined in the spring of 1976 by Dr. Richard Garwin, of IBM's Watson Research Laboratory, a defense consultant and a member of the scientific advisory board of the Joint Strategic Target Planning staff:

> . . . So far as our capability to destroy the Soviet Union is concerned, we can do that with 10 percent of the Minuteman force. . . . In the 1960s when the Defense Department asked for the ABM system, saying without it, our deterrent would disappear . . . they neglected to tell you that the vast majority of Minuteman

were not targeted against any industry and population at all. They were targeted against relatively low value, military targets, simply because in the process the important targets were assigned first, and then warheads do not go unassigned. If they have to be launched, they would be launched against military targets . . . The Soviet attack would use up excess missiles, missiles which were built to penetrate ABM systems, and which were then assigned to military targets of very little value.

Now, I will give you not a probable conversation between a military planner and a civilian leader but one that is more probable than the one proposed by the Defense Department. The scenario that the Defense Department has advanced at times goes that the Soviet Union destroys all the Minutemen and then they say to the United States, "Surrender, we hardly killed anybody."

. . . and the President of the United States, seeing he has no Minutemen left, somehow chooses to surrender.

This scenario ignores the fact that the vast number of our warheads are on the Poseidon force and not in the Minuteman, and our military capability is, in fact, little affected if one ranks all the targets in value. But the prelude is completely unnecessary. The Soviet Union could say, without destroying Minuteman, "Look here, Mr. President, surrender or we will destroy American cities."

It wasn't necessary to destroy Minuteman in order to say that. The compelling nature of the argument would be just the same. The President has all the options left in the first case, as he has in the second. They could launch some weapons at some cities, and then say, "Now you see what nuclear weapons will do to your population, why should we waste them on your military forces? But we mean business; we are implacable, and if you fire back, we will destroy all of you."

And the question is . . . who believes what? What is inevitable in this system? That is the problem with the questioning that began with President Nixon in 1970, where he belittled our existing military capability (in my opinion, much to the detriment of the U.S. position in regard to its allies and neutrals), by pretending that he had no options between the total destruction of the Soviet Union, which would not do us any good, and doing nothing. . . .

Is it credible that President Nixon was unaware that our Minuteman forces had, right then, the technical capability of being launched as individual missiles or in small numbers against any target complex prespecified by the President?

. . . The Defense Department leaped in to suggest all kinds of weapons programs to fill this gap which did not exist.[23]

Obviously, something more than a desire to avoid Soviet cities was involved in the Nixon/Schlesinger campaign for more nuclear "options," by which they really meant, "weapons." As former Kennedy Administration national security advisor McGeorge Bundy observed during a speech in 1979, "The Republicans appeared to believe that a significant counterforce capability was desirable, and they regularly did battle with the straw man of a strategy of city-busting only."[24]

The change in targeting doctrine—the first major revision of the SIOP in 14 years—was contained in President Nixon's 1973 National Security Decision Memorandum (NSDM) 242 and Secretary Schlesinger's subsequent guidance document, the Nuclear Weapons Employment Policy issued in April 1974. President Carter's 1977 Presidential Directive (PD) 18 essentially reaffirmed the strategic objectives set forth in Nixon's NSDM 242, but called for a further review of targeting options.* Although these documents remain classified, the broad outlines and intent of the new targeting doctrine were explained by Secretary Schlesinger in 1974.[25]

He noted that the ABM Treaty** had "effectively removed the concept of defensive damage limitation (at least as it was defined in the 1960s) from contention as a major strategic option." This development, in conjunction with the growth of the Russians' own deterrent capabilities beyond the capacity of the United States to take away," has called into question American willingness to employ its nuclear forces "in response to anything less than an all-out attack on the United States and its cities," a concern remarkably like that expressed by the Gaither panel in 1958.[26]

Secretary Schlesinger was particularly concerned about the U.S. ability to deliver an appropriate nuclear response to threats against allied forces. To the extent that these threats could be deterred by the prospect of nuclear retaliation, Schlesinger observed, they demanded more limited responses and "advanced planning tailored to such lesser responses."[27]

"If you ask the people who do SIOP planning, they will tell you that we can always do selective strikes, if that is what is wanted," Schlesinger testified. "But there had not been a sufficient examination of the details so that one could say definitely that we had practicable options."[28]

Asked on another occasion whether the President had the option of ordering a limited strike against missile silos, Schlesinger responded, "He does hypothetically in that he could ask SAC to construct such a strike in an emergency."

> But in order to have that kind of capacity one has to do the indoctrination and planning in anticipation of the difficulties involved. It is ill-advised to do that under the press of circumstances. Rather one should think through the problems in advance and put

---

*The review Carter requested was completed in the spring of 1980 and the conclusions incorporated in PD 59, the broad outlines of which were leaked to the press on August 5, 1980, a few days before the Democratic convention.

**The 1972 ABM Treaty limited the deployment of anti-ballistic missile defenses to two areas—one for the defense of the national capital and the other for the defense of some ICBMs. A 1974 Protocol further limited both parties to a single area of deployment.

together relevant, small packages which a President could choose under the circumstances in which they might be required.[29]

Under just what circumstances might these small packages of nuclear weapons be invoked? "Conventional conflicts could escalate into nuclear exchanges," Schlesinger noted. "Indeed, some observers believe that this is precisely what would happen should a major war break out in Europe."[30] As Schlesinger subsequently made clear in his Congressional testimony, the United States would be the one doing the escalating.[31]

The credibility of this first-use threat, Schlesinger noted, depends to some extent on the relative invulnerability of U.S. strategic systems, particularly land-based ICBMs which, because of their greater accuracy and more effective command and control apparatus, pose a more credible threat of escalation than do submarines or bombers.

"There are many ways" Schlesinger wrote in March 1974, "other than a massive surprise attack, in which an enemy might be tempted to use his strategic forces to gain a major advantage or concession." Nuclear threats to our strategic forces, he pointed out, "might well call for an option to respond in kind against the attackers' military forces," and in some circumstances, "a set of hard targets might be the most appropriate objective for our retaliation."[32]

In addition to the prospect of such limited counterforce attacks, Schlesinger noted that he could not "preclude the massive surprise attack on our force . . . although I regard the probability of such an attack as close to zero under existing conditions."

Indeed, "close to zero" was probably an overstatement. By the mid-seventies, the Pentagon's surprise-attack scenario had become even more fanciful. Since a surprise attack was no longer credible militarily, as it could no longer disarm the U.S. deterrent, an overtly political element was introduced into the script. In 1970 President Nixon worried publicly about "the Soviet threat to the *sufficiency* of our deterrent" and followed that up a year later with the assessment that the Soviet Union might be seeking forces which could destroy "*vital elements* of our retaliatory capability." As before, the scenario begins with a Soviet surprise attack on our land-based missiles, non-alert bombers, and submarines in port, but this time the Russians issue an ultimatum threatening retaliation against American cities if the United States responds with its sea-based deterrent. Since the attack on U.S. land-based systems is only partially successful and ignores alert bombers and submarines on patrol, it does not appreciably change the deterrent situation. Why would the Russians take the risk?

U.S. sea-based forces could retaliate against a broad range of Soviet targets, and the United States could issue a counter-ultimatum—that the Soviet strikes against U.S. cities would result in full-scale retaliation against Soviet cities. Particularly after killing millions of Americans in the initial counterforce attack, the Russians could not be sure that the United

States would control its response, *even if it wanted to*. As the newsletter of the Federation of American Scientists observed in 1974, "The entire scenario is bizarre — enormous risks for no point. . . . One can only imagine that the Joint Chiefs have been smoking pot."[33]

Secretary Schlesinger had an alternative explanation for the persistence of such highly improbable scenarios. They were useful, he said, "in testing the design of our second-strike forces."

> We have arrived at the current size and mix of our strategic forces not only because we want the ultimate threat of massive destruction to be really assured, but also because for more than a decade we have thought it advisable to test the force against the "higher-than-expected" threat. *Given the built-in surplus of warheads generated by this force-sizing calculation,* we could allocate additional weapons to non-urban targets and thereby acquire a limited set of options, including the option to attack some hard targets."[34] (emphasis added)

In other words, since the scenario by which the Soviet Union strikes first at U.S. nuclear forces is a "higher-than-expected threat," that is, a hypothetical threat that is not really taken seriously, a primary purpose of the surprise attack scenario must be to generate a surplus of U.S. warheads which can then be assigned to military targets in the Soviet Union. Whether by conscious design or because of the incentives built into the system by which these calculations are made, accepting the existence of a counterforce potential by the Soviet Union automatically leads to the acquisition of that potential by the United States. Given the importance of such an outcome, it is worth reviewing these calculations in some detail.

TOTAL FORCE = FORCES LOST IN SOVIET FIRST STRIKE
+ COUNTERFORCE RETALIATION
+ ASSURED DESTRUCTION RESERVE
+ POST-WAR RESERVE

What this equation says is that the United States should have a strategic force large enough to absorb a first strike, to retaliate against Soviet military targets while holding an "assured destruction" capability in reserve, and then if the latter should be required, finish the war with a certain percentage of the force intact. By this calculation, the requirement for warheads, and systems to deliver them, can be immense. The size of required U.S. forces is quite sensitive to the number, size and accuracy of the warheads assumed to be in the hypothetical Soviet attack. An increase in the size and effectiveness of the Soviet attack would greatly increase the size of the U.S. force that would be needed to absorb the attack, and then retaliate. Posing a growing Soviet threat has been one of the methods used by the Pentagon to document the requirement for MX.

It is doubtful whether the United Sates is able to gather and interpret crucial information concerning Soviet strategic forces. The record is not very reassuring. When the Congressional Joint Committee on Defense Production released the Gaither report in 1976, the committee commented that the missile gap:

. . . like so many other weapon system gaps before and since, failed to materialize as expected. Indeed, the Kennedy Administration, which had campaigned partly on the missile gap, was later constrained to admit that this chasm never existed and that at the time of the Gaither report, the Soviet Union probably had fewer than a dozen operational ICBMs. . . .

The nonexistent missile gap and the recommendations for expanded military and civil defense spending that issued from it were based on unduly alarmist views of Soviet capabilities and on predictions of spectacular progress in the future, much in the same way that today's recommendations are based on simplified linear projections of current Soviet programs.

The recommendations of the Gaither Committee were based on a number of other expert forecasts that proved erroneous. For example, the breakthrough in ASW (Antisubmarine Warfare) has yet to occur, despite billions of dollars spent on this problem by the United States alone. This would suggest that, while insurance or hedges against certain hypothetical threats is clearly necessary, we must be careful indeed in selecting the most likely threats, lest the premiums on the insurance outweigh its benefits.

The committee gave a particular example of how an exaggeration of the Soviet threat became the determining factor in the size of U.S. strategic forces.

In the one area where the Gaither recommendations were ultimately implemented — improving the breadth and depth of the strategic nuclear weapons arsenal—the result has been not stability but a dynamic arms competition.

Indeed, the increase in nuclear weapons arsenals has allowed the United States to adopt a new or modified strategy that is implicit in the Gaither report. This is the strategy of nuclear warfighting or limited nuclear war. . . . sheer vertical proliferation of nuclear warheads, coupled with technological improvements in accuracy, targeting and yield-to-weight ratios, now permits nations to consider *fighting* rather than *deterring* nuclear wars, since they have adequate weapons to fire some while holding others in reserve.[35]

Earlier the Pentagon claimed that MX was necessary because of the increasing numbers and hardness levels of Soviet targets which needed to be attacked in order to preserve deterrence. Following this argument an increase in the damage criteria which define "assured destruction" will also increase U.S. strategic force requirements. In the case of economic targets, since the criteria are set as a percentage rather than as some finite number, Soviet economic growth alone generates a requirement for additional warheads.

An even more dramatic increase in the total number of warheads comes from an increased demand for accuracy. While one warhead on a hard target may yield a 65 per cent overall probability of damage, to achieve 95 per cent can very often require three, a situation of very obvious diminishing returns. A 95 per cent probability of damage to Soviet strategic forces would still leave the U.S. quite vulnerable to Soviet retaliation. The requirements for a counterforce attack on the Soviet Union, buttressed by claims of a growing Soviet threat and an expansion of U.S. targets, can generate an almost insatiable demand for warheads.

Conclusion

U.S. strategic doctrine has come a long way in an attempt to stay in the same place. The evidence points to a continuing desire on the part of U.S. military policy makers to maintain some level of nuclear superiority over the Soviet Union, and in particular to maintain superiority in the ability to attack hardened military and industrial targets. At the same time, there has appeared to be a continuing effort to obfuscate this objective, either by denying its existence or by treating it as a response to alleged Soviet superiority. The MX, as we argue in the next section, is the latest weapon to fit this design.

Footnotes

1. *Air Force Magazine,* May 1979, p. 26.
2. Ibid.
3. Calculated as follows: Ten per cent of the Triad is 35 bombers carrying 236 EMT; 66 Poseidon SLBMs carrying 69 EMT; 105 ICBMs carrying 97 EMT. Total number of delivery vehicles is 206; total EMT is 402; number of weapons is 1,385. The United States has about 2,053 strategic nuclear delivery vehicles and 27,000 nuclear warheads; the Department of Defense has calculated that 400 EMT would kill about 30 per cent of

Soviet population (74 million people) and destroy 76 per cent of Soviet industry. The equivalent of 100 one-megaton weapons would kill 37 million Soviet citizens and destroy 59 per cent of Soviet industry. See "New Weapons/Old Doctrines: Strategic Warfare in the 1980's," text of a talk by Dr. R.L. Garwin presented to the American Philosophical Society, November 1979, p. 5.

4. For a convenient summary of declared U.S. doctrines, see "The Evolution of U.S. Declaratory Strategic Policy," By Ben T. Plymale, *Journal of International Relations*, Fall 1977, p. 242.
5. Data on U.S. deployment from "The Conventional Roots of the Nuclear Arms Race," draft monograph by Randall Forsberg, Director, Institute for Defense and Disarmament Studies, Brookline, MA, pp. 54–55. Dr. George Rathjens notes that early war plans specified "three objectives to be served by nuclear weapons: the 'Bravo'-'blunting'-mission, involving delivery of weapons against military targets in the Soviet Union to blunt its ability to launch nuclear strikes; the 'Delta'-'destruction'-mission aimed at the destruction of Soviet war-making potential, the analogue of the strategic bombing efforts of the Second World War against Germany and Japan; and the 'Romeo'-'retardation'-mission to interdict and delay an expected movement of Soviet forces into Western Europe.... there was conflict over allocation of effort to the three missions; arguments about which allocation would have the most favorable effect on war outcome—significantly not about whether allocating more resources to, say, the 'Delta' mission would enhance deterrence." See G.W. Rathjens, "Nuclear War between the Superpowers" in Griffiths, Franklyn and Polanyi, eds., *The Dangers of Nuclear War*, Toronto, 1979.
6. Henry Kissinger, "NATO: the Next Thirty Years," *Survival*, XXI,6 (November/December 1979) p. 265.
7. quoted by Plymale, *op. cit.*, p. 243.
8. *Deterrence and Survival in the Nuclear Age* (The "Gaither Report" of 1957), declassified in 1973, printed for the use of the Joint Committee on Defense Production, Congress of the United States, USGPO, Washington, D.C., 1976, pp. 16–19.
9. Ibid. p. 18.
10. *Department of Defense Annual Report*, Fiscal Year 1981, p. 68.
11. quoted in *FAS Public Interest Report*, February 1974 (newsletter of the Federation of American Scientists, Washington, D.C.).
12. quoted in Plymale, *op. cit.*
13. Extract from FY 1966 Posture Statement of Secretary of Defense Robert McNamara, cited by James Schlesinger in testimony before the Committee on Foreign Relations, U.S. Senate, Subcommittee on Arms Control, International Law and Organization, March 4, 1974, hearing on *US-USSR Strategic Policies*, USGPO, Washington, D.C. 1974, p. 27.
14. Ibid.
15. The Soviet "Yankee"-class submarines carrying the 1,750-mile range SS-N-6 missile entered service in 1968-69. Their survivability was compromised from the beginning by their large "acoustic signature" and limited patrol area, facilitating detection by vastly superior U.S. naval forces equipped for ASW (anti-submarine warfare).
16. Plymale, *op. cit.*, p. 246, Mr. Plymale is a former Deputy Director, Defense Research and Engineering, Strategic and Space Systems.
17. Ibid.
18. Kevin N. Lewis, "The Prompt and Delayed Effects of Nuclear War," *Scientific American*, July 1979, p. 39.
19. Interview with a former member of the Joint Strategic Target Planning Staff, April 1980.

20. Cited by Secretary of Defense James Schlesinger, *Annual Report of the Department of Defense,* Fiscal Year 1975, p. 35, hereafter cited as *FY 1975 Posture.*
21. *Civil Preparedness and Limited Nuclear War,* Hearings before the Joint Committee on Defense Production, 94th Congress, Second Session, April 28, 1976, USGPO, Washington, D.C. 1976, p. 57.
22. *U.S.-USSR Strategic Policies,* op. cit., p. 8.
23. *Civil Preparedness,* op. cit., pp. 55, 26, 56.
24. "The Future of Strategic Deterrence," *Survival* XXI,6 (November/December 1979) p. 271.
25. For a discussion of PD 59, see section titled "Extended Deterrence" in this study
26. *FY 1975 Posture,* p. 37; U.S.-USSR Strategic Policies, p. 9; FY 1975 Posture p. 38.
27. *FY 1975 Posture,* p. 38.
28. *Counterforce Attacks,* op cit., p. 37.
29. *US-USSR Strategic Policies,* p. 9.
30. *FY 1975 Posture,* p. 38.
31. *US-USSR Strategic Policies,* p. 13.
32. *FY 1975, Posture,* p. 28.
33. *FAS Public Interest Report,* February 1974.
34. *FY 1975 Posture,* p. 35.
35. Joint Committee on Defense Production, Congress of the United States, *Deterrence and Survival in the Nuclear Age* (The "Gaither Report" of 1957), U.S. Government Printing Office, Washington, 1976, pp. 1,3.

    See also Les Aspin, "Debate Over U.S. Strategic Forecasts: A Mixed Record," *Strategic Review,* VIII, 3 (Summer 1980), William T. Lee, "Debate Over U.S. Strategic Forecasts: A Poor Record," Ibid.; Les Aspin, "A Rebuttal," Ibid. On other aspects of the Soviet threat see Fred Kaplan, *Dubious Spector: A Second Look at the 'Soviet Threat,'* Washington and Amsterdam, Transnational Institute, 1980, second edition, and Alan Wolfe, *The Rise and Fall of the 'Soviet Threat': Domestic Sources of the Cold War Consensus,* Washington, Institute for Policy Studies, 1980.

3.
Origins and Early History of the MX

The Air Force began thinking about a mobile ballistic missile as long ago as the late 1950s. At that time, strategic thinkers were beginning to consider seriously the possibility that America's nuclear forces were vulnerable to a Soviet first strike. The so-called missile gap became a major issue, first in the secret Gaither report (1957), and then publicly during the 1960 Presidential campaign.

It was also a period of intense interservice rivalry for control of strategic nuclear missions and budgets. The Navy was trumpeting the virtues of its "virtually invulnerable" Polaris submarine. Anxious not to be left behind, the Air Force unveiled a plan in June 1960 for 60 missile trains—five missiles on each train—to roll randomly around the nation's rail network so that the Russians could never pinpoint their targets.

Throughout the summer of 1960, the Air Force's "Project Big Star" tested the rail mobile concept. In December of that year, Secretary of the Air Force Dudley Sharpe approved plans for 30 trains with three missiles each as the first phase of the project. According to one recent account, "the Boeing Corporation immediately began designing the missile trains."[1] But December was also the month John Kennedy picked Robert McNamara as his Secretary of Defense. McNamara became publicly dubious about the "missile gap;" he told the Air Force he was "deferring" the development and deployment of missile trains.[2]

The Air Force immediately began casting about—unsuccessfully—for solutions to McNamara's objections to missile trains. These were, chiefly: insufficient command and control, the high risks of sabotage, collision, and fuel explosion, and nuclear spillage. As the Air Force explained to Congress 15 years later, the "random movement" as opposed to "multiple shelter" concept for land-based missiles was eliminated for two connected reasons: "Random deployment over a large portion of the United States [on trucks and trains] could create a severe public interface problem. Deployment of ground-based random mobile [missiles] in a relatively limited area, on the other hand, leaves the transporter vulnerable to a low-level attack."[3]

In 1963 the Air Force began studying the "Improved Capability Missile" — designated WS-120A — which had evolved by 1970 into a concept known as ICBM-X. Its size and guidance were first defined in 1967: it would be larger, with much greater throw-weight* than the Minuteman III then under development, and would carry more warheads. These warheads would be individually guided, and the new missile would have high performance, solid-fuel rocket motors with a guidance system capable of adjusting itself to the position of the missile. This last feature was considered essential for a mobile missile, which would be moved back and forth between vertical and horizontal positions. Through FY 1968, the Pentagon provided some $53 million for studies and technology development related to the new missile. By 1970 this total had risen to some $250 million; this figure, however, considerably understates the true amount spent on advanced ICBM technology during this period. Budget line items for Minuteman III and Advanced Ballistic Reentry Systems (ABRES) both included developments of direct relevance to an improved ICBM.[4]

In 1967 the Air Force came forward with a new concept for mobile land-based missiles which, it was claimed, had none of the "public interface problems" of the train idea or the vulnerabilities of a movable system confined to a limited area. Rather than constantly moving around on trucks or railcars, the missiles would be shifted periodically among a large number of silos strengthened to withstand nuclear explosions. It was a form of shell game; an enemy could locate the silos but would have to guess which ones contained the missiles.

During his final months as Secretary of Defense, McNamara decided to subject the Air Force's concept to open competition, inviting proposals from the other services in order to examine them all in what became known as the *Strat-X Study*. The *Strat-X* analysis killed the Air Force's proposed new shell-game system; it concluded that the Russians conceivably could develop sensors to detect which silos actually contained missiles.

The study considered the Navy's underwater long-range missile

---

* The maximum weight of the warheads, guidance unit, and penetration aids which can be delivered by a missile over a particular range and in a stated trajectory.

40   Origins and Early History of the MX

system (ULMS) and ship-launched missile system (SLMS), however, to be feasible concepts, and the Navy was instructed to continue working on them. When the Navy discovered it did not have enough money to pursue both developments, it shelved the SLMS project in favor of ULMS. This became the massive, extraordinarily expensive Trident submarine. In 1967 McNamara directed the Navy to begin development of a stellar inertial guidance system for the Poseidon missile, with the objective of improving the accuracy of the small yield (40kt) Poseidon warheads so that they would have some capability against hardened military targets.[5]

Its scheme postponed, the Air Force began to take another look at silo-basing. In June 1968 the journal *Space/Aeronautics* reported, "The new Minuteman III silos being planned are sized not only for existing missiles, but for larger missiles as well, so that each new system will have even more potential for growth." In 1969 the Air Force revealed that it had five advanced ICBM concepts under study: "Ranger," the rail or truck mobile ICBM; "Nemesis," an ICBM positioned deep underwater; "Vulcan," to be launched from superhardened silos 1,000 to 3,000 feet underground in abandoned brimstone mines; "Janus," a multi-purpose missile, named for the two-faced Roman god of doorways, which could serve as both an ICBM and an ABM; and WS-180, an Advanced Minuteman.[6]

In June 1970 USAF planners made it known that they wanted to have "the capability of striking targets at ICBM ranges with a circular error probability as low as 600 feet in a five-mile-an-hour prevailing wind at reentry. Target date for such a capability is in the post-1975 period." Fearful that, in the words of *Aviation Week*, "any approval for ULMS might strip it of its prized ICBM responsibility," the Air Force floated the concept of a "flying submarine" as a possible counter. Characterized as a "long-range air-to-surface strategic missile system," the concept envisioned the use of a Lockheed C-5A heavy transport airplane to carry and launch 10 to 12 missiles with a range of 5,500 miles.[7] Thus was born the "air mobile" concept, which drifted in and out of favor for the next decade, ultimately losing out, in the summer of 1979, to a horizontal variation* of the original shell-game concept rejected by the Strat-X team.

In the early seventies, however, Minuteman vulnerability was still regarded as a relatively long-term threat. A more immediate threat to the land-based ICBM came not from the Russians but from the grand designs of the U.S. Navy. The Navy's proposed ULMS system, observed *Aviation Week* in July of 1970, "poses a potential threat to the Air Force's present monopoly on the ICBM arsenal, a fact of which USAF is well aware. But according to independent Pentagon and industry

---

*The vertical plan called for the missiles to be housed upright in silos; they would be easy to launch but difficult to move in and out of the silos. In the horizontal plan, the missiles could be moved more quickly from shelter to shelter.

observers, including some within the Air Force, that service's planners and those of its contractors have been unable to produce a tenable solution for deployment of a mobile land-based ICBM."[8]

The Navy, on the other hand, had some persuasive arguments in favor of moving the bulk of U.S. long-range missiles to sea. Even assuming sudden dramatic advances in Soviet anti-submarine warfare (ASW) capabilities—not a very likely development—the survival time of ULMS would be measured in hours or days instead of minutes.

In addition, a shift to a sea-based deterrent would lessen the possibility of damage to the United States in a counterforce exchange. The 6,000-mile range ULMS, the Navy argued, would create a virtually insoluble problem of submarine detection for the Russians, increasing at least tenfold the area that would have to be searched to locate the submarine. Not only would ULMS have a greatly expanded area from which to launch attacks, but it could attack from virtually every direction. Navy officials pointedly observed that Minuteman could be launched only "through a small pie-shaped sector across the top of the world."[9]

Moving the missiles to sea, the Navy contended, would also help stabilize a crisis: a surprise attack upon the United States would then result in no military advantage, thus eliminating whatever incentives there might be for such an event.

The attacker would be confronted with the prospect of devastating retaliation from a large, relatively invulnerable force; such a deployment would emphasize that the United States does not need to resort to a first-strike or a launch-under-attack doctrine to ensure its own security.

The Navy's justification for ULMS (renamed Trident in 1971) was not without contradictons, however. The admirals simultaneously argued: (1) the Poseidon/Polaris force was invulnerable; (2) Trident was needed because it was quieter and therefore less detectable; (3) the Trident must be made capable of higher speeds—producing more noise—in order to escape from enemy forces after it was detected; and (4) higher speeds required a larger reactor, which in turn required a larger submarine, increasing magnetic and acoustic signatures.

There was an obvious solution to all these difficulties, one which would obviate the necessity for the Trident submarine altogether: if more powerful fuel were used in the Poseidon missile, the missile's range would be increased, widening the patrol area available to U.S. submarines. Nevertheless, the military planners considered that the increase in the percentage of the U.S. strategic arsenal based at sea resulting from the Trident program would be a prudent hedge against the potential vulnerability of the land-based leg of the Triad in the 1980s. The Trident program received its first large-scale funding in 1973. The following year the Air Force began advanced development of the MX, explaining that a heavier throw-weight, more accurate, potentially mobile ICBM, was needed to offset possible Minuteman vulnerability in the 1980s.

It should be noted that only the last of those characteristics—mobility

— was required in response to the vulnerability problem. Similarly, an extended-range missile was all that was required to increase dramatically the survivability of the submarine force. In both cases, larger, more expensive, and theoretically more capable systems were proposed; their characteristics bore little intrinsic relation to the nature of the anticipated threat.

With an eye to the Navy's burgeoning Trident program, the Air Force during the early seventies toned down its earlier emphasis on silo vulnerability and began talking instead about Minuteman's enduring capability. The Soviet counter-silo threat receded as rapidly as it had been conjured up. In January 1973 the USAF's Deputy Chief of Staff for Research and Development, General Otto J. Glasser, remarked in an interview that there was no specific timetable for completing the next round of MX studies because "it isn't at all clear that we can reasonably credit the Soviets with any near-term capability that could wipe out our ICBM force as a strategic entity." Air Force calculations indicated, the General said, that "the task of laying on a precise attack with high confidence of success may be as difficult, or more difficult, than solving the ASW problem."

The problem of a successful attack against the entire force, General Glasser observed, "appears insurmountable from the Soviet point of view. Everything that can be reasonably extrapolated from present Soviet capabilities confirms that, no matter how we set the scenario, a sufficient number of Minuteman missiles can be expected to survive to carry out the system's assigned assured-destruction role."

This did not mean that an even more survivable system would not be needed at some future date. It was "obvious" to most Air Force planners, said General Glasser, "that there is nothing more mobile than an aircraft, and that no mobile system shows greater operational and cost-effective advantages than an air-mobile strategic system."

If airborne mobile systems had not been emphasized in the past, Glasser remarked, "then we must attribute this to the only defect in Air Force thinking that we might be guilty of — our concern about cost, and therefore, the desire to incrementally and inexpensively improve what we have, rather than go after brand-new, completely innovative systems such as the Navy's Trident program."[10]

But in fact the Air Force was doing both. There was nothing incremental or inexpensive about the B-1 bomber and cruise missile programs, and the list of incremental improvements to Minuteman is impressive. Beginnning in the early 1970s, the Air Force began deploying a new generation of warheads and guidance systems that gave 550 Minuteman III missiles greater accuracy, and in some instances more explosive power as well. Between 1980 and 1983, the Mark 12 warhead on 300 Minuteman III missiles will be replaced by the more powerful Mark 12-A, which is also the warhead planned for the MX, increasing the hard-target kill probability of each Minuteman III warhead from 55 per cent to 70 per cent. By the mid-1980s, predicts House Armed Services Committee member Les Aspin, guidance "will probably be further improved through further testing and refinement to reach its theoretical peak of accuracy — about 490 feet CEP.* With this improvement, those Minuteman IIIs with the older MK-12 warheads will have a 70 per cent chance of destroying Soviet missile silos in a single shot; those with the newer, more powerful MK12-A warheads will have an 83 per cent chance."[11]

Another "incremental" improvement to Minuteman completed during the 1970s was the command data buffer system, an electronic system linking the Minuteman III launch-control centers to the individual silos. Previously, each missile was programmed for a very limited number of targets. To change the tape in the missile's computer, SAC headquarters in Omaha had to produce a new targeting tape and a SAC retargeting team had to visit each silo and insert the new tape by hand in the missile computer, "a time-consuming and highly cumbersome process," according to one veteran Air Force observer, "especially during or following a nuclear attack."

Command data buffer overcomes this problem by linking all 550 Minuteman III launch control centers to SAC headquarters and to their individual silos through an electronic system that is secure, hardened against electromagnetic pulse, blast, and shock, and reportedly, "operable on the minimum amount of power that can be expected to be available during and after a nuclear attack."

According to General Glasser, after a nuclear attack the system allows the Air Force "to survey what's left of our own force and to retarget and reassign with the speed of light. As the planners revise SIOP on a continuous basis, they will be able to modify the targeting of the force to match these changes in SIOP."[12]

And finally, the Air Force pushed through a Silo Upgrade program, increasing the blast resistance of most Minuteman silos from 300 to about 2,000 pounds per square inch at a cost of some $1.4 billion.[13]

While all this Minuteman activity was underway, the Air Force took advantage of the inherently loose statutory authority surrounding such line items as "advanced ICBM technology" and "advanced ballistic reentry systems (ABRES)" to begin development of the MX. In May 1974, for example, while the first request for an MX advanced development program was still pending before House and Senate Armed Services Committees, the Air Force announced two contract awards — one for $19.6 million to Aerojet Solid Propulsion Co., a subsidiary of General Tire and Rubber, for "the design and fabrication of one second-stage propulsion system that could be applicable to USAF's proposed MX advanced intercontinental ballistic missile," and the other for $4.6 million to United Technologies to develop and demonstrate a "high deflection, low

---

*A measure of missile accuracy. It is the radius of a circle around a target in which 50 per cent of the missiles aimed at that target will land.

torque, moveable nozzle system for the MX booster stage employing advanced carbon composite material."[14] The contract awards were legitimate, the Air Force claimed, because the funds to be expended had already been appropriated by Congress as part of the continuing development of Minuteman. Contracts were awarded for MX work throughout the mid-1970s on these budget lines.

In October 1974, the Air Force demonstrated the feasibility of the air-mobile concept by successfully dropping (and briefly igniting) a Minuteman I missile from a Lockheed C-5A.[15] But in February 1975 Secretary Schlesinger rejected the air-mobile concept in favor of further exploration of land-based approaches, in particular the multiple protective shelter and the buried trench.[16]

In May 1976 the Ford Administration submitted a budget amendment requesting $317 million for an additional 60 Minuteman III missiles. The Senate Armed Services Committee noted that this request implied "a higher confidence by the Defense Department in the continued survivability of our silo-based ICBMs," and cut the $84 million FY 1977 MX request by $32.4 million. The committee reported that this action was "designed to insure that the MX does not go into full-scale development before the Defense Department has resolved contradictions in its testimony about future ICBM survivability and has demonstrated a clear need for a particular mobile-basing alternative."[17]

When asked in the course of a Senate Armed Services subcommittee review of the MX program whether there was "a discrete number of missiles which it is generally agreed represents the minimum number of surviving missiles that must be addressed," the Pentagon's Deputy Director for Strategic and Space Systems, John B. Walsh, replied:

> That number has not been explicitly addressed. . . . It isn't until we start production that we have to make a decision. The later we can make the decision the better off we are because [of] the better knowledge we will have of the precise target structure that has to be addressed by these missiles.[18]

Walsh noted that the Pentagon's projections of the number of Minuteman missiles expected to survive a Soviet counterforce attack in 1985 varied across a wide range:

> This spread reflects our inability to precisely surmise Soviet capabilities and is characteristic, not only of 1976 and 1985, but of the intervening years as well. Therefore, whether Minuteman remains a viable, survivable force depends upon one's definition of these terms, the actual threat which emerges, and the ability of the Soviets to achieve the precise time-on-target control required for multiple RV [re-entry vehicle] attacks.[19]

Walsh observed that Department of Defense computations of Minuteman survivability were "based on the unsophisticated and unlikely assumption that a Soviet planner might elect to concentrate his attack on U.S. silos, while ignoring the more important requirement of attacking all legs of the Triad to reduce their mutually reinforcing capability of retaliation against any form of attack."[20]

Walter LaBerge, then Assistant Secretary of the Air Force for Research and Development, reiterated the point. While expressing his belief that "we need to have protection against the possibility that the silos become vulnerable," LaBerge testified:

> I think there are good reasons to believe, however, that we can use this missile in the economical silo-basing mode for quite some time. . . . it depends in its survivability as shown here on the Triad relationships; namely, that one must understand . . . that the other portions of the Triad are available, and therefore, a direct attack on the land-based system will draw support for the other two pieces.[21]

LaBerge's testimony was inherently contradictory. If Minuteman depends for its survival on the retaliatory capability of the other two legs of the Triad (i.e., on not being attacked), then concern over what might happen to Minuteman silos in the event of an attack is irrelevant. However, "even under the most pessimistic assumptions," the Department noted in a written response to the committee, "substantial numbers of missiles would survive."[22]

When asked, "Is the concern for the increasing vulnerability of Minuteman the primary and deciding factor pacing the MX program?" the Department replied:

> No. While an attack on Minuteman with projected Soviet ICBM capabilities in the mid-1980s could decrease Minuteman silo survivability, it is not the primary factor pacing MX development. Hardening and dispersal of Soviet economic recovery targets, the existing shortage of high-quality weapons, and a near [deleted] increase in "superhard" Soviet targets between now and the mid-1980s have been the deciding factors in the pace of the MX development program.[23]

The contradictions did not end here, however. Since Minuteman vulnerability was not the key determinant of MX development, the subcommittee inquired, "How much of a factor, in the motivation of the MX program, is the need to show some form of ICBM reaction to the new Soviet ICBM programs?" The Department of Defense provided the following response:

> The pace, character, and scope of Soviet strategic programs influence our own strategic programs to some extent, but these are not the primary considerations in establishing our requirements. . . . The motivation for the MX program then is threefold: (1) to respond to expanded Soviet strategic capabilities, considering the contribution each of our systems makes toward meeting our retaliatory requirements; (2) to advance technology and incorporate these advances into deployed systems thereby improving total force effectiveness; and (3) to accomplish an orderly modernization of our strategic forces by replacing older ICBMs with newer, more capable

systems.[24]

To the extent that these requirements are considered to be independent of one another, then requirements (2) and (3) would continue to provide a justification for the MX regardless of Minuteman's survivability or the scale and pace of Soviet ICBM programs. Publicly, the decision to proceed with the MX was tied to Soviet restraint in building up its new ICBM forces. Within the Pentagon, however, the MX missile was non-negotiable. "We prefer to deploy the MX in existing silos," the Defense Department informed the Senate Armed Services Committee in March, 1976. "If the Soviet threat develops in a way which could prejudice silo survivability, then we can proceed to deploy ICBMs in an alternate basing mode."[25]

"SALT II ceilings would not prevent stimulation of MX deployment," the Air Force testified, "because they would not inhibit the Soviets from efforts to achieve technological improvements such as accuracy and more MIRVs per booster."

The ceilings would only restrict the gross number of missile launchers and heavy bombers. We could detect Soviet efforts to achieve greater capability and take appropriate action. Conversely, we could also detect that they were not seeking these improvements, either because they were trying to strengthen detente, or because they were putting their development efforts in other fields. Either way, we could make an appropriate response.[26]

Lest anyone conclude, on the basis of the above statement, that the MX program depended on what the Russians might or might not do, the Department of Defense hastened to add that "the need for MX remains, *regardless of further Soviet effort,* in order to counter Soviet initiatives which are now ongoing and thus to insure our deterrent capacity.[27] (emphasis added)

The "ongoing initiatives" which the Department of Defense identified as sufficient justification for the MX were "increased numbers, hardness, and dispersal of Soviet economic . . . targets," and a projected increase in "super-hard" "time-sensitive" targets between "now and the mid-1980s." In other words, regardless of the capability of the missiles the Soviets decided to deploy in their superhardened silos, the Air Force needed a silo-busting missile. This requirement was viewed as the result of Soviet military and industrial hardening programs and the shift in U.S. nuclear weapons employment policy toward the targeting of many individual "economic recovery resources." These developments produced, according to SAC Commander Richard Ellis, "an annual average increase in the target list of approximately 10 per cent over the past several years."[28] Thus the MX was conceived in order to threaten Soviet retaliatory capability as well as to remedy "the existing shortage of high-quality weapons" needed to accommodate the shift in doctrine.

Footnotes

1. "The Shell Game Strategy," by Robert Schrum, reprinted from *Politics Today* (undated) in the *Congressional Record*, July 9, 1979, S.8944.
2. Ibid.
3. "Committee on Armed Service, United States Senate, FY 1977 Authorization, *Hearings, Part 11*. p. 6403 (USGPO, Washington, D.C., 1976).
4. *Aviation Week and Space Technology*, June 22, 1970, p. 222; *Space/Aeronautics*, January 1970, p. 69.
   Space/Aeronautics, January 1968, p. 103.
5. *Space/Aeronautics*, June 1970, p. 26.
   Committee on Armed Services, United States Senate, FY 1980 Authorization, *Hearings, Part 1*, p. 358.
6. *The Superwarriors*, by James W. Canan, New York, 1975, p. 162; *Space/Aeronautics*, January 1970, p. 69.
7. *Aviation Week*, June 22, 1970, p. 22.
8. *Aviation Week*, July 20, 1970.
9. *Armed Forces Journal*, February 14, 1970; on the origins of ULMS, see Norman Polmar and Captain D.A. Paolucci, USN (Ret.), "Sea-Based 'Strategic' Weapons for the 1980s and Beyond," *U.S. Naval Institute Proceedings*, May 1978.
10. Edgar Ulsamer, "MX: The Missile System for the Year 2000," *Air Force Magazine*, March 1973, reprinted in the *Congressional Record*, March 12, 1973, p. E1464.
11. Les Aspin, "Judge Not By Numbers Alone," *Bulletin of the Atomic Scientists*, June 1980, p. 29. Aspin's calculations are based on a figure of 2500 psi for Soviet silo hardness.
12. Ulsamer, op. cit.
13. Aspin, op. cit, p. 30.
14. *Aviation Week and Space Technology*, May 6, 1974, p. 20.
15. DMS Inc., *Missiles/Spacecraft,* Advanced ICBM, 1978, p. 3.
16. *Aviation Week,* February 17, 1975; after the great oil price rise of 1973–74, the air-mobile concept with a certain percentage of the missiles on airborne alert became prohibitively expensive.
17. *Aviation Week*, May 31, 1976, p. 13.
18. Senate Armed Services Committee *FY 1977 Authorization Hearings, Part 11, Research and Development*, p. 6266.
19. Ibid., p. 6518.
20. Ibid., p. 6518.
21. Ibid., p. 6273.
22. Ibid., p. 6527.
23. Ibid., p. 6520.
24. Ibid.
25. Ibid., pp. 6523, 6521.
26. Ibid., p. 6522.
27. Ibid.
28. Senate Armed Services Committee, *FY 1980 Authorization Hearings*, p. 397.

4.
The Pentagon's Case for the MX—An Evaluation

The Pentagon bases its case for the MX on four arguments:
(1) It argues that the Minuteman ICBM force will soon be vulnerable to a Soviet surprise attack. The MX will deter such an attack by confronting the Soviet Union with a new land-based system capable of absorbing the attack and launching a retaliatory second strike against super hardened Soviet military targets.
(2) The land-based MX is purportedly needed as a hedge against the possible vulnerability of the remaining two legs of the strategic Triad: bombers and cruise missiles carried by bombers; and ballistic missile submarines.
(3) The MX, argues the Pentagon, will offset recent Soviet expansion in strategic forces, in order to maintain "essential equivalence" between the two superpowers. Even if the MX does not physically achieve this aim, the mere undertaking of such a massive project will convince the Russians of our serious intentions and prevent further Soviet adventurism.
(4) Finally, the MX is seen as extending the concept of nuclear deterrence. The MX, it is argued, will give the United States more flexibility in deploying and targeting its strategic forces and thereby confront the Soviet Union with a variety of possible responses should the Soviets attempt some military action against American interests short of an all-out attack on the United States itself.

We consider each of these four arguments below, examining both its failures of logic and its inconsistencies with other past and present justifications for expansion of U.S. strategic nuclear forces.

Minuteman Vulnerability and Deterrence of a Massive Surprise Attack

According to the Department of Defense, within a year or two (of 1980) we can expect the Soviets to have enough reliable, accurate and well-armed ICBMs to threaten most of our Minuteman and Titan silos using only a relatively small proportion of their ICBM force.[1]

As numerous expert observers — including Defense Secretary Brown — have noted, however, an increase in Soviet "hard target Kill capability" is not synonymous with the ability to conduct a coordinated massive attack on the entire U.S. ICBM force. "The Soviets would face great uncertainties," wrote Secretary Brown, "in assessing whether they would have the capability we fear — and still greater uncertainties as to its military or political utility."[2] A partial listing of these uncertainties includes the following:

(1) **Accuracy** The Russians could not be sure that results achieved with test missiles over test ranges could be duplicated by operational missiles on trajectories never traversed before. Accuracy is usually measured by "Circular Error Probable" (CEP), defined as the radius of the circle around the target within which half of the warheads are expected to fall. A small CEP — 450 feet is projected for MX, 600 feet for the large Soviet ICBMs — describes a highly accurate warhead.

But the size of the circle might remain the same while the center drifts, so that the warheads form a tight circle around a false target. This is a problem known as bias. Long-term Pentagon consultant Richard Garwin feels that bias is a serious problem which severely limits the accuracy of ICBMs.

In every ICBM you have an inertial package. Accelerometers and gyros and things like that are mounted in your missile. You've got to fire your missiles from operational silos to points in your enemy's country. . . . You've never done this before and you have to base your calculation on test shots. . . . Judging from how far each test shot falls from the target, you adjust your accelerometer or your gyro, to compensate for the inaccuracy, until in the end your test shots are landing within the prescribed area. But every time you fire a new-model missile over the same range or the same missile over a slightly different range, the bias changes. Sometimes it is greater, sometimes it is smaller, but it has never been calculated beforehand.

So you have to go back to readjusting the gyros and so on to try and eliminate the novel bias. But if we were firing operationally, both we and the Russians would be firing over a new range in an untried direction . . . and a whole new set of random factors would come into play—anomalies in the earth's gravitational field, varying densities of the upper atmosphere or unknown wind velocities. They may adjust and readjust in testing and eventually they might feel sure that they have eliminated the bias. But they can never be absolutely certain. We certainly cannot be, and . . . there is no reason to suspect that [the Soviets] are any more successful than we are at dealing with the problem. If you cannot be sure that you would be able to hit the enemy's silos, then there would be no point in even trying—because the idea is that one side could wipe out the other's missiles before they are launched in a first strike.[3]

(2) **Reliability** The Soviets could not be sure what percentage of their total force would fail to launch, fail during boost phase, or fail to detonate upon reaching the intended targets.

(3) **Timing and Fratricide* Effects** The difficulties in succeeding in a multiple-warhead attack on silos are well-known. Warheads are extremely sensitive to debris in the air, changes in wind currents, and shock waves; they can be destroyed or knocked off-course by such phenomena. Nuclear explosions would produce debris and shock waves that would travel rapidly between silos and to substantial heights. The Russians would have to time their attack with tremendous precision; their warheads would either have to strike all the targets in a silo complex almost simultaneously or else sweep through the complex in a manner allowing them to stay ahead of the growing nuclear clouds; furthermore, they would have to do so for each U.S. silo complex. Given the dispersion of missile bases in the Soviet Union, such timing is probably impossible to achieve. And since a massive attack can never be tested, the Russians are likely to be very doubtful that they could do it, and for that reason alone they would be extremely reluctant to attempt it.[4]

Additional missiles to compensate for rocket failures must be reprogrammed very quickly, in view of the nuclear effects noted above, a task that requires a sophisticated retargeting capacity which the Russians reportedly do not have and are unlikely soon to acquire. Reprogramming cannot overcome failure to deploy the RVs properly, or failure of the RVs themselves. Even detecting such failures requires a sophisticated satellite assessment system which the Soviet Union does not possess, and it would take half an hour or more from launch time until the detection of failure, too long to prevent a retaliatory launch of the surviving missiles.

It has been suggested that the Russians might overcome this deficiency by targeting a second round of warheads for reliability only. In other words, if the first weapon fails to arrive or detonate at the target, a second warhead, timed to arrive within a few seconds of the first, will destroy the target. If the first warhead functions, the second will be destroyed. This

---

*"Fratricide" occurs when the explosion of one warhead destroys or damages other warheads before they reach their targets. The exploding warhead destroys its "brothers."

tactic, while theoretically possible, is costly in warheads, requiring more than one Soviet warhead to destroy one Minuteman or Titan warhead, thereby undercutting whatever "rational" basis might exist for the attack. Furthermore, this scenario assumes that the first warhead, while eliminating the second RV, actually destroys the target. Since actual performance diverges from expectations, this may not occur, making the outcome of such an attack highly uncertain.

(4) **Launch on Warning** The DoD contends that if nothing is done to counter Minuteman's vulnerability, the United States will be forced to launch nuclear weapons on warning of an attack, creating a hair-trigger atmosphere at a time of severe international tension. According to Secretary Brown's FY 1981 Annual Report:

> ... It is one thing (and by no means an easy one) to have an operational capability to launch nuclear weapons, without warning or under attack. It is quite another matter to be obliged to launch them in order to avoid losing them to the attacker. The latter posture, with its vulnerability to accidents and false alarms and still more with its premium on hasty action rather than deliberate control, is unacceptable to the United States. In a given situation, the President may decide to order a launch, with or without warning. The duty of the Department of Defense is to plan and procure systems so that the force can ride out an attack if that is what the situation calls for, and what the President directs. It is not our duty to force his hand.[5]

As Undersecretary of Defense for Research and Engineering, William J. Perry testified in 1980, "We always have had an LUA (Launch-Under-Attack) option for the President." In fact, Undersecretary Perry noted that "recent changes have, we believe, removed significant impediments to exercising that option."[6] So the issue is not the possible resort to launch-under-attack *per se*, but whether, in the absence of the MX, the President would be obliged to use it.

The MX system is being designed to assure the survival of 1,000 warheads after a surprise attack in the 1990s and beyond. The survival of these 1,000 warheads, out of a projected 1990s inventory of 12,000 to 15,000 nuclear warheads available for retaliation, would not exactly "oblige" the President to launch on warning of an attack. Furthermore, MX would only survive the first round. After absorbing an initial large-scale attack, enough shelters would be destroyed to permit the Russians to concentrate their second strike on those that remained, requiring the MX to be launched under attack to avoid destruction in its shelters.[7]

With respect to Minuteman, just as in the case of the MX, if even the slightest doubt persisted about the nature of the incoming attack, the President would not be obliged to launch, having at his disposal thousands of other nuclear weapons on board submarines and bombers equipped with cruise missiles. The fact is, however, that the massive scale of an attack aimed at destroying Minuteman—or for that matter

MX—would offer fairly unambiguous warning, or else be preceded by a preliminary "blinding" attack on our early warning satellites. It is highly unlikely that the latter attack would itself escape detection by the various U.S. warning systems.* This is not to argue in favor of reliance on a launch-under-attack system, but only to note that the vulnerability of Minuteman does not compel reliance on such a system any more than the MX would preclude its use. Similarly, it is not necessary to replace Minuteman with the MX if the purpose is to avoid adopting an unstable launch-on-warning posture.

(5) **U.S. Retaliation** A more powerful inhibiting factor than any of the uncertainties cited above is the uncertainty surrounding the prospective U.S. response to a massive Soviet counterforce attack.

Even under pessimistic assumptions, such as 90 per cent of the present land-based force being destroyed in a Soviet first strike, 105 missiles would survive carrying 215 warheads, including 170 kt, 340 kt, 1.2 mt and 9 mt sizes.** The 340 kt Mark 12A on the Minuteman III has counterforce capability. Even this comparatively small force constitutes a powerful deterrent; the smallest of these weapons is 13 times the size of the bomb that destroyed Hiroshima. What makes this arsenal even more potent is that a large submarine and bomber force would also survive and be available for a second strike aimed at a variety of Soviet targets.[8]

By 1985, when Minuteman is presumed by some observers to be very vulnerable, the U.S. submarine fleet will have on the order of 6,000 deliverable warheads. Assuming that the 60 per cent of the force on patrol survives a surprise attack (this percentage would increase with warning), a force of about 3,600 warheads would be available for second-strike retaliation from the sea-based deterrent. Assuming a very generous (to the Russians) 90 per cent probability of kill in a one-on-one attack on U.S. ICBMs leaves a force of 215 warheads. A 25 per cent bomber alert rate (this is generally considered a peacetime minimum) would guarantee the survival of roughly 500 out of the projected force of some 2,000 air-launched cruise missiles in service by 1985. Adding these already programmed surviving forces together yields a long-range missile force of 4315 warheads, hardly a negligible number, to execute the full range of limited response items.[9]

---

*These include the ground-based Space Detection and Tracking System (SPADATS), now in the process of being supplemented by the construction of the global five-site Ground-based Electro-Optical Deep Space Surveillance (GEODSS) system; the Ballistic Missile Early Warning System (BMEWS), currently being upgraded; and other ground-based radar. See *The FY 1981 Department of Defense Program for Research, Development, and Acquisition,* Statement by the Honorable William J. Perry, Undersecretary of Defense for Research and Engineering, 96th Congress, 2nd Session, 1980.

**A kiloton is a measure of the yield of a nuclear weapon, equivalent to 1,000 tons of TNT. A megaton is equivalent to a million tons of TNT.

During the 1980s, the Trident missile force will be upgraded. Trident I accuracy is already in the process of being improved from the present 1,500 ft. CEP to 750 ft., giving each of the missiles' 100 kt warheads a 31 per cent chance of destroying hardened Soviet silos. This is, in effect, the program shelved by the Nixon Administration during the period of the SALT I negotiations because it was deemed incompatible with the goals of crisis stability and arms control. The Defense Department rejected a similar accuracy improvement program for Minuteman in 1971, noting, "It is the position of the United States *not* to develop a weapon system whose deployment could reasonably be construed by the Soviets as having a first-strike capability. Such a deployment might provide an incentive for the Soviets to strike first."[10] The Trident II is still in research and development. The Navy has let it be known, however, that it plans to speed development of the Trident II to make it a hard-target killer, and to make it available by 1989, when full deployment of the MX is projected. The Navy expects to develop a submarine-launched missile that can "achieve the same accuracy now possible only with fixed land-based ICBMs launched from presurveyed sites."[11]

In the mid- and late-1980s, the increased accuracy of submarine-launched missiles will enable any U.S. SLBM, including the relatively small Poseidon with its single 40 kt warhead,* to have the capacity to destroy some hardened targets. A more powerful, more accurate and more secure replacement for Minuteman cannot be justified, therefore, on the grounds that the loss of Minuteman would eliminate U.S. options to attack Soviet hardened targets. It would not, and if the present modernization of the submarine force continues or is accelerated, then U.S. options will increase even if nothing is done about Minuteman.

Similar reservations were stated by Secretary Brown:

. . . An attack intended to destroy U.S. silos could kill at least several million Americans and would leave untouched at least the alert bombers and at-sea SSBNs with thousands of warheads. The Soviets might — and should — fear that, in response, we would retaliate with a massive attack on Soviet cities and industry. The alleged 'irrationality' of such a response from a detached perspective would be no consolation in retrospect and would not necessarily be in advance an absolute guarantee that we would not so respond. In any event, any Soviet planner, considering U.S. options, would know that, besides massive retaliation, the surviving U.S. forces would also be capable of a broad variety of controlled responses aimed at military and civilian targets and proportioned to

---

*This could be obtained in theory, through the use of the NAVSTAR satellite, Global Positioning System (GPS) or Ground Beacon System (GBS), possibly in conjunction with precision-guided Maneuvering Re-entry Vehicles (MARVS).

the scale and significance of the provocation . . . Indeed, with ALCMs deployed on the surviving alert strategic bombers, we would still have a very substantial capacity to destroy remaining Soviet silos, though with some hours of delay.

In short, the vulnerability of MINUTEMAN is a problem, but even if we did nothing about it, it would not be synonymous with the vulnerability of the United States, or even of the strategic deterrent. It would not mean that we could not satisfy our strategic objectives. It would not by itself even mean that the United States would lack a survivable hard-target kill capability or that we would necessarily be in a worse post-exchange position in terms of numbers of weapons, payload, or destructiveness.[12]

Footnotes

1. Department of Defense *Annual Report,* FY 1981, p. 85.
2. Department of Defense *Annual Report,* FY 1979, p. 63.
3. "The Myth of ICBM Vulnerability," *Defense Week,* August 11, 1980, pp. 4–6.
4. For a convenient summary of the operational and physical factors affecting a counterforce attack, see Lt. Col. Joseph J. McGlinchey, USAF and Dr. Jakob W. Seelig, "Why ICBMs Can Survive," *Air Force Magazine,* September 1974, p. 82.
5. Department of Defense *Annual Report,* FY 1981, p. 88.
6. Senate Armed Services Committee Authorization Hearings, FY 1981, Part 2, p. 6361.
7. Interview with Seymour Zeiberg, Deputy for Space and Strategic Systems, Department of Defense, April 1980.
8. Department of Defense *Annual Report,* FY 1980, p. 117; Daniel Seligman, "Our ICBMs Are In Danger," *Fortune,* July 2, 1979, p. 52; 1985 force level projections from "Statement of Paul Nitze, Annex II, U.S.-USSR Systems," in *Military Implications of the Treaty on the Limitation of Strategic Offensive Arms and Protocol Thereto (SALT II Treaty)* Hearings before the Senate Armed Services Committee, Part 3, October 1979, pp. 896-899.
9. Ibid.
10. quoted in *FAS Public Interest Report,* February 1974.
11. *Aviation Week and Space Technology,* June 16, 1980, p. 91.
12. Department of Defense *Annual Report,* FY 1979, pp. 63–64.

5.
Hedging the Triad

A second line of argument used to justify the MX is that a survivable land-based ICBM is essential to the preservation of a Triad of strategic forces, and that the Triad, in turn, is essential for maintaining deterrence of nuclear war. Since 1960, preserving the Triad has meant maintaining a diversified force of land-based ICBMs, intercontinental bombers, and submarine-based missiles.

The MX is seen as needed to hedge against weaknesses in the submarine and bomber forces that might crop up in the 1990s and beyond. Many experts have questioned the existence of such serious, potential problems; even if they exist, there are a variety of far less expensive solutions that are available now or could be available in the next decade. Moreover, the argument that SLBMs will be vulnerable to Soviet attack in the future appears to have a partisan flavor, proposed passionately by Air Force supporters and opposed equally vehemently by the Navy and most independent observers.

The Triad

The current distribution of strategic nuclear forces among bombers, submarine-launched ballistic missiles (SLBMs), and ICBMs is as much an accident of interservice rivalry and defense budget politics as it is the fulfillment of some conscious design for the forces necessary to deter nuclear war. If the Navy, for example, had gone ahead in the mid-sixties with the deployment of ballistic missiles carried on surface ships, fitted with flotation collars, and simply launched from the water, we might have had a Quadrad. Or if carrier and land-based aircraft that are capable of carrying nuclear weapons and are based in Europe, the Middle East, or Asia, are included in the strategic forces (they are included in the SIOP), as the Soviets have frequently demanded, then the United States already has a Quadrad. The deployment of cruise missiles on submarines and surface ships would make this a Pentad. The impending deployment of Air-Launched Cruise Missiles (ALCMs) gives the air leg two branches: one that requires bombers to penetrate enemy air space in order to drop bombs; the other allowing aircraft to launch cruise missiles from afar. The point of raising these possible combinations of forces is only to emphasize that the current Triad is primarily an historical rather than a logical concept.

If the Triad has any origins apart from the bitter interservice battles over strategic weaponry in the late 1950s and pressure from Congressional and contractor interests, they can be traced to a need to diversify in case ICBMs and SLBMs should fail. As Dr. Herbert York, a former director of Defense Research and Engineering, has observed, there would have been no reason for building a Triad if we could have assured ourselves in advance that any one of the systems would maintain its viability indefinitely.[1] In other words, given a sufficiently secure, reliable, and accurate delivery system, there is no logical reason why we could not maintain deterrence by fielding just one type of system, as we did with our bomber fleet during the 1945-55 decade.

What is important about the Triad is not the particular existing mix of weapons but rather the general principle of diversity, which provides a hedge against unforeseen technical failures as well as technological breakthroughs by the enemy. However, a triad of forces will not automatically be more reliable than a dyad or monad. It merely guarantees that any single failure will affect only a portion of the total force. While the probability of three simultaneous catastrophic failures might appear less than the probability of one or two such failures, such an outcome actually depends on the individual reliability of the weapons involved.

Thus, another way to increase the overall effectiveness of the strategic arsenal would be to reduce the probability of failure in one or more of the existing legs. Strengthening one of these might be less expensive and less destabilizing than adding new weapons or legs to the total force. For example, improvements already underway in the submarine and bomber force—the longer-range Trident I missile and the introduction of ACLMs—could compensate for Minuteman's vulnerability.

Similarly, to the extent that technological breakthroughs can be anticipated and compensated for, the need for a Triad of deployed forces is correspondingly diminished. If the Russians require—as does the United States—twelve years to develop and deploy a new system, this would leave ample time to develop responses before the alleged "'breakthrough" threatened the deterrent capability of U.S. forces.* There is no logical reason, for example, why the existing force of ballistic-missile submarines could not perform the nuclear deterrent function presently performed by the Triad. If further guarantees are required, then plans for both the cruise missile and a mobile ICBM could be continually updated, so that the missiles could immediately be put into production and deployed within five to seven years. At the same time, an anti-submarine warfare countermeasures program could continue. In view of the probable success of the latter, it is likely that the cruise missile and MX options would never have to be taken up. If a serious threat to the submarine force did arise, all that would be necessary to counter it would be the production of either cruise missiles or mobile ICBMs, and only enough of them to offset the anticipated degradation of the submarine force.

The position taken above requires the acceptance of one important and, in view of the awesome effects of nuclear weapons, not unreasonable assumption: that the number of nuclear weapons required for deterrence is finite and, as it happens, quite limited. Given the millions of casualties involved in an exchange of only a few hundred nuclear warheads, the present practice of tying the requirement for strategic forces to the growth of the Soviet economy and military would seem to be a gross exaggeration of what is necessary for deterrence. How can it be that 9,000 weapons**—the approximate number contained in the present SIOP—are required when it has been calculated that the equivalent of 400 one-megaton weapons would end the U.S.S.R's existence as a modern industrial nation?

The huge number is apparently derived from the planners' assumption that *each* leg of the Triad must be able to strike back effectively at the U.S.S.R. after a massive Soviet surprise attack. Even if one accepts the need for the diversity and technological hedging inherent in the notion of the Triad one need not accept the requirement that each leg of the Triad have a survivable assured destruction capability—indeed, there is no sound logical reason to do so.

In 1974 Secretary of Defense Schlesinger suggested "a switch away from what I will call the canonical logic of the Triad. . . . To some extent,

---

*Although this unforeseen breakthrough argument is very often invoked to justify the Triad, it is interesting to note that only twice in this century has technical surprise—the development of radar and the atomic bomb—conferred what most people would consider a "decisive" contribution toward the outcome of a conflict, and even here the evidence is mixed.

**Representing 1,434 surviving EMT under the most pessimistic assumption of a Soviet Surprise attack on U.S. forces on "day-to-day" alert.

I think the rationale of the Triad was a rationalization."² In his posture statement for FY 1975, Schlesinger noted that the Pentagon's purpose in continuing an appropriate mix of bombers, ICBMs and SLBMs "is not to provide an independent assured destruction capability in each element of the strategic forces, as some people have presumed."

> Rather, it is to achieve a sufficient degree of diversification in our forces to hedge against both foreseeable and unforeseeable risks, and to enable us to continue to make available to the President a reasonable range of strategic options. . . . By maintaining an appropriate mix of the three, however, we can maximize their collective strengths and minimize the effects of their individual weaknesses, thus ensuring that *the force as a whole is not inherently vulnerable to any one type of attack or any one type of defense.*³ (emphasis added)

This was not the view of the Carter Defense Department, judging by the very heavy emphasis that Undersecretary Perry and other defense spokesmen placed on the steady erosion of Minuteman's hypothetical post-attack retaliatory capability. The seemed to assume that this state of affairs would soon deprive the Minuteman force of all usefulness, or worse yet, convert it into a positive liability.

It must be noted that this view cannot logically co-exist with the Pentagon's favorite scenario of a Soviet surprise attack on the Minuteman force. For decades, U.S. and NATO nuclear doctrine has emphasized the "nuclear umbrella" concept of potential first-use of nuclear weapons. Naturally, it follows that if a nuclear weapon is to be used first, its deterrent value does not come only from its ability to survive an attack! In fact, one might argue the opposite — that a technically vulnerable nuclear weapon system which is nonetheless capable, as Minuteman is, of being launched under attack, is very likely to make a potential enemy even more cautious about doing anything which might lead U.S. authorities to believe their force was in jeopardy. As Secretary Brown observed during Congressional testimony in 1979, the relationship between increased survivability and deterrence is not as cut and dried as one might think:

> Certainly a survivable system, a system that can ride out attack, further reduces the incentive of the other side to strike at it. At the same time you have to recognize that you are paying for that extra dimension, and the knowledge that the U.S. might launch under attack also is a deterrence, a different kind of deterrent, and it is kind of hard to evaluate the two against each other. You might, for example, conclude that having a survivable system might encourage them to strike because they know we will not strike back so quickly, that we might think about it for awhile. It is this kind of speculation, and the speculative nature of this kind of examination, that makes it very hard to say how a nuclear war would go.⁴

IBM scientist R.L. Garwin went into more detail during testimony before the House Armed Services Committee in February 1979:

Some appear to believe that a vulnerable Minuteman force is to be avoided at all costs — that a vulnerable strategic system is worse than none at all. This ignores two important aspects of the strategic forces — the first being that each of the individual missiles, launching platforms, or forces is embedded in a complex of others, so that a vulnerable Minuteman force (or a Poseidon or Trident submarine vulnerable in a U.S. port) is not *the* United States retaliatory force and therefore does not impel preemptive attack.

The second point ignored is that many believe there are uses for strategic offensive forces besides retaliation to destruction of the nation. Such a use is, in fact, put forward in the scenario by which the Soviet Union destroys the vast majority of U.S. silo-based ICBM forces without being able to destroy the aircraft or the SLBM forces and without destroying intentionally the U.S. population and industry. For this purpose, unless the U.S. struck first, it would make no difference whether the missiles used by the Soviet Union were in a vulnerable or an invulnerable basing structure. Thus, even without "launch-under-attack" . . . a vulnerable force could have a useful role to play, especially at levels of engagement well below those corresponding to all out nuclear exchange (and dubbed by their supporters "flexible response").[5]

Will the Oceans Be Transparent?

Senior Department of Defense officials are well aware of the above arguments. Their statements about needing MX to preserve the land-based leg of the Triad have shifted in the direction of arguments about the possible decline in the future deterrent value of the *other* legs of the Triad.

The Defense Department's annual report for FY1981 notes that:
. . . We can live temporarily with the vulnerability of one Triad leg, so long as the other two are in good working order. But we would be ill-advised to accept that vulnerability as a permanent condition in light of what could happen to the survivability of the other two legs. Indeed, right now, considering the momentum behind current Soviet strategic programs, it is not unreasonable to assume in such a case:
— the Soviets would be tempted to greatly expand their efforts to neutralize the effectiveness of the bomber and SLBM legs;
— our acquiescence in Minuteman vulnerability would encourage them to increase the resources dedicated to that enterprise; and
— they would be able to transfer resources from their ICBM program for this purpose.
In other words, if we stand still, and do not repair the vulnerability of ICBMs, we may find that the bombers and then the SLBMs have become vulnerable as well.[6]

Minuteman is far from "neutralized," even in its pending vulnerable state. How likely is it that the Soviet Union will be able to neutralize the two remaining legs of the Triad? Future Soviet developments in air defense have already been countered by the impending deployment of air-launched cruise missiles (ALCMs).

Today the ABM treaty limits Soviet use of an ABM system against incoming missiles. More important, it is impossible for the Soviet Union to produce and deploy such a system without substantial advance warning, especially on a scale that would be needed to counter the U.S. strategic forces that will be in place during the remainder of the 1980s, and this is before adding MX.

As the MX encountered stiffening resistance from members of Congress, residents of the prospective Nevada-Utah basing area, and a broad cross-section of the scientific community — including a number of prominent weapons consultants — Pentagon leaders began to make the case for a new mobile land-based missile by publicly spreading doubts about the survivability of the Navy's submarine force.

During a nominally off-the-record breakfast session with reporters in April 1980, Undersecretary Perry remarked that Soviet anti-submarine warfare technology was advancing so rapidly that the Navy's new Trident submarine as well as the older Poseidon would probably become vulnerable by the 1990s. As for U.S. capabilities, according to one knowledgeable observer, "[Perry] said . . . that if given the billions of dollars needed to mount such an effort, he could find all the Soviet submarines in the ocean and destroy them."[7]

For the public record, Dr. Perry has stated that detecting submarines represents less of a technical challenge than finding a single missile within a complex of 23 shelters. Responding to a question from Representative Norman Dicks before the House Defense Appropriations Subcommittee on May 15, 1980, Perry stated:

. . . I know how to detect submarines. It is difficult and expensive. But I at least know ways of doing it. I can describe to you four different ways in which I can take systems which have already been designed, and take them out into the ocean and detect submarines.

It is more of an economic problem, as to how many systems you have to build and the great expense of deploying them, rather than a technical problem involved in submarines.

It is because of that economic problem, then, that we continue to work on more effective ways to detect submarines. We are looking for a way which is economically feasible. (Deleted)

So in submarine detection, our improvements are a matter of degree in order to make them economical. That is the kind of breakthrough we are looking for there. We don't lack for ideas about how to detect submarines, and we don't lack for the techniques for actually doing it.

MR. DICKS. You are saying we lack techniques for being able to determine where a missile is in one of 23 shelters?

DR. PERRY. For each of the techniques which our most ingenious surveillance people, of whom I consider myself one, have been able to think of so far, we have a simple counter. That doesn't mean a year or five years from now somebody might not think of a new one.[8]

At other times, Dr. Perry has been a bit more modest in his claims, telling the Senate Appropriations Subcommittee on Military Construction in May 1980, for example, "We have designed techniques for submarine detection that, if deployed, could detect their submarines in ten years time."[9]

"Submarines are invisible today," Perry remarked to a large audience of citizens concerned about the MX in Salt Lake City last spring. "By the 1990s . . . my judgement is that we ourselves will be able to detect and locate Soviet submarines at sea at that time period. I have no reason to believe that the Soviets will not be able to do a similar thing."[10]

For its part, the Navy is, in the words of one high-ranking officer, "extremely unhappy" over Perry's statements. Although it does not believe that U.S. submarines will remain invulnerable, or nearly so, forever, it does not believe that the Soviets are anywhere close to achieving the capability suggested by Dr. Perry. "The Soviets are a long way from that," observes one recently retired admiral and DoD consultant with an intimate knowledge of Soviet anti-submarine warfare capabilities. "I have a great deal of respect for Dr. Perry," he remarked, "but I think his statements are farfetched and influenced by political concerns about the MX."[11]

Another high-ranking naval officer notes, "You may assume that we have examined the things [Dr. Perry] is referring to, and we do not see the prospects for either an acoustic or non-acoustic breakthrough as realizable as early as the 1990s."[12]

The Navy's displeasure with Dr. Perry's statements was so acute that Admiral Thomas B. Hayward, Chief of Naval Operations, apparently accused civilian Pentagon officials of undermining the Navy's strategic programs, in order to win support for the MX. Secretary Brown, according to press reports, "acknowledged that senior Pentagon aides . . . may have exaggerated the vulnerability of the Navy's strategic submarines" and promised Admiral Hayward that Pentagon officials would refrain from similar public statements in the future.[13]

This intramural squabble, however, is not the end of the story. Since the Soviet anti-submarine warfare "breakthrough" argument was, by a number of accounts, the one which clinched President Carter's approval of the large-diameter, land-based MX missile (which will not fit in the Trident submarine's launch tubes), its validity should be explored. First, it is ironic for the Pentagon to justify the MX by hypothesizing Soviet breakthroughs in the very area of the arms race in which the U.S. leads by the widest margin.[14] Second, covering the possibility of such a breakthrough does not require the immediate construction of an enormous missile system in the middle of the Western desert, but simply a steady research program on methods to counter anti-submarine warfare, which we have already. Third, should the Soviets actually develop a capability to detect U.S. submarines over the next decade, it would be at least eight to 12 years before they could deploy it efficiently enough to threaten the entire submarine force, leaving plenty of time for the United States to implement appropriate countermeasures, such as a new mobile ICBM, or some other system.

The overwhelming advantage which the United States has maintained in anti-submarine warfare has probably played a major role in Soviet planning decisions, particularly the decision to rely on land-based ICBMs as the major component of their strategic forces. Unlike the United States, political pride and a continuing sense of technological inferiority prevent the Russians from advertising their vulnerabilities. If, as the Carter Administration claims, the MX program is the consequence of the Russian rejection of Carter's March 1977 "Deep Cut" proposals—which imposed big reductions on ICBMs but did not even address sea-based forces — then the need for the MX and the anti-submarine warfare capabilities are indeed linked, but not in the way Undersecretary Perry suggested. We may need the MX not because the Russians are so good in anti-submarine warfare, but because we are. Our effectiveness in this area has discouraged the Soviets from moving a larger percentage of their nuclear deterrent out to sea, where the SLBMs would have a greater chance of surviving, although they would carry fewer warheads. These less accurate SLBMs would not pose a first-strike threat to the U.S. Minuteman force.

In fact, limiting the growth of the Soviet heavy ICBM force and moving the Soviets out to sea has been one of the avowed goals of the U.S. SALT negotiating position. But with continuing massive investment by the United States in improved anti-submarine warfare forces since the mid-sixties, why should the Russians move to sea if our hunter-killer submarines and submarine-hunting aircraft are there to greet them?

Summary

Proponents of the MX have argued that the new system is needed to halt the decline in effectiveness of the U.S. strategic Triad. A replacement for Minuteman would arrest the deterioration of the land-based leg of the Triad. Moreover, a more survivable ICBM would provide a hedge against the possible vulnerability of the air and sea legs of the Triad.

This rationale is unconvincing for three reasons. First, the existence of a Triad is an historic, not a logical phenomenon; the real issue is whether U.S. strategic forces are capable of deterring a possible Soviet attack. Even if Minuteman becomes vulnerable, the U.S. arsenal is quite large, diverse, and powerful. Second, Minuteman is far from useless, even in a pending vulnerable state. As numerous experts, including Secretary

Brown, have stated, the Minuteman force will remain as a fundamental element of our nuclear deterrent even as its vulnerability supposedly increases. Finally, arguments that the MX is needed to counter deterioration of the air and, in particular, sea-based forces, run counter to the facts. There are, moreover, far less expensive means of hedging against the possibility of deterioration than building such a costly new system as the MX.

Footnotes

1. Dr. Herbert York, interview, May 1981.
2. *U.S.-USSR* Strategic Policies, op. cit., p. 25.
3. Department of Defense *Annual Report*, FY 1975, p. 49.
4. House Defense Appropriations Subcommittee, FY 1980, Part 1, p. 596.
5. Testimony of R.L. Garwin before the Committee on Armed Service, U.S. House of Representatives, Feb. 7, 1979, typescript. p. 23.
6. Department of Defense *Annual Report,* FY 1981, p. 88.
7. Edgar Prina, "Sub Vulnerability Stressed as M-X Battle Continues," *Seapower,* June 1980, p. 22.
8. House Defense Appropriations Subcommittee, FY 1980, Part 7. p. 309.
9. Public hearing held May 6, 1980.
10. *Bill Moyers' Journal,*op. cit.
11. Personal interview, July 1980.
12. Quoted by *Prina,* op. cit., p. 23.
13. Richard Burt, "Brown Admits Aides Distorted MX Issue," *New York Times,* October 5, 1980.
14. Testifying before the Senate Armed Services Committee in February 1980, at about the same time as he began to issue dire warnings about the looming threat to U.S. ballistic missile submarines, Dr. Perry noted that the Russians "are in the early development phase of new submarine detection systems which by the early nineties could have *some* level of effectiveness against our *current* nuclear submarines." (emphasis added) In other words, if the U.S. submarine program stood still for 12 years or so while the Soviet Union continued to develop their ASW systems, by the

end of that time the Russians *might* be able to threaten *some* of the U.S. SSBN force. With a longer-range missile already being fitted into existing submarines, and a new, longer-range submarine (Trident) entering the force in the 1980s, there is almost no chance of the Russians catching up in the 1990s or soon thereafter. Perry also stated: "From our understanding of the R&D programs in the U.S.S.R. and the technologies involved, we believe the Russians have litle prospect of overcoming their detection and tracking problems (deleted)." Senate Armed Services Committee Authorization *Hearings* for FY 1981, Part 2, pp. 507, 627. In 1978, then Navy Secretary Graham Claytor stated the point more bluntly, remarking that "The qualitative edge that we hold over the Soviets in both equipment and personnel is awesome." George Wilson, "U.S. Leads in Sub-Hunting — Moscow Can't Match Computerized Sound Systems," *Washington Post,* May 28, 1978. See also Joel S. Wit, Advances in Antisubmarine Warfare, *Scientific American,* February 1981.

6.
Essential Equivalence

The Pentagon has also claimed that the MX is needed to match the massive buildup in the Soviet ICBM force. Since the 1960s, the Russians have constructed large numbers of missiles capable of carrying multiple warheads, and they are now reportedly improving their guidance systems. Thus, according to the Pentagon, the Soviet Union is creating the necessary combination of accuracy, power, and warhead numbers to have a war-fighting nuclear arsenal. In order to stay even, the United States needs a new, large, accurate land-based missile.

A close reading of official statements, however, indicates that the objective is not to match the Soviet Union weapon for weapon. Military planners admit that a combination of weapons different from that of the Soviet Union will keep the United States even, or ahead, and that the introduction of ALCMs and Trident submarines and missiles will give the United States substantial strength vis-a-vis the Soviet Union. Rather, the argument is that the Soviet missile buildup has altered the world's perceptions of the relative strength of the United States and the U.S.S.R. The MX is needed as a political statement—perhaps even a symbol—denoting American willingness to prevent the Russians from gaining the upper hand in contested areas of the globe.

According to Secretary Brown's FY 1980 *Annual Report* to the Congress, "We now recognize that the strategic nuclear forces can deter only a relatively narrow range of contingencies, much smaller in range than was foreseen only 20 or 30 years ago." This supposed acceptance within the Pentagon of limitations on the use of strategic nuclear forces is belied not only by the abundance of new counterforce nuclear weapons programs — and a corresponding enthusiasm for so-called "limited" nuclear options — but also by Dr. Brown himself, who acknowledged that "a strategy and a force structure designed only for assured destruction is not sufficient for our purposes. At the same time, we have to admit that we have not developed a plausible picture of the conflict we are trying to deter."

The proponents of counterforce and damage-limiting campaigns, he writes:

. . . Find it difficult to tell us what objectives an enemy would seek in launching such campaigns, how these campaigns would end, or how any resulting assymmetries could be made meaningful. We are left instead with large uncertainties about the amounts of damage that would result from such exchanges, about escalation, and about when and how the exchanges would terminate.[1]

One solution to the dilemma, according to Brown, would be to ignore the problem altogether by designing our forces "on the basis of essential equivalence, assuming we know what is meant by the term."[2]

Indeed, the term is inherently ambiguous. If by "essential equivalence" one means "equivalence is essential," then this would require that U.S. capabilities be equal to the Soviet Union's when measured by such indicators as numbers of delivery systems, throw-weight, and equivalent megatonnage. This is the interpretation preferred by most of those commentators, legislators, and DoD officials who favor the MX and other additions to the strategic arsenal.

However, "essential equivalence" can just as plausibly be taken to mean "essentially equivalent," meaning that the United States should maintain nuclear forces which are roughly equivalent to those of the Soviet Union in their overall deterrent effect. Secretary Brown took this position: "A more reasonable interpretation [than strict numerical equality] demands that judgements be made, and would require us to be ahead by some measures if behind in others."[3]

As means of comparing relative military capacities most of the numerical indicators are misleading or irrelevant. The great irony about nuclear weapons is that, unlike conventional forces, one cannot improve either deterrent or war-fighting capacities simply by building more of them, for the magnitude of the destruction caused by nuclear weapons is so great that the point of diminishing returns is very rapidly reached.[4] As Harold Brown observed in March 1975. "One need be only moderately sophisticated to see that beyond a certain number of offensive weapons, so long as the retaliatory ones on the other side are relatively invulnerable, one does not gain in real military capability."[5]

This reasoning also applies when comparing qualitative characteristics, such as the relative ability of U.S. and Soviet weapons to destroy a hardened missile silo or command and control center. Once targeting improvements allow for the weapons to land reliably within the "lethal radius"—defined by the power of the warhead and the hardness of the target—further refinements in accuracy do not increase the destructive capability of the force. They do, however, allow for reductions in yield, thereby lessening damage to areas away from the target. In theory, this reduces the chances for further escalation. A reduction in damage to surrounding areas, however, may produce the opposite effect, since the weapons would cause less damage to civilian areas, thereby increasing chances for escalation in a crisis.

Pentagon analysts and other proponents of nuclear war-fighting scenarios contend that the balance of abilities to limit unintended damage is a key element in the credibility of U.S. threats to use nuclear weapons in a crisis. Since, it is argued, the Soviets are developing war-fighting options, the United States must also do so to maintain essential equivalence. Others, however, emphasize that, despite improvements in targeting accuracy and an increase in the range of options available for the use of nuclear weapons, the fundamental situation between the two superpowers has not been altered. Since we are inescapably in a situation in which "the Soviets can kill an enormous number of Americans and the Americans can kill an enormous number of Russians," Dr. Wolfgang Panofsky, a leading United States scientist, has emphasized, "we have to make a basic policy that we give absolute priority to the prevention of nuclear war over the ability to fight one."

The difficulty is that this is a very hard priority statement for military people to accept and as soon as you start hedging and say yes, but if war breaks out anyway, then we must be able to do this and that, then it feeds back on the probability of the threat itself. This is a basic dilemma of the nuclear age and you cannot get around it by trying to compare the judgments of different people as to what the . . . scenarios of nuclear war might be.[6]

Secretary Brown's formulation of essential equivalence, which has also been used by other Administrations, seems to draw a major distinction between itself and the policy of developing full-fledged nuclear war-fighting capabilities; this divergence is, in fact, more apparent than real. Dr. Brown not only failed to indicate those measures of strategic power in which, as he put it, a "reasonable interpretation" would require us to excel, but he also neglected to specify any yardstick for measuring *how much* of each of these measures *is enough*. Since U.S. and Soviet nuclear forces are highly asymmetrical, the United States can quite easily concede to the Russians superiority in certain measures of strategic power—numbers and explosive power of ballistic missiles, for example—without in any way restricting our own inexorable movement toward the ability to wage a nuclear war based on our superior detection, guidance, and command and control capabilities.

"There is no obvious solution to our dilemma at this juncture," Brown lamented in February 1979. He thought that the best we can do is to adopt what he has dubbed the "countervailing strategy." This strategy, of which only the name is really new, consists of insuring that "whatever the nature of the attacks we foresee, we have the capability to respond in such a way that the enemy could have no expectation of achieving any rational objective, no illusion of making any gain without offsetting losses."[7] As a definition of strategic nuclear doctrine, the sheer breadth and vagueness of this formulation can scarcely be considered an improvement over essential equivalence. Moreover, it appears to run directly counter to DoD's recent recognition that the strategic nuclear forces "can deter only a narrow range of contingencies." Brown's countervailing strategy would, in reality, appear to be a far-reaching mandate for the use of nuclear forces across a broad range of contingencies. Because of its breadth and lack of precision, the countervailing strategy—as one "reasonable interpretation" of essential equivalence—does not provide an adequate analytical basis for establishing strategic military requirements.[8]

Pentagon officials respond to this criticism by asserting that "essential equivalence" is really a political rather than a military concept.[9] In view of asymmetries between the United States and the U.S.S.R. and the fact that it would be inefficient if not counterproductive slavishly to imitate Soviet capabilities, Brown noted, "To plan our forces, and measure their adequacy, simply on the basis of essential equivalence, would give no assurance that the forces would perform their essential deterrent functions." Given the inherently foggy nature of the concept, this is hardly surprising. But rather than throwing out essential equivalence entirely, Brown paid obeisance to the concept while admitting that no one really agrees on what it means. "We must insist on essential equivalence with the Soviet Union," he concluded, "to *symbolize* the equity that both sides accept in this realm."[10]

Although he rejected the view that nuclear superiority confers greater freedom of action in a crisis—"It is simply a myth that from the standpoint of responsible policymakers, the United States has suffered a major loss of leverage because of the Soviet nuclear buildup"—Secretary Brown left the door open to the argument that nuclear forces are necessary for America's foreign policies. He suggested that the United States "must respond to the *perceived* differences that follow from a world of strategic parity." This is necessary because it is "conceivable . . . that some parts of the Soviet leadership see these matters in quite a different light." In other words, even though U.S. leaders have concluded that nuclear superiority does not confer any real military advantage, the Soviets may believe that it does; thus, to prevent this "misperception" from emboldening Soviet foreign policy, the United States must continue to increase its nuclear arsenal.[11]

Buying more nuclear weapons to manipulate Soviet foreign policy in a direction favorable to U.S. interests would appear to have very little to do with the avowed primary objective of deterring a nuclear attack upon the United States and its allies. The MX, and other strategic modernization programs currently contemplated or underway — all with first strike capabilities—are just as likely to *create* misperceptions as to dispel them. For example, the Russians are as likely to "misperceive" that they could become subject to preemptive attack as they are to feel constrained not to occupy Iran with their conventional forces.

The "misperception" that the United States could launch a preemptive attack might result in a full-fledged Soviet launch-on-warning posture, with the accidental or purposeful launch of Soviet missiles during a crisis, ending in the deaths of millions of Americans.

The enormous existing stockpile of nuclear weapons systems is more than adequate to convey American threats of nuclear escalation to the Russians. It is difficult to see how the MX and other additions to the strategic arsenal will add to the credibility of such threats—if such threats are credible at all. As many students of the strategic balance have noted, the success of these threats hinges more on the significance of the interests at stake for each side than on perceived differences in nuclear capability, or, in Harold Brown's phrase, "on a weakness of will more than a weakness of weapons systems."[12] It is even more important, however, to question the wisdom of a national "defense" doctrine that would compensate for the decade-long failure to develop a rational energy policy by risking the lives of millions of Americans in a nuclear war.

The key argument, then, offered to justify the need for essential equivalence — and hence, the MX — is based on the hypothesis that "many countries make comparative judgments about our strength and that of the nuclear balance. It is in this regard that essential equivalence is particularly relevant."

> We need forces of such a size and character that every nation perceives that the United States cannot be coerced or intimidated by Soviet forces. Otherwise the Soviet Union could gain in the world, and we lose, not from war, but from changes in perceptions about the balance of our nuclear power. As long as our relationship with the Soviet Union is more competitive than cooperative—and this is clearly the case for the relevant future — maintaining essential equivalence of strategic nuclear forces is necessary to prevent the Russians from gaining political advantage from a real or perceived strategic imbalance.[13]

It is easy to assert such an intimate correlation between the strategic force balance and the achievement of foreign policy goals, but virtually impossible to demonstrate. One recent investigation of the subject, conducted under the auspices of the Brookings Institution, notes that, in general,

> . . . the data do not support propositions as to the importance of the strategic balance. . . . Our data would not support a hypothesis that the strategic weapons balance influences the outcome of in-

cidents in which both the United States and the U.S.S.R. are involved.[14]

In spite of this non-existent, or at least unproven, link between the strategic balance and the success or failure of American foreign policy, U.S. leaders continue to treat such a linkage as self-evident.

The MX and Essential Equivalence

Without building the MX, we are told, we will fail to maintain essential equivalence, a situation that could lead to Soviet political gains. In the wake of the Soviet invasion of Afghanistan, the Carter Administration leaned heavily on this particular argument to win popular approval of the MX, particularly in meetings with local residents of the "Designated Deployment Area" in Utah and Nevada. "In these days of heightened international tension and thinly disguised aggression on the part of the Soviets," remarked Air Force Undersecretary Antonia Chayes to a large gathering in Ely, Nevada,

> . . . it becomes less difficult to explain the need for stronger military capability. Soviet moves in Afghanistan over the past several weeks have worked like a cold bath, to emphasize the critical importance of our military strength, both strategic and conventional.
>
> The successful deployment of the MX, with full and careful concern not only for the effectiveness of the system, but for the quality of those communities affected by it, is one way we can demonstrate this resolve.[15]

Unconvinced by such arguments, one Nevada resident pointedly asked the Air Force representatives, "If you had the missile in place and ready to fire right now, how would that affect the situation in Afghanistan?" Another Air Force spokesman failed to answer the question directly, responding instead with a statement about the overall importance of maintaining a "strong nuclear umbrella."

A similar stance was taken a few weeks later by deputy Assistant to the President for National Security Affairs David Aaron during a televised debate on the MX in Salt Lake City. In addition to citing the Soviet invasion of Afghanistan and the expansion of the Soviet ICBM force as rationales for the MX, Aaron also disputed the notion that the MX was a first-strike weapon.

> The MX, as we have planned to deploy it, is not a first-strike weapon. It will not give us a first strike to destroy the Soviet deterrent. It will not even give us the capability to destroy the Soviet ICBM force in the sense that they will not have anything left over in their force. So that whole concern I think is exaggerated.[16]

Although it is technically the case that the planned deployment of 2,000 MX warheads will not *by itself* allow for the targeting of two warheads per Soviet silo to compensate for failures in reliability—which would allow some Soviet survivors—it is also true that the MX in conjunction with the 900 counter-silo Mark 12A warheads already programmed for the Minuteman III force would provide such a theoretical capability. Indeed, under the existing SALT limit of 820 MIRVed ICBMs, the Russians have no guarantee that the current program to improve the accuracy and yield of Minuteman ICBMs will not be extended to an additional 320 missiles, and their 960 warheads. This is considered unlikely only because an equivalent and more survivable capability can be obtained by improving the accuracy and yield of submarine-launched missiles.

Clearly, with the nominal capacity for a counterforce attack available in both its SLBM and ICBM forces, the United States will have a force that could be aimed at Soviet ICBM silos, Aaron's assurances notwithstanding. The White House cannot have it both ways, inferring a "practical threat" to U.S. ICBMs from Soviet capabilities while discounting the threat to the Soviet Union posed by U.S. programs merely because such programs are "intended" for retaliation only. If intentions are to be inferred willy-nilly from capabilities, then the argument must be allowed to work in both directions.

Debate moderator Bill Moyers also asked Aaron whether he agreed that "If we do not build the MX we will be perceived by the Soviets as vulnerable." Once, again, confusion ensued.

David Aaron: Yes, I certainly do. . . . I just don' think it's very prudent for any of us, when you really think about eterring a nuclear war . . . to depend upon the good will of the Soviet Union not to exercise an option that it has.

Bill Moyers: But do we really want to spend $60 to $100 billion dealing with perceptions of vulnerability? Aren't there better ways of sending messages to the Soviets and to our allies? [Moyers then suggested a conventional buildup in the Persian Gulf region as a more effective response to Soviet challenges in that area.]

David Aaron: I wish we were just talking about perceptions of vulnerability. The facts are facts. They have the systems, they have the capabilities. And I think we have to pay attention to Winston Churchill, when he says that he never argues with arithmetic. Now, this doesn't mean that we shouldn't try to meet the problems of the Persian Gulf and elsewhere [i.e., with conventional forces]. We should, and we can. But without the fundamental strength of our strategic nuclear deterrent, if we can't deter nuclear war, if our deterrent has been undermined, then we're going to have more crises, we're going to have more contingencies that we have to meet, not fewer ones. So, there's no substitute for a strong nuclear deterrent.[17]

Aaron indulges in the same confusion and interweaving of U.S. strategic objectives that has bedeviled public and even official discussions of nuclear weapons since 1945. Year after year, the American public has been induced to support ever higher levels of strategic weapons in the belief that these weapons were needed to deter the Soviets from launching nuclear attacks on the United States or its allies, when all along the reality has been that the Pentagon procured these weapons with the intent of deterring the Soviet Union, its allies, and its clients from launching conventional attacks on U.S. forces, allies, clients, and interests worldwide.

Aaron contends that Minuteman vulnerability is not a perception but a fact, and this fact threatens to "undermine" the ability of the United States to deter nuclear war. One would hope that the passing acquaintance of most Americans with the enormous destructive potential represented by the remainder of America's nuclear arsenal would cause them to reject the scare tactics of Washington officials whose chief concern is not lessening the danger of nuclear war, but rather enhancing their ability to employ nuclear threats in the conduct of U.S. foreign policy.

Footnotes

1. Department of Defense *Annual Report*, FY 1980, p. 76.
2. Ibid.
3. Ibid.
4. SALT critics have made much of alleged Soviet "superiority" in two "key indicators" of the strategic balance — Counter-Military Potential (CMP = $nY.67/CEP^2$) and Area-Kill Potential (Equivalent Megatonnage (EMT) = $nY.^{48}$.) As Dr. R.L. Garwin has observed, "One can argue that the indicator of CMP is seriously flawed. Once the accuracy of the weapon is sufficiently good to provide a high single-shot kill probability against the target, improved accuracy does not increase the capability of the force. Yet halving the CEP would multiply this particular *indicator* of CMP by a factor (of) 4! Furthermore, as regards both the CMP indicator and area-kill indicator, neither takes into account the declining marginal utility of a force rationally applied against a target structure. Finally, a force with an area-kill capability indicator less than that of a second force may in fact be considerably superior, if it is composed of a large number of small weapons (rather than a smaller number of large weapons) so that an individual weapon does not needlessly 'destroy' largely undeveloped area surrounding the principal 'area target.' " Letter from R.L. Garwin to "SALT connoisseurs," June 28, 1979, containing his comments on the strategic forces tables of Paul Nitze at a meeting of the Council on Foreign Relations in Washington, June 27, 1979.
5. *Civil Preparedness,* op. cit., p. 137.
6. Ibid., p. 70.
7. Department of Defense *Annual Report,* FY 1980, p. 76.

8. Secretary Brown advanced four criteria in support of his countervailing strategy:
   > We must have forces in sufficient numbers and quality so that they can: (1) survive a well-executed surprise attack; (2) react with the timing needed, both as to promptness and endurance, to assure the deliberation and control deemed necessary by the National Command Authorities (NCA); (3) penetrate any enemy defenses, and (4) destroy their designated targets. [Department of Defense *Annual Report,* FY 1980, p. 77.]

   These criteria are quantitatively imprecise and are so general as to be applicable to any weapon system, strategic or tactical, nuclear or conventional.
9. "In addition to their purely military capabilities," Secretary Brown observed in a January 1980 discussion of essential equivalence, "strategic nuclear forces, like other military forces, have a broader role in the world." [Department of Defense *Annual Report,* FY 1981, p. 68.]
10. Department of Defense *Annual Report,* FY 1980, p. 76.
11. Ibid.
12. Department of Defense *Annual Report,* FY 1981, p. 68.
13. *Civil Preparedness,* op. cit., p. 131. Although most reasonable analysts would agree that beyond a certain numerical level — long since attained by both sides — further additions to nuclear arsenals do not appreciably enhance mutual perception of the willingness to use nuclear weapons, as Barry Blechman has trenchantly observed, the quest for nuclear superiority can not be totally divorced from the credibility of first use threats:
    > Some argue, however, that the *threat* of nuclear war should be integrated more centrally into U.S. foreign policy; . . . . To the extent that the United States must rely on nuclear weapons, it is argued, agreements which seek to enshrine strategic nuclear parity as a permanent condition of U.S.-Soviet relations are misguided; rather, the United States must turn its resources and technology to the quest for strategic supriority. Not that success in this goal is seriously contemplated; none but the most naive believe that such an end is attainable. Nonetheless, the argument runs, by placing itself formally in a posture of seeking nuclear superiority, the United States would be demonstrating a willingness to manipulate the risk of nuclear war for political objectives, thus lending credibility to the nuclear threats implicit in its foreign policy. In short, only in an environment of wide-open U.S.-Soviet nuclear competition can the United States' *necessary reliance* on nuclear weapons to underpin its foreign policy be supported successfully.

    See Barry M. Blechman, "Do Negotiated Arms Limitations Have a Future?" *Foreign Affairs,* Fall 1980. pp. 111–12.
14. Department of Defense *Annual Report,* FY 1981, p. 69.
15. Barry Blechman and Stephen S. Kaplan, *Force Without War: U.S. Armed Forces as a Political Instrument,* The Brookings Institution, 1978, pp. 128–29.
16. Speech by Air Force Undersecretary Antonia Chayes at MX Environmental "Scoping" Meeting, Ely, Nevada, January 14, 1980.
17. *Bill Moyers' Journal,* Public Broadcasting System, April 24, 1980.

7.
Extended Deterrence

The fourth major argument used to support the MX is that adding the new system to the U.S. nuclear arsenal would expand the range of options available to U.S. planners. One such option is the use of nuclear weapons in a limited conflict. The acquisition of what has become known as a war-fighting capacity is seen by some as necessary to offset similar Soviet developments (see previous section, "Essential Equivalence").

Military planners also see the ability to fight, or at least threaten to fight, a limited nuclear war as an extension of tactical nuclear and conventional deterrence. U.S. conventional forces are supported by the threat to use tactical nuclear weapons should the tide of battle turn against us in an actual conflict. Now the Pentagon seems to feel that it needs a war-fighting threat at the strategic nuclear level, to back up the tactical nuclear threat. A strategic nuclear force, goes its argument, based upon the doctrine of assured destruction is inadequate to this task; what is needed are weapons with the accuracy and explosive power to threaten hardened military targets. The MX is the weapon for this purpose.

Extended Deterrence

The view that the MX is necessary for the purpose of threatening nuclear escalation in a conventional crisis is increasingly put forward by analysts both within and outside the Department of Defense. "I believe the time has come for very serious rethinking about fundamental strategic assumptions," said President Carter's special Assistant for National Security Affairs Zbigniew Brzezinski. Dr. Brzezinski was concerned about "the requirements of effective bargaining during crises under the likely conditions of the 1980s" and "the requirements of effective and politically focused conflict management."

> I think you see already the beginning of a serious review manifesting itself in the Secretary of Defense's posture statement, in being able to respond to nuclear threats in a flexible manner, in the serious thought being given to our nuclear targeting plans, in the much higher emphasis being placed on command and control capabilities. . . . The United States, in order to have effective deterrence, has to have choices which give us a wider range of options than either a spasmodic nuclear exchange or a limited conventional war. Anything less than that will give the Soviet side greater flexibility and staying power in the event of a sustained crisis. We have to avoid a situation in which they would be able to bargain and we could not. This would be dangerous to us.[1]

Dr. Brzezinski was implying that the Russians have or will develop a greater capacity for flexible nuclear options than the United States. This is not so. The United States has many more accurate, lower-yield warheads, potentially deliverable by a greater variety of systems, than does the Soviet Union. Thus, Brzezinski's fear must be rooted in the nature of the potential crisis itself, in particular the balance of conventional forces within a given theater, and the role which Soviet perceptions of strategic parity are likely to play in their willingness to back down. Some light was shed recently on this subject by General David C. Jones, Chairman of the Joint Chiefs of Staff.

> Because the mission of our strategic forces extends beyond merely deterring an attack on our cities to encompass U.S. interests and allied forces overseas, there could be a reverse of the (1962) Cuban situation where they might have a strategic advantage combined with local conventional force advantage.[2]

Under such conditions, General Jones suggested, the outcome would be likely to prove detrimental to the United States unless leaders were willing to take great risks. The solution, according to the Joint Chiefs chairman, is a stepped-up strategic force modernization program with the MX as the priority. This would compensate for the Soviet Union's (purported) local superiority in conventional forces by undermining Soviet confidence in strategic parity and increasing their fears of U.S. nuclear escalation. "The focus must be on this nation having the capability actually to fight sustained nuclear war," he concluded, "including all the ingredients that entails."[3]

How might the MX actually be deployed? A senior advisor to the Department of Defense has suggested a scenario that could lead to the United States being the first to use its strategic weapons:

The sequence begins when the Soviet Union launches a massive invasion of the Persian Gulf region using conventional forces, rapidly overwhelming whatever U.S. conventional forces are in the region. U.S. nuclear forces—such as carrier-based aircraft—stationed in the area are largely destroyed before Washington can make a decision on their use. The United States' difficulties are compounded by the fact that, if we use tactical weapons against Soviet forces in oil-producing countries, the resulting damage to the oil fields and civilian populations will seriously impair our post-war relations with those countries. In this situation, and in light of the U.S.S.R.'s own nuclear capacities, the U.S. tactical nuclear threat cannot be considered particularly decisive or credible.

What the Joint Chiefs think they need in this situation, according to the advisor, is a strategic nuclear force capable of threatening the prompt destruction of all Soviet forces relevant to their Middle East operation—such as ammunition and supply depots, bomber, airlift, and missile bases, and so on—while limiting damage to the rest of the U.S.S.R. The Russians, realizing that nuclear escalation on their part would only widen the damage to their homeland, would back down and withdraw their forces from the Middle East. Better yet, having made these calculations in advance they would refrain from launching the incursion in the first place.

This strategy requires an accurate nuclear weapon system with a short flight time and excellent command and control. A land-based ICBM would provide such a system. The MX's ability to absorb any Soviet retaliatory attack further enhances the credibility of the U.S. nuclear first-strike threat. This is probably the kind of scenario Brzezinski had in mind when he worried publicly about the United States' "ability to bargain in the context of a severe crisis." And it is in this context that the Pentagon sees Minuteman's hypothetical vulnerability as a serious issue. Minuteman vulnerability does not affect the deterrence of Soviet surprise attacks upon the United States, but, say the military planners, it does lessen the credibility of U.S. nuclear threats against Soviet forces in a severe crisis involving American overseas interests.

In the words of Secretary Brown,

No enemy should be left with the illusion that he could disable portions of our nuclear forces—CONUS [Continental United States] *— based or overseas — as a preliminary to attacks in specific theaters with his general purpose forces. The latter can and should be targeted.* Under many conditions, moreover, [his general purpose forces] may be more time-urgent targets than residual missiles. So might the command and control, war-reserve stocks, and lines of communication necessary to the conduct of theater compaigns. In some circumstances, we might also wish to take war-related industries under attack, especially those decoupled from cities.[5]

This view is supported by General Richard H. Ellis, the Commander in Chief of SAC and Director of the Joint Strategic Target Planning Staff.

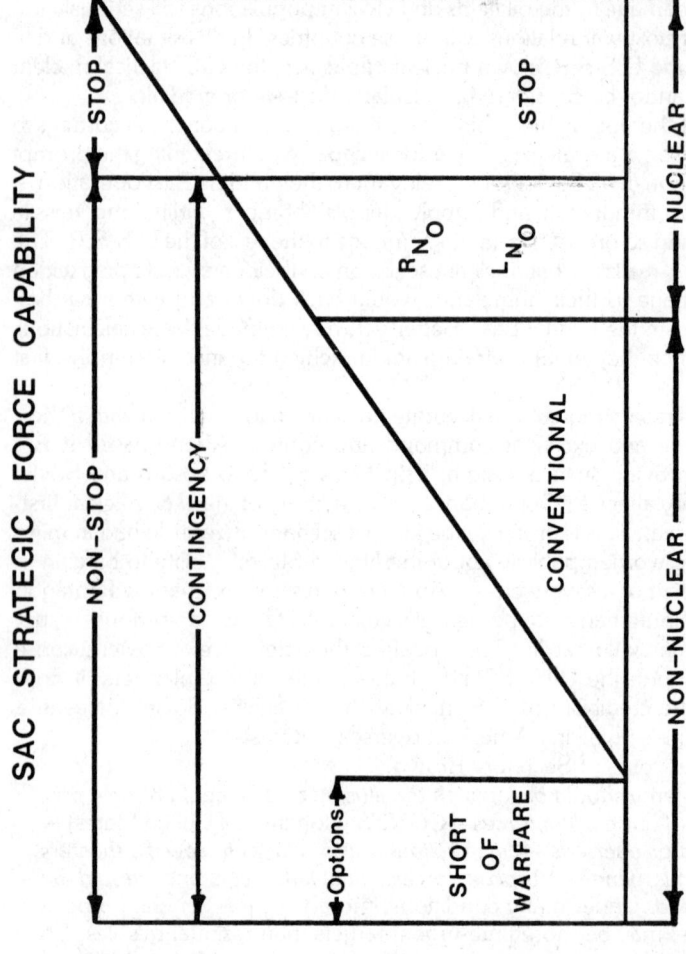

Chart provided by Gen. Ellis to illustrate the concept of deterrence as a "single entity" composed of a continuum of escalatory options. RNO and LNO stand for "Regional" and "Limited" nuclear options, respectively.

Noting that his "gloomy assessment [of the balance in surviving warheads after a U.S.-Soviet counterforce exchange] does not mean that strategic nuclear war is imminent," General Ellis testified that "SAC can and will continue to have the capability to inflict massive destruction on Soviet economic and military targets under any condition of war initiation. However, *it does mean the Soviets can undertake peripheral political and military actions without considering possible nuclear consequences to the same degree that was necessary in the past.*"[6] (emphasis added)

The conviction appears to be widespread within the national security establishment that without the capability to threaten a controlled strategic nuclear escalation after an attack — a capability, think the planners, provided chiefly by the current Minuteman force — the United States will have to face an increased Soviet challenge to its global interests. According to General Ellis:

> Today, we find the Soviets using their increased strategic capabilities as a "nuclear umbrella" in the pursuit of global activities we were able to deter when we had the undisputed nuclear shield. *Because of this, deterrence can no longer be neatly divided into subgroups such as conventional and nuclear. It must be viewed as an interrelated, single entity.*
>
> In response, SAC is developing new options which provide the National Command Authorities (NCA) with additional flexibility to respond to future crises and conflicts in a timely and controlled manner. In addition to nuclear adjustments, we are exploring a range of non-SIOP (contingency) options for SAC forces (see chart).
>
> Participation in these evolving contingency options is not intended to diminish the SIOP mission but to assure the most effective use of SAC resources. Strategic forces are uniquely capable of supporting general-purpose force missions. The ability to execute contingency plans and procedures using SAC assets — particularly the manned bomber — markedly improves U.S. war-fighting capability. SAC aircraft can provide rapid long-range force projection in the conventional and theater areas while retaining their contribution to the SIOP, if so tasked.[7]

In "Summary Remarks" prepared for the Senate Armed Services Committee on the state of the nation's strategic nuclear forces for FY 1981, Ellis noted that the Carter Administration's renewed emphasis on defense "must continue and be accelerated, where practical, *if we are to protect our global interests.*"[8] (emphasis added) The immediate question posed by his testimony is that, if increased deployment of conventional and "dual-purpose" forces are required to protect U.S. interests in the Persian Gulf-Indian Ocean area and elsewhere, why not accomplish this task without paying an extra $50-$115 billion for the supposed advantage of posing a more credible threat of escalation to strategic nuclear war? This threat continues to exist in any case, both directly, from the broad

U.S. array of strategic nuclear weapons bearing some 9,000 warheads, and indirectly, by way of the 20,000 U.S. tactical nuclear weapons, several hundred of which are deployed with carrier task forces such as those presently patrolling the Indian Ocean-Arabian Sea area.

The answer to this question is to be found in the Pentagon's apparent conviction that the threat of first-use of tactical nuclear weapons is not credible unless backed up by the threat of strikes against military targets using strategic weapons. In other words, the intent of the MX would appear to be, in the first instance, to make the world safe for U.S. conventional forces, or failing that, to allow the United States first-use of tactical nuclear weapons while successively deterring: (1) a Soviet nuclear or chemical response on the battlefield; (2) Soviet theater-wide attacks with its medium-range nuclear missiles and bombers; (3) Soviet use of its intercontinental strategic forces against allied military targets in the United States and overseas.

During Congressional hearings in 1976 on a proposed resolution banning U.S. first use of nuclear weapons, Rep. Richard Ottinger of New York posed a series of questions which highlight the dangers and uncertainties of current U.S. nuclear doctrine, and the possible role which the Pentagon planners are seeking for the MX.

MR. OTTINGER. . . . Let us take Europe, and there is a conventional attack on Europe. We decide that the way to protect against that is to use tactical nuclear weapons with the authority of the President. There are really two questions. The Russians have the power to respond to that nuclear response. They can respond to it either with tactical weapons, or strategic weapons.

Do you think that we would take that risk? Would we use the tactical weapons, knowing that they might come back with a strategic strike, *or do you think that we would go for the strategic strike right away?*[9] (emphasis added)

The MX appears to be the Pentagon's answer to Representative Ottinger's question. It would provide a counterforce capability which suggests that the United States would indeed "go for the strategic strike right away." The Pentagon hopes that the Russians will be deterred from launching attacks with their conventional forces in Europe and elsewhere, and thus the U.S. will not have to face the dilemma posed by its reliance on tactical nuclear weapons. If our nuclear arsenal fails to deter a Soviet conventional attack, leading to the use of tactical nuclear weapons, then the purpose of the MX would appear to be to limit the scale of the Soviet response by threatening the swift destruction of Soviet military capabilities, nuclear and conventional.

Does the MX offer the prospect of a further reduction in the probability of strategic attack upon the United States? If the rationale for the weapon is as described above—and there is mounting evidence that this is indeed the Pentagon's actual view[10]—then, clearly, reducing the probability of a nuclear attack on the United States was never intended to be the primary mission of the MX. Rather, the primary mission of the MX is to reduce the probability of Soviet conventional attacks, or support for such attacks, on far-flung U.S. geopolitical interests, by 'backing-up' the U.S. threat to use tactical nuclear weapons in areas of the world where our conventional forces are unable to protect or further our interests.

The Conventional Balance

The present reliance on first-use of nuclear weapons in U.S. strategy diverts attention and resources from the problems posed by a far more probable range of threats, involving conventional forces as well as terrorism, guerilla warfare, and so on. In this respect, over-reliance on nuclear weapons would appear to weaken rather than strengthen U.S. defense of its vital interests. According to MIT arms expert William Kaufmann, ghost-writer of the Defense Secretary's annual posture statement, no matter how the issue of strategic force modernization is resolved, "It is essential that the United States and its allies finally acknowledge that the strategic and tactical nuclear forces will only deter the use of nuclear force by others, particularly the Soviet Union."[11]

"If they do not face this reality," Kaufmann writes, "there is no assurance that they will get on with the serious business of coping with the more likely and imminent dangers."

"Such candor undoubtedly has a price," Kaufmann observes, requiring that the United States and its allies "develop a conventional posture that can stand up to attack without nuclear crutches." Such candor would also confirm to the Soviet Union, Kaufmann notes, U.S. acknowledgement of the existence of a "nuclear stalemate and mutual nuclear deterrence." Such an acknowledgement is by no means universal. The 1980 Republican Party Platform, for example, states, "We will build toward a sustained defense expenditure to close the gap with the Soviets and ultimately reach the position of military superiority that the American people demand."[12]

Any attempt to seek nuclear superiority "over a moderately competent and determined adversary," Kaufmann observes, would be "a wasteful and futile exercise" because nuclear weapons "are not simply another explosive."

> Their use makes it extremely difficult not to kill large masses of people very quickly. They do not fit well into traditional concepts of how wars can be fought and hence deterred.
>
> At the tactical level attempts have been made by the United States, as well as by the Soviet Union, to force them into the traditional mold. But all analyses of this kind of warfare, unless they are quite abstract, suggest that both the battlefield and the rear areas of the belligerents would be rapidly reduced to chaos.

At the strategic level what may be more plausible and feasible types of exchanges have been invented. But even these have an air of artificiality. They usually lack a political beginning or ending. More often than not, the war is stopped after several volleys, residual weapons are counted and compared, and the side with the larger numbers is declared the victor. Even where, in the hypothetical campaigns that are more seriously conducted, some more exploitable form of leverage begins to emerge, it looks at best precarious and dangerous to exploit for any purpose commensurate with the costs already incurred and the risks ahead.[13]

Kaufmann notes that it is important to be clear about what acceptance of a nuclear stalemate means.

> . . . The U.S.S.R. may prove more tenacious in defending its alleged interests . . . than it was in Berlin and Cuba, when the superiority that was nominal to Americans may have seemed operational to the Russians. But that is all the more reason for dropping the pretense that nuclear weapons will somehow extricate the United States from the confrontations and hazards of the future. They will not. Only adequate non-nuclear capabilities will.[14]

What are those non-nuclear capabilities? Professor Kaufmann, who for years has had access to all the data on U.S. forces and intelligence on foreign threats, observes, "The Soviet conventional posture at present is not nearly so out of proportion to that of the United States and its allies as is popularly supposed." Although Soviet ground forces of roughly 1.8 million men are roughly double U.S. active-duty personnel,

> . . . Most Soviet divisions are less than fully manned, many of them are less capable and ready than the U.S. National Guard and Reserve divisions, and there remain questions about how much equipment of what vintage is held by the less ready Soviet divisions.
>
> In peacetime, many of the Soviet divisions appear to lack many of the support forces that would permit them to sustain a military operation for more than a couple of weeks. As was evident in Afghanistan, it takes the Soviet establishment a substantial amount of time — months rather than weeks — to organize a small operation against a weak and relatively disorganized country. The forces, once in occupation, seem to devote as much as 40 per cent of their manpower to combat service support — that is, primarily to logistic and maintenance functions.[15]

Kaufmann notes that the Soviet tactical air forces are no larger than comparable U.S. forces, and that, while some late-model Soviet aircraft may be the equivalent of the more advanced F-4s and F-5s, "they are not on a par with the newer U.S. aircraft. Beyond that, Soviet pilots are less well-trained than their American counterparts, fly fewer hours, and exercise less initiative because of the constraints imposed by Soviet ground control."

Concerning naval forces, Kaufmann points out that while the Soviet Union now deploys an oceangoing fleet that "at least superficially rivals that of the United States," Soviet surface combatants "appear to carry only small reserves in missiles and ordnance; their cruising range is limited. . . ." Although larger ships are under construction, "it will be some years before significant numbers are deployed." As for the much touted Soviet anti-ship cruise missile threat, "It is not clear how accurate these missiles would be when fired at targets over the horizon."

Kaufmann notes that U.S. land-based and fleet aircraft "should be able to do well" against any surface combatant that "ventured from under the cover of Soviet land-based aircraft." Of the four Soviet fleets,

> . . . Two of them—in the Black Sea and the Baltic—are virtually landlocked, and even the Northern and Pacific Fleets would have to pass through narrow waters and a number of man-made barriers to reach U.S. and allied surface combatants and merchant ships. Soviet attack submarines armed with torpedoes and cruise missiles are similarly divided and would have similar problems reaching their targets.[16]

While military strategists see the Backfire bombers assigned to Soviet naval aviation as a bigger threat to U.S. maritime capabilities, Kaufmann notes that the United States is countering them with a program of cruisers equipped with the AEGIS ship-borne anti-aircraft system. This new system is designed to track large numbers of planes and cruise missiles and coordinate the defense against them. In areas such as Japan and the Greenland-Iceland-UK gap, Kaufmann suggests that land-based aircraft will also be used against the Backfire.

Although the Russians can be expected to continue to develop the elements of long-range power projection, Kaufmann observes that they "have little capability for this kind of activity at present."

General Jones made the following appraisal, effectively supporting Kaufmann's analysis:

> U.S. combat forces for distant projection are generally superior to corresponding Soviet forces. U.S. amphibious forces are much stronger than their emerging Soviet equivalents. U.S. tactical aviation, including sea-based aviation, is better; the lack of tactical air capability *at a distance* is a serious Soviet deficiency. U.S. naval forces are generally superior to Soviet forces. Soviet naval forces are hampered by poor sustainability at long distances from port and by greater vulnerability to air and submarine attack.

General Jones continued his observations, noting that Soviet capabilities to project military power "are minimal at present."[17].

"If the Soviet Union is so constrained," Kaufmann asks, "why does so much pessimism exist about the ability of the United States to cope with its capabilities by conventional means?" The main reason, he says, is that what U.S. planners "expect the Soviet Union to be able to do some years hence — and what the United States must allow for in its defense programs — they credit the Soviet Union with being able to do now."[18] To Kaufmann's explanation one might add that there is a penchant for exaggerating the extent of the Soviet threat in order to provide a justification for the projection of American power into areas rich in oil and strategic minerals.

War-Fighting

The notion of a counterforce missile capable of actually fighting a nuclear war dominates the rationale behind MX. The MX's counterforce capacity comes from the large number of MIRVed warheads it can carry and, most importantly, from the increased accuracy of each warhead. It is accuracy that allegedly distinguishes MX from its land-based predecessors and from its sea-based contemporaries.

But the claimed level of accuracy may be more theoretical than real. As we detailed in section 4A, there are severe problems that would be encountered in actually carrying out a controlled nuclear strike. These problems include: (1) fratricide, where one incoming warhead detonates and destroys those following; (2) reliability, where the percentage of missiles that actually reach their targets cannot be known in advance; and (3) bias, where a missile traverses a brand-new flight path in an actual attack and encounters a variety of physical phenomena that cause it to drift from its planned trajectory. These all severely lower the chances of a successful attack.

No matter how overwhelming accuracy and superiority of numbers look on paper, the figures do not translate automatically into reality, a fact often ignored by counterforce enthusiasts. Any responsible leader whose advisors told him that he had the option of launching a disarming strike would have to be extremely doubtful of its success. This very lack of assurance is in itself a form of deterrence, and it has been present almost from the very moment the Russians detonated their first atomic bomb in 1949.

Even if technical problems could be overcome, there is no way that a missile attack could be limited to military and military-industrial targets. An attack on such targets in the Soviet Union would put some sixty warheads in the vicinity of Moscow. Following a similar attack on the United States, there would be an extremely heavy fallout pattern over the Eastern seaboard. But there are, of course, military targets located near major population centers, as are most industrial targets. Since it is impossible to separate military from civilian targets in a nuclear attack the potential for escalation would be very high. As McGeorge Bundy cogently pointed out, "There may be room for argument about this 'military' target or that one, but niceties of targeting doctrine do not make the weapons themselves discriminating."[19]

Bundy also noted that, to a certain extent, American analysts have fallen prey to their own rhetoric. While "stable mutual deterrence at the strategic level" was the accepted policy in the Kennedy and Johnson Administrations, "the heavy rhetorical emphasis on continuing American superiority was misleading," he wrote.

We did assert that we had strategic superiority and we did assert that having it made a difference. What we did not say so loudly was that the principal use of this numerical superiority was in its value as reassurance to the American public and as a means of warding off demands for still larger forces.

In a similar fashion, we may have spread confusion by using the measuring stick of assured destruction to demonstrate that the deterrent power of our strategic forces was more than adequate. This measurement lent itself to the erroneous conclusion that the population itself would be the preferred target of any actual attack . . .[20]

Such considerations seem to be falling on deaf ears.* Evidence was provided by Undersecretary Perry in testimony on the MX program before the Senate Armed Services Committee. Asked to provide a brief summary of present U.S. targeting doctrine, Perry's statement clearly denotes a very broad role for the use of nuclear threats in U.S. foreign policy. "The fundamental objective of our Nuclear Targeting Doctrine," Perry wrote, "is to deter nuclear and conventional attacks, or coercion attempts under threat of such attacks against the United States, its allies and any nation important to U.S. interest." In contrast to a doctrine which envisions the use of nuclear weapons solely in retaliation for deliberate nuclear attacks on the U.S. and its allies—the popular view of U.S. nuclear doctrine—the Pentagon's renewed emphasis on a strategy of "extended" deterrence, controlled escalation and the possibility of fighting a nuclear war has the effect of increasing the options for using a nuclear weapon. Although it is not easy to calculate the effect of this strategy on the probability of nuclear war, it is only common sense that a dramatic increase in the number of pre-planned nuclear contingencies, if backed up by the relevant weaponry, must increase that probability.

"Should deterrence fail and conflict occur," Perry informed the Senate committee, the objective of U.S. nuclear targeting doctrine is to "assure the United States a position of power and influence" and "limit the conflict and its consequences as to the United States and its allies. To the extent escalation cannot be controlled in general war, maximize the postwar U.S. political, economic, military power relative to the enemy, (deleted)."[21]

---

*Even if, with MX, ALCMS, Trident I and II missiles, and improved command and control, the United States should obtain the technical capacity to fight a limited nuclear war, there would still be a missing component. A civil defense capacity is an essential accompaniment to a nuclear war-fighting strategy in order to limit damage to the civilian population. Without such a capacity, Soviet threats to U.S. military targets would become nearly synonymous with threats to the civilian population. Under assured destruction doctrine, since cities were the hostages, civil defense, like the ABM, was not needed.

In his FY 1981 Annual Report, Secretary Brown contended, "There is no contradiction between this attention to the militarily effective targeting of the large and flexible forces we increasingly possess . . . and our primary and overriding policy of deterrence." Unfortunately, the beneficial effect of counterforce targeting on deterrence is not the open-and-shut case which Secretaries Brown and Perry presume it to be. It is indeed ironic that one of the most persuasive critics of the concept of fighting a nuclear war was until a few years ago a Cal Tech president by the name of Harold Brown. "There are various possible purposes for strategic nuclear forces," Brown observed during an address to members of the Institute of U.S. Studies of the Soviet Academy of Sciences in March 1975.

Some of them are overlapping, or at least not wholly mutually exclusive. Most of them are in my opinion illusory. The principal possible purposes I see are: deterrence (in various forms); coercion; war-winning and its relative, nuclear war-fighting . . . My own view is that unless the United States and the Soviet Union can agree—at least tacitly — that of these only deterrence is feasible for either of them with respect to the other, and that they will structure their forces so as to not undermine that objective in pursuit of other objectives, further progress in strategic arms limitation will be severely hampered, and perhaps not possible. Deterrence is, first of all, the perceived capability and intention of retaliating so as to destroy a substantial part of the population and industrial capacity of any nation initiating a nuclear attack on oneself. By this capability and intention, deterrence has the objective of preventing any such attack from being launched.

. . . To the extent that deterrent capability exists—and as I have suggested, that is a very large extent indeed — the side that is "losing" a countermilitary exchange can call a halt by invoking deterrence—the threat of counter industry/population strikes. This is a deficiency in the concept of "war-fighting." In the confusion of nuclear war, the distinction between classes of targets is very unlikely to be preserved anyway. Even if it were, the secondary effects of strikes on "military" targets are likely to be enormous because military targets include military and communication headquarters, which are almost invariably co-located with population and industrial centers. Thus even a thermonuclear exchange that succeeded throughout its course in being directed at military targets would leave tens of millions of dead on each side and the bulk of productive capacity destroyed through direct effects, not to mention the disruptive secondary effects of such destruction.

. . . . Providing that no one is deceived into thinking that the existence of forces, options and plans for a strategic countermilitary exchange makes survival of either the United States or the U.S.S.R. in a nuclear war at all likely, or into forgetting that the fatal and almost certain outcome is the explosion on the cities of both countries of nuclear weapons, the existence of such plans and the development of such forces is an acceptable idea. *However, to the extent that it erodes deterrence, this contingency planning could increase the likelihood of catastrophe. For that reason it ought to be severely limited. My own view is that the facts of the indefensibility of each of our countries against nuclear attack by [the] other, and the open-ended nature and unlimited costs of a countermilitary strategy are clear.* I therefore conclude that counterforce capabilities, especially because the limitations on their effectiveness are not matched by limitations on their cost, will not be carried very far on either side. Facts do in the end prevail, whatever doctrine may assert.[22] (emphasis added)

While Brown's conclusions may have changed, the logic of his argument remains intact. The attempt by the United States to attain a superior capacity to employ counterforce threats, which appears to be a major rationale behind MX, will result only in a heightened arms race and a less stable world.

Footnotes

1. *New York Times,* March 30, 1980.
2. *Air Force Magazine,* May 1979, p. 46.
3. Ibid.
4. Personal interview, April 1980.
5. Department of Defense *Annual Report,* FY 1980, p. 78.
6. "Strategic Nuclear Forces Report," Introductory Remarks by Gen. Richard H. Ellis before the Senate Armed Service Committee, February 20, 1980, p. 3.
7. HASC Authorization Hearings for FY 1981, Part I, p. 10-11.
8. Ibid., p. 5.
9. An unofficial answer to Ottinger's question was provided by Vice-Admiral Gerald E. Miller, U.S. Navy retired, and former Deputy Director of the Joint Strategic Target Planning Staff:
   "My feeling is that we would approach the situation with an escalatory policy. We have demonstrated that in recent years as our basic approach to warfare. I think that it would be very difficult to start with nuclear weapons in any scenario." See *First Use of Nuclear Weapons: Preserving Responsible Control,* Hearings before the Subcommittee on International Security and Scientific Affairs of the Committee on International Relations, House of Representatives, 94th Congress, Second Session, U.S.GPO, Washington, 1976, p. 78.

10. See the discussion surrounding the unofficial release of the contents of Presidential Directive 59 in August 1980, for example:

> The Carter Administration has adopted a new strategy for nuclear war that gives priority to attacking military targets in the Soviet Union rather than to destroying cities and industrial complexes. . . .
>
> The revised policy . . . requires American forces to be able to undertake the precise, limited nuclear strikes against military facilities in the Soviet Union, including missile bases and troop concentrations . . . [and] to develop the capacity to threaten Soviet political leaders in their underground shelters in time of war. (Richard Burt, "Carter Said to Back a Plan for Limiting any Nuclear War," *New York Times,* August 6, 1980.)
>
> The MX ICBM, Pentagon Officials say, is "highly consistent" with the Administration's nuclear targeting policy as spelled out in Presidential Directive 59.
>
> For one thing . . . MX will be survivable because of its multiple protective shelter concept. Also, they say, it will "improve our capability to respond against targets which require high accuracy." (*Aerospace Daily,* August 22, 1980, p. 301.)

See also Department of Defense *Annual Report,* FY 1982, Section I, chapter 4.
11. William W. Kaufmann, "Defense Policy," in *Setting National Priorities,* Brookings Institution, 1980, p. 297.
12. Republican Platform statement quoted in the *Washington Post,* July 16, 1980.
13. Kaufmann, *op. cit.,* p. 295.
14. Ibid, p. 299.
15. Ibid, p. 300.
16. Ibid., p. 301. Kaufmann goes on to detail the problems facing the Soviet submarine fleet: "Soviet nuclear submarines are admittedly faster than most U.S. nuclear submarines, and the new Alpha-class titanium alloy submarine has demonstrated impressive speed and deep-diving characteristics. However, all Soviet submarines carry limited numbers of torpedoes and cruise missiles; they are also very noisy. All would have to run the gantlet of various U.S. early warning systems, mines, and anti-submarine aircraft, quiet submarines armed with high-speed torpedoes, and surface combatants equipped with sophisticated detection gear and anti-submarine helicopters (of which there will be around 200 abroad surface combatants)." Ibid.
17. Gen. David C. Jones, USAF, *United States Military Posture: An Overview For FY 1981,* p. iii.
18. Kaufmann, *op. cit.,* pp. 302, 303.
19. McGeorge Bundy, "The Future of Strategic Deterrence," speech to IISS conference, September 1979, excerpted in *Survival,* XXI, 6 (November–December 1979), p. 269.
20. Ibid., p. 270.
21. Senate Armed Services Committee, Authorization Hearings, FY 1980, Part 3, p. 1437.
22. Harold Brown, "Strategic Force Structure and Arms Limitation," talk given before the Institute of U.S. Studies of the Soviet Academy of Sciences, Moscow, March 1975, reprinted in *Civil Preparedness.*

8.
Multiple Aim-point Basing: A Pointless Idea

In September 1979, after evaluating and discarding more than 20 alternative basing modes for the MX, the Carter Administration and the Air Force finally settled on the "horizontal shelter" variant of the long-standing "multiple aim-point system" (MAPS) shell-game* concept. This proposal consisted of an MX mounted on a "Transporter-Erector-Launcher" (TEL) vehicle which would shuttle the missile among 23 semi-underground garages built at 7,000-foot intervals around a large (five miles by two miles) oval "racetrack."[1]

The MX racetrack system represented a rather hasty design evolution from the previous leading candidate—a vertical silo MAPS concept—endorsed by the Defense Science Board and the Air Force as well as leading conservative critics of the Carter Administration's SALT policies. During the winter of 1978-79, this concept was found to suffer from a number of defects. A plausible case could be made that a vertical MAPS

---
*The multiple aim-point system provides an enemy with a multiplicity of targets to hit to ensure destroying the U.S. missile force. Since most of the shelters will be empty, a shell game is established; the enemy must hit all of the aim points to ensure destroying the one with the missile. The Air Force changed the name of the system, and now calls it a Multiple Protective Shelter (MPS) system. The notion of Nevada and Utah being filled with aim points for Soviet missiles did not sit well with residents of those states.

violated SALT prohibitions against the deliberate concealment of missile launchers and the construction of new fixed-site launchers.[2]*

In announcing the change to a MAP system with horizontal shelters and the ability to shift the missile rapidly among those shelters, the Carter Administration preferred to emphasize the military requirement for mobility rather than the unverifiability of MAPS under SALT. The improvement in design, Carter Administration officials contended, would allow the MX to be moved quickly if located by the enemy. The shift from vertical shelters, containing infrequently moved missiles, to horizontal garages housing a fully mobile TEL vehicle alleviated, but by no means eliminated, the potential verification difficulties of the system. Unlike vertical silos, Carter Administration officials reasoned, concrete garages could not be mistaken for "launchers" under Salt II. However, the Russians could only verify the system accurately because we would build in a number of cooperative measures, including verificaton ports in the roofs of the shelters, final assembly areas open to satellite inspection, and a system of barriers to assure the entry of only one TEL/missile combination per racetrack. The objection to this arrangement is obvious: what if the Russians decide to deploy a similar system, but refuse to provide the cooperative measures essential for adequate U.S. verification?[3]

During the winter of 1979-80, the MX/MAPS concept underwent still further evolution. Analysis revealed that the "dash" capability—the ability to move the missiles quickly from shelter to shelter — greatly increased the land requirements and cost of the system while adding little to its security. The TEL vehicles would be enormous, each weighing a million pounds. They would carry large mobile home-like structures called "visibility shields" to disguise their movements and would require 210-foot long garages. Critics pointed out that within the flight time of a Soviet SLBM—five to seven minutes as opposed to 30 minutes for an ICBM—the TEL moving at a maximum speed of only 30 miles per hour could reach reach only two shelters on either side of its previous position. If the Soviets had located that position, they would not have to attack all 23 shelters but only five, well within the range of current Soviet capabilities.[4] Although Soviet SLBMs in all likelihood would be unable to move in close enough to mount such an attack without first being detected by U.S. antisubmarine systems, this hypothetical design weakness was in fact no more improbable than the Soviet surprise attack scenario which prompted the search for a mobile-basing mode in the first place.

---

*SALT II places ceilings on the number of ICBM launchers each country can have. Launchers include intercontinental bombers and submarine launch tubes, as well as ICBM silos. In order to simpligy verifications of launch sites, which is primarily done through satellite photographs, the United States and U.S.S.R. have agreed to count each ICBM silo as a launcher. Presumably, the garage-like MX shelters would not be considered as launchers by the Soviet Union.

There was, however, a more practical and immediate problem. "Assuming that mass simulators* will be required," Dr. Perry noted in February 1980, "and the evidence is very convincing at this point, we have encountered the tough technical problem of providing this capability while preserving the ability to dash from one shelter to another shelter. The problem is that the baseline design requires that the mass of the entire transporter-erector-launcher (TEL) must be simulated. This requires a simulator so large that it effectively fills the shelter interior, thus blocking the entry of the dashing TEL. . . . Fortunately, we are looking at a variant of this design known as horizontal loading dock. In that design, only the mass of the missile and its launcher mechanism must be simulated, thus making this problem much more manageable. That design does provide the ability to perform a manned dash from a loop road position to a shelter.[5]

Thus was born the Carter Administration's final attempt at a workable MX basing design. In the horizontal loading dock concept, only the missile erector launcher (MEL) would be moved in and out of a smaller, and therefore less expensive, shelter and the transporter itself would act as a mobile surveillance shield. Since the oval layout had been decided upon mainly to maximize the number of shelters within range of the TEL, it too was discarded, in favor of a "linear road" design.

The open ends of the road meant that the original 7,000-foot spacing between shelters required by the closed loop design — in order to preserve the option of adding additional shelters — could be reduced to 5,000 feet. Additional shelters, if required, could be added to either end of the proposed road, or additional roads could be constructed. The more efficient land utilization of the "dragstrip" concept, the Carter Administration claimed, would reduce the required land area by some 2,000 square miles. If, in spite of such elaborate efforts to conceal the missiles, the Russians still managed to detect their position (as some U.S. strategists suspect that they will), a certain number could be kept on the strip or in the transporter garage, on alert status, ready to rush to another shelter upon warning of an attack. The difficulty with this approach was that it made the system ultimately dependent on warnings for its survival. "In effect," testified Undersecretary Perry, "it was a concept similar to the B-52s where a certain percentage of them were kept on strip alert." His explanation was ironic, as one of the key features of land-based ICBMs — which the Air Force contended it was trying to preserve — was "independence from strategic or tactical warning for pre-launch survival."[6]

---

*Mass simulators are, in effect, fake missiles. They need to be large enough, heavy enough, and dense enough to fool Soviet satellite sensing devices into thinking they could be a real missile. If each shelter houses a simulator or a missile, and if the vehicle transports simulators as well as missiles, the Soviet Union will never be sure where the real missile is.

Multiple aim-point schemes share a number of crippling defects.

(1) **MAPS offers no real protection.** MX proponents state that MAPS would once again make ICBMs invulnerable to a Soviet attack. This assertion is somewhat misleading. MAP basing does not effectively protect ICBMs from the effects of a nuclear attack. In fact, with multiple shelters hardened to 600 pounds per square inch (psi) or less — it would be extremely expensive to harden all 4,600 shelters beyond this point — the MAPS offers less real physical protection to the missile than the present silos hardened to 2,000 psi. Rather than withstanding the effects of a nuclear attack, MAP is designed to make such an attack prohibitively expensive to conduct, by forcing the Russians to expend many more warheads in an attack than they could expect to destroy. "Thus," testified Secretary Brown, "a rational enemy, if starting from a position of near-parity, would be deterred from attacking preemptively since one result of such an attack would be to shift the relative balance [in remaining warheads] against him."[7]

If this crude model of deterrence is indeed the real rationale for MAPS, then it is very difficult to see what MAPS adds to the deterrent equation that is not already provided by the far more tangible prospect of devastating retaliation by the many survivable components of the existing Triad of strategic forces.

The official justification for MAPS amounts to a tautology. An allegedly "rational" enemy not already deterred by the enormous uncertainties surrounding the outcome of any nuclear attack or by retaliation from other strategic forces, would be classified, almost by definition, as *irrational*, and therefore oblivious to the allegedly "unfavorable" cost-exchange scenarios posed by MAPS systems. Indeed the deficiency of any system composed of fixed land targets is, simply, that it can be attacked. In the case of the proposed MX system, this deficiency is magnified by the possibility of the Soviet Union attaining the ability to detect the relatively small number of missiles within the multiple shelter complex. If we cannot be totally confident that the MX will stay concealed — and the provision of various mobility options indicates that there is already some doubt on this score — then whatever adverse consequences are now alleged to ensue from Minuteman vulnerability would soon be replicated — indeed, magnified, because of the scale of the investment — by the proposed MX/MAPS system. As Dr. Jeremy Stone, Director of the Federation of American Scientists, has observed, "Congressmen have a right to be nervous when two different methods of security are proposed with neither sufficient by itself [concealment through deception on the one hand and through movement on the other]".[8]

(2) **MAPS invites a saturation attack.** Even supposing for a moment that MAP basing would help deter an attack against American ICBMs, the Pentagon's perennial question should then be posed, "What are the consequences of this system should deterrence fail?" MAP basing

invites a saturation attack on a central portion of the continental United States, more than tripling the scale of the attack over what would be required to attack just the current Minuteman system (some 6,600 warheads compared with the 2,000 required to attack Minuteman alone.) The 4,600 warheads needed to attack the MX system deployed in the arid Great Basin environment would generate huge radioactive dust clouds that would, depending upon prevailing weather patterns, spread lethal fallout over wide and densely populated areas.

The Office of Technology Assessment has calculated that between 2 million and 20 million Americans would die within the first 30 days after an attack on the present Minuteman and Titan silos. "This range of results is so wide," the OTA study noted, "because of the extent of the uncertainties surrounding fallout." In 1975, the Department of Defense estimated that an attack consisting of two 550-kiloton warheads against each of 1,054 American ICBM silos would result in 4,000,000 to 5,600,000 fatalities.[9]

During hearings before the House Interior Subcommittee on Public Lands in January 1980, Utah Representative Dan Marriot observed:

One of the big issues we continue to hear from those who are against the system is that what this system is going to do is make Utah a red dot on the Soviets' target list and, as a result, the entire state could be destroyed if in fact the Soviets decided to try to knock out all those missiles. Can you respond? . . . What would be the loss in the State of Utah in terms of our citizenry?

Marriot's query was followed by successive official attempts at obfuscation. The first to respond was Undersecretary of the Air Force Antonia Chayes:

I think you have to recognize the unfortunate fact that 6,000 Soviet warheads would make our entire country a target. Even if an area does not receive a direct hit, there is fallout, and all of the West would be facing the kind of fallout that would come from a direct hit on cities.

There are other targets presently in Utah, very important high-value military targets, which would not be exempt from the strike.

I think that that is the kind of nightmare vision that one can have, but I do not think that the positioning of the MX system in Utah or Nevada or any other place is going to make a great deal of difference in terms of vulnerability. But the failure to have an MX system may say something about the possibility of in fact having a "nuclear war."[10]

Since Undersecretary Chayes' answer was unresponsive to his question, Representative Marriot repeated it. Dr. Seymour L. Zeiberg, the Deputy Undersecretary of Defense for Strategic and Space Systems, replied that the presence of the Dugway Proving Grounds, Hill Air Force Base, and other installations in Utah "would create sufficient motivation for the Soviets to target the area in the case of a general war on the scale associated with attacking our land-based ICBMs."

Moreover, in a war, according to that scale, there would be sufficient targets in the areas west of Utah and Nevada, in particular California, such that the fallout, drifting from California eastward would have a devastating effect. So my personal judgement, a little bit off the top of my head, because I do not have the numbers in front of me, is that the presence of the MX in Utah would not add very much to the vulnerability that would exist in Utah in the circumstances were such a large-scale war started by the Soviets.

Mr. MARRIOT. Are you saying that because of Hill Air Force Base in Ogden and Dugway Army Depot, we are already as vulnerable as we are going to be? An attack on the MX system would not add to our problems there in case of an all-out attack?

Dr. ZEIBERG. Yes, as far as targets to the west of Utah. The fallout would be a function of what occurs upwind of where you are. Targets in Nevada, targets in California, all would be struck, and the weapons that are there would create fallout that would drift eastward. Under normal wind conditions the fallout would probably get there in considerably less than a day and therefore still be very hot. As a result the fallout would be fatal to many people.

Representative Jim Johnson of Colorado noted that Zeiberg's answer again did not respond to the question. Recalling the OTA study of the previous year, Johnson again asked: "If there is the theoretical preemptive strike against MX, what would be the casualty rate there?"

Dr. ZEIBERG. I do not know of that study, but I would venture a judgement that the answer you get would be somewhat larger than the 20 million because . . . the amount of fallout scales with the number of warheads so an attack on MX, therefore, would cause proportionately more fallout and more fallout deaths that result from it.

Mr. JOHNSON. It would be an increase over the projection for the Minuteman?

Dr. ZEIBERG. . . . I do not believe that looking at the problem in isolation is meaningful. I believe if the Soviets would attack Minuteman or attack MX, they would at the same time attack all other important military facilities that we have . . . and you have to consider the deaths and devastation that would occur from that total attack, not looking at any one element.

Mr. JOHNSON. I do not disagree with that, but I think you are not in agreement with the theory of the preemptive strike which would be limited to the Minuteman which is one of the justifications for building the MX.

Dr. ZEIBERG. By no means is that a justification. Nobody thinks that the Soviets would pinpoint Minuteman over all of our military assets and say I will go shoot that out and thereby gain a military advantage. Part of the story gets somewhat misrepresented. . . . The idea of an isolated attack on Minuteman is not held to be credible by me or other senior people in the Defense Department or the administration.[11]

The above testimony is clearly inherently contradictory; it is yet another example of the Pentagon's attempt to twist reality in its defense of the MX. It is simply untrue that the MX will fail to add significantly to the hazards of radioactive fallout from a nuclear attack. In the absence of the MX, for example, Hill AFB is the only strategic military target in Utah; it could be destroyed with one low-yield nuclear weapon. There are currently no such targets in Nevada, five SAC bases in California, none in Oregon, three SAC bases and a submarine base in Washington, one SAC base in Idaho, and 18 Titan missiles in Southern Arizona based in unhardened silos. In other words, the present number of strategic military targets west of the Rockies could be destroyed with about 60 relatively low-yield warheads. Locating the MX in the Great Basin would increase the weight of this attack at least a hundredfold.

Moreover, Zeiberg's assertion that "part of the story gets somewhat misrepresented" is disingenous, since one does not see either him or his colleagues, predecessors, or successors at the Pentagon rushing to amend the public impression, fostered by official statements and friendly journalists, that U.S. "prompt hard-target counterforce capability" (i.e., Minuteman) might be the object of a limited Soviet counterforce attack. Indeed, over the last decade senior officials have worried repeatedly in public that: the Soviet Union could develop forces aimed at destroying "*vital elements* of our retaliatory capability (Nixon, 1971);" that there were "many ways other than a massive surprise attack in which an enemy might be tempted to use his strategic forces. . . . (Schlesinger, 1974);" that "threats . . . to a portion of our forces are certainly conceivable . . . we cannot count on others to refrain from inventing ways to attack a limited but vital set of targets. . . . (Rumsfeld, 1976);" or that "no enemy should be left with the illusion that he could disable portions of our nuclear forces. . . . (Brown, 1979)."

In short, the Pentagon is trying to have it both ways, raising the specter of limited counterforce attacks in order to justify the MX, and then denying the plausibility of such scenarios when citizens and legislators express concern about their possible consequences. Moreover, the contention that all Soviet counterforce attacks would be full-scale does not mesh with Zeiberg's own assessment of the adverse political consequences allegedly flowing from the knowledge that "a major portion of the most responsive portion of our Triad is at risk." According to the Chairman of the Joint Chiefs of Staff, a bolt-from-the-blue attack on U.S. strategic forces is adequately deterred by the "substantial retaliatory capability that would survive such an attack," quite apart from Minuteman.[13] Hence the adverse political consequences feared by Zeiberg and others must derive from the impact of Minuteman vulnerability on the outcome of some lesser nuclear exchange. In Zeiberg's words, "We would be less inclined to face down" the Soviets (i.e., threaten nuclear first use) if our capacity for limited strategic nuclear options (i.e., Minuteman and/or MX) could be destroyed in a preemptive attack, or in retaliation, if such options were ever used.

To the extent that a limited nuclear exchange, growing out of a severe foreign policy crisis involving conventional and theater nuclear forces, is considered a more probable threat than an all-out attack on opposing strategic forces, then deployment of the MX in the Great Basin of the western United States increases both the probability and severity of a nuclear attack on this region.

(3) **MAPS means an open-ended commitment.** By the 1990s the Russians could deploy, in theory, the equivalent of 6,160 Mark 12-A (340 kt) warheads. Likewise, assuming that Soviet accuracy at that time is equivalent to the projected accuracy of the MX (400 ft. CEP) the Soviet Union could achieve a single-shot kill probability of 99 per cent against the MX shelters hardened to 600 psi, the design hardness of the Carter Administration's horizontal shelter scheme. Assuming an 80 per cent reliability for Soviet missiles, the Russians could expect to destroy 79 per cent of the shelters; that is, all but 42 of the MX missiles. Compensating for 20 per cent unreliability of the initial strike by targeting an additional 920 warheads, and distributing them uniformly across the MX fields, would further reduce the number of survivors, although it would not eliminate them completely. Unlike a silo-based system, in which each target is both hardened and contains a missile, the MAP system does not require a two-on-one attack to overcome the effects of hardness and unreliability. Since there is only roughly a 4 per cent chance that each surviving shelter contains a missile, the penalties for failure in the MAP system are considerably diminished. Similarly, a 100 per cent reduction in accuracy (from 400 to 800 ft. CEP) yields a 20 per cent decline in kill probability against shelters but a 42 per cent decline against silos.[13]

Twenty to forty missiles—the number which could be expected to survive the postulated attack—is less than 4 per cent of today's silo-based ICBM force. This number of survivors is *worse* than that generated by the most pessimistic scenarios of silo-based ICBM vulnerability. In the case of the DoD's example of a two-on-one 500 kt attack on Minuteman, using the same accuracy and reliability assumptions as the MAP case above, some 57 missiles would survive, about 5.5 per cent of the present silo-based force. Twenty to forty surviving MX (10 to 20 per cent of the force) is equal to 101 to 202 surviving Minuteman, in terms of surviving warheads. In other words, the massive investment in the MX system is equivalent to a gain of only 5-15 percentage points in the ratio of surviving silo-based ICBMs. Clearly, without the limits imposed by SALT II, which would prevent such a massive Soviet expansion as that postulated above, the planned MAP system does not offer a degree of protection against feasible increases in the Soviet counterforce threat commensurate with its immense cost and environmental impact.

The system would be obsolete even before it is completed, requiring additional deployments of shelters and missiles, or an ABM defense of those shelters containing the MX missiles. Thus, a commitment to the MAP basing mode would be building a future vulnerability, a vulnerability which is already generating strong pressures for abrogation of the ABM treaty, one of the last remaining barriers to an all-out arms race. In the words of Brigadier General Guy Hecker, the Air Force's former Special Assistant for MX,

> Another step we could go . . . *before we go to* [more] shelters . . . would be adding a ballistic missile defense device using existing shelters as a home. That is, an interceptor missile, but using all the existing facilities that we have in the deployment area there. That would only come about if SALT was totally obviated, and I hope that does not happen, but should it be obviated, then the arms race could go on to proportions the whole nation would be astounded by.[14]

It should be noted that it is American defense officials, legislators and aerospace executives—not the Russians—who are making noises about possible abrogation of the ABM Treaty.

(4) Verification problems and breaking out from treaty limitations. During a Congressional hearing in 1979 Secretary Brown was asked why the DoD was still pursuing various air-mobile basing schemes if the MAP system was indeed permitted by SALT, as the Administration contended. Brown responded that the key question was not

> . . . whether MPS [i.e., MAPS] is permitted by SALT, but rather whether verification can be mutually assured assuming both sides deploy a MPS system, and, in our case, can we adequately bound the threat to ensure survival of MPS.
>
> Our confidence in achieving either or both of these with MPS has been seriously questioned both within and without DoD. For that reason, we think it was and is prudent to develop an additional option to MPS.[15]

A year later the Air Force provided the following assessment of the verifiability and expansion potential of a Soviet horizontal MAP system:

> Without the incorporation of cooperative measures such as verification ports and procedures for the observable assembly and introduction into the deployment area of missiles and associated launch equipment, the Soviets could readily deploy additional launchers and missiles covertly into their multiple protective structure system. Such a deployment would be easier to detect in a SALT II environment. Even with SALT cooperative measures, the possibility would exist for the covert stockpiling of additional missiles that could be overtly deployed following the abrogation of expiration of a SALT agreement.[16]

With or without SALT constraints, the Russians would be free to construct a MAP or some other mobile system of their own, and to assert unilaterally, as has the United States in the case of MX, that it is verifiable. Whether it actually would be verifiable is another matter, as numerous defense experts have testified.

Moreover, in view of the current anxiety over Minuteman, if the Russians were to build a MAP or mobile ICBM system under the constraints of a SALT agreement, there would probably be no way to assure today's MX advocates that the Soviet Union would stay at agreed-upon levels after the expiration of the agreement. In the case of the MAP system, where the purchase of additional missiles is a relatively small percentage of total cost of the system, there could well be tremendous pressures on both sides to deploy more missiles in the already constructed shelters.

5. **Police state in the desert.** To maintain security and prevent missile locations from being compromised, the Air Force is planning an extensive electronic surveillance system "interconnected to security alert facilities distributed throughout the deployment area." Each security alert facility "will be located within the specified security police response travel time to the various protective structures." Although the Air Force claims that "a basic principle guiding MX program planning is to permit public use of the MX system road network," it also notes that the security system will require "monitored access to the areas outside the fenced protective structures. Some constraints on public access are anticipated during launcher movements which are undertaken to ensure preservation of location uncertainty."[17]

In the event of a security alert, General Hecker testified, access to the roughly 14,000 square miles encompassed by the deployment area "could be operated in a staged manner so all the people who have traditionally done business in there could be issued passes and could continue to operate." Other persons "from outside or inside the State, with or without beards, would be denied access."[18]

6. **Can MX/MAP Withstand a Nuclear Attack?**

According to the usual Pentagon criteria, the deterrent value of a system should be assessed not only by the results of computer-generated counterforce exchanges but also by the degree of confidence which can be placed in these results. Unlike submarine-launched missiles, 55 to 66 per cent of which are assured of surviving a surprise attack by virtue of their concealment in the world's oceans, the MX system's survivability is predicted on a purely hypothetical ability to withstand a nuclear attack. Since the system can never be tested, even partially, under actual operating conditions, a large measure of uncertainty surrounds estimates of the ability both of components and of the overall system to withstand nuclear effects — radiation, blast, heat, ground shock, debris, and electromagnetic pulse. Consider, for example, the question of how far apart MX shelters must be located in order to withstand the effects of explosions at neighboring shelters. According to General Hecker, "there is a wide range of uncertainty as to the exact effects of a one-megaton weapon detonated at ground zero. Since we do not have atmospheric testing, it is hard to garner this data against the hardness of a particular silo." Expert opinion, apparently, is divided.[19]

The September 1979 racetrack system proposal called for an initial 7,000-foot spacing between shelters to allow for future spacing of 3,500 feet with additional shelters, in case the Russians increase their warheads to mount an attack on all the shelters. Since the attacking RVs would be of lesser yield,* the Air Force reasoned, the spacing between shelters could also be proportionately less. In October the initial distance between shelters was reduced to 6,000 feet, with 3,000-foot spacing projected for additional shelters. In May 1980 the initial spacing was reduced still further, under environmental pressure, to 5,200 feet. But with this spacing, testified Gen. John W. Hepfer, Director of the Air Force's Ballistic Missile Office, "Electromagnetic pulse does become an area of concern, and we need to take a good look at that. There is an effect that when you get near the detonation, which we will be, there is what they call source region EMP. And there is an EMP concern relative to that effect."[20]

The Air Force is concerned that the buried power lines which supply electricity to the shelters will conduct the EMP surges associated with nuclear explosions into the missile power supply, damaging various electronic components. This problem might be overcome by adding fuel cells as a buffer at each shelter. Incoming electrical power would be converted at the shelter's support facility to chemical energy and pumped to the fuel cell in the shelter, where the process would be reversed to provide power to the launcher and missile. But this solution merely replaces one uncertainty with another, as MX program officials are reportedly unsure whether innovative fuel cell technology is sufficiently developed to meet the MX program requirements.[21]

Summary

Any plan for a land-based MX in a MAP deployment is seriously flawed because:

* it fails to provide adquate protection for the missiles, raising the prospect of the MX being just as (theoretically) vulnerable as Minuteman is today;

* it invites a massive attack on the central continental United States far in excess of what would occur now should deterrence fail;

* it must be expanded to retain its effectiveness, or defended with an ABM system, which would require abrogation of the ABM

---

*The Soviet Union can add warheads by reducing their size, and explosive power, in order to fit more warheads on each missile. This is known as fractionation.

treaty and ignite an interactive offensive-defensive arms race of unparalleled dimensions and expense;

* it is difficult to verify with any high degree of confidence and, with its tremendous costs sunk in deployed launch points and command and control systems, it encourages mutual fears of destabilizing "breakout" from treaty limitations or historic levels of deployment;

* it requires elaborate and prolonged deception in order to maintain MX survivability, an activity whose secrecy and security demands are incompatible with an open and democratic society; and

* it is subject to the same severe operational uncertainties as any other system required to "ride-out" or "absorb" a nuclear attack, and thus does not significantly increase confidence in the number of post-attack retaliatory forces.

Footnotes

1. *The MX Missile System,* Oversight Hearings before the Subcommittee on Public Lands of the Committee on Interior and Insular Affairs, House of Representatives, 96th Congress, First and Second Sessions, Serial No. 96-30, p. 59, hereafter cited as *MX Missile System.*
2. Strobe Talbot, *Endgame: The Inside Story of SALT II,* New York, 1980, p. 172.
3. See testimony of Dr. William Perry, Senate Armed Services Committee [SASC] Authorization *Hearings* for FY 1980, Part 6, p. 35351.
4. Sidney D. Drell and Richard L. Garwin, "SUM: The Better Approach to ICBM Basing," Draft Manuscript #4, 04/25/80, p. 16.
5. SASC Authorization *Hearings* for FY 1981, Part 2, p. 605.
6. SASC Authorization *Hearings* for FY 1981, Part 6, p. 3690; Letter from Air Force Chief of Staff General Lew Allen to House Armed Services Committee [HASC] Research and Development Subcommittee Chairman Melvin Price 12/29/78, cited in R.L. Garwin Testimony before the HASC, 02/07/79, p. 34 (draft).
7. "Statement on the MX System by the Honorable Harold Brown, Secretary of Defense, before the Subcommittee on Military Construction of the Committee on Appropriations, House of Representatives, March 25, 1980," p. 4.

8. Prepared Statement of Dr. Jeremy Stone, Director, Federation of American Scientists, in the *The MX Missile System*, op. cit., p. 537.
9. *The Effects of Nuclear War*, Office of Technology Assessment, May 1979, p. 84; *Civil Preparedness*, op. cit., Appendix III, "U.S. Civilian Nuclear Fatality Estimates for Various Counterforce Attack Scenarios," p. 158.
10. *MX Missile System*, op. cit., p. 100.
11. Ibid., pp. 101–103.
12. "United States Military Posture: An Overview by General David C. Jones, USAF, Chairman of the Joint Chiefs of Staff, for FY 1981," p. iii.
13. Data for the preceding analysis of MAP vulnerability drawn from the following: "Statement of Paul Nitze, Annex II, U.S.-USSR Systems," in *Military Implications on the Limitation of Strategic Offensive Arms and Protocol Thereto* (SALT II Treaty) Hearings before the SASC, Part 3, October 1979, pp. 896-899; TRW ICBM System Effectiveness and Survivability Slide Rule, TRW Defense and Space Systems Group, 1978; *MX Missile System*, op. cit., p. 122. *Air Force Magazine*, Nov. 1980, p. 119.
14. Ibid., p. 63.
15. House Defense Appropriations Committee *Hearings* for FY 1980, Part 1, p. 601.
16. SASC *Hearings* for FY 1981, Part 2, p. 589.
17. E-Systems' Greenville, Texas, division has received a study contract for an MX electronic security system based on its experience in developing and operating a security system in the Sinai Desert between Egypt and Israel, See "Sinai Technology Applied to MX," *Aviation Week and Space Technology (AW&ST)* August 18, 1980, p. 24; "MX Siting Area Decision Paper," Preliminary Draft, ICBM Program Office, August 1979, p. 12.
18. *MX Missile System*, op. cit., p. 62.
19. Ibid., p. 63.
20. HDASC, *Hearings* for FY 1981, Part 7, p. 357.
21. *AW&ST*, Oct. 6, 1980, p. 27.

Multiple Aimpoint Basing

9.
Conclusion: Is the MX Needed

The United States Department of Defense is proposing the production and deployment of the MX missile system. The system would include 200 missiles, each with ten warheads and an improved guidance system. The MX would carry more warheads and be more accurate than the missile it would replace, the Minuteman. Present plans call for the MX to be based in the Nevada-Utah desert. Each missile would be shuttled along a roadway and placed in one among a series of 23 hardened, underground shelters. Both because the missile would be mobile, and because its precise location would not be known to outsiders, the MX would be difficult for the Soviet Union to destroy in the event they launched a strike against U.S. ICBMs.

The elaborate and extremely costly basing scheme is seen as necessary to secure the system from a Soviet attack. CEP's investigation of the basing scheme leads us to the conclusion that the system would not provide the degree of protection needed. Only if SALT II ceilings prevented the proliferation of Soviet warheads would there be some chance of the scheme being effective in its objective. The Reagan Administraton has stated that it will not seek the ratification of SALT II, and that it will proceed with MX before seeking additional arms limitation agreements with the Soviet Union. Without SALT, there is a high probability of a race between the United States and the U.S.S.R. with the former building shelters and the latter warheads aimed at the shelters. Larger and larger portions of the desert would be destroyed and more and more money would be spent. There is a good chance that the United States would then resort to a ballistic missile defense system, undercutting the ABM treaty with the U.S.S.R. The net result of all this activity would be that neither side would be any more secure than it is today.

In addition, if the system should fail to deter the Soviet Union from launching an attack on the United States, the MX would invite a level of attack far in excess of what would now occur if deterrence should fail. Thus, while the scheme seems to provide little guarantee of halting further growth in arms, failure of the system would have even more severe consequences than failure of existing systems.

It is also CEP's conclusion that the issue of the missile is of even greater importance than the issue of the basing mode. Most public debate has assumed that the missile will be built but that the question to be decided is how to base it. Our research suggests that the fundamental rationale for the MX has little to do with enhancing our ability to deter a Soviet nuclear attack on the United States, and has little to do with the argument that we need to protect our land-based missile force from a potential Soviet first strike. Over the years, the Pentagon has put forward four basic arguments in support of the MX missile. We found each to be faulty.

(1) The MX, according to the Pentagon, is needed to replace Minuteman, a missile housed in fixed silos, that is becoming vulnerable to a surprise attack from increasingly accurate Soviet missiles. The problems with this argument are manifold. There are immense technical difficulties concerned with pulling off a successful first strike against targets as small and protected as missile silos. Even without such problems, a strike against Minuteman would leave the United States with a huge nuclear force for retaliation — submarine-based missiles, bombers carrying nuclear bombs and cruise missiles, shorter-range nuclear missiles and aircraft based in Europe and on carriers, and even a portion of the Minuteman force, 10 per cent of which, according to the Pentagon, would survive a Soviet first strike. Thus, even a successful attack on Minuteman would leave enough in the U.S. arsenal to obliterate the Soviet Union as a functioning society. What could the Soviets possibly gain by launching a surprise attack on Minuteman silos? This suggests the real rationale for MX lies elsewhere.

(2) A second argument frequently put forward is that MX is needed to hedge against vulnerabilities in the other two legs of the strategic Triad, submarine launched missiles and bombers. If planes and submarines become more vulnerable to improvements in Soviet air defenses and anti-submarine warfare, then a secure land-based missile would be even more important as a means of preserving the deterrent power of the U.S.

nuclear arsenal. The problem with this reasoning is that the introduction of air-launched cruise missiles has already increased the survivability of bombers, since they will not have to enter Soviet air space in order to deliver a nuclear warhead. In addition, the United States has a huge lead in submarine missiles and anti-submarine warfare. Our submarine missiles can be protected by maintaining an effective counter to Soviet anti-submarine warfare programs, rather than by an expensive new land-based missile. Moreover, the need for a triad of strategic forces is more a product of history, especially interservice rivalries over nuclear weapons budgets, than of logic. A more secure deterrent force can be attained in a variety of ways such as protecting our missile-carrying submarines from Soviet detection efforts and a full triad may not be needed.

(3) It has also been argued that the MX is needed to maintain parity with the Soviet Union, in light of the expansion and modernization of Soviet nuclear forces. Since the nuclear forces of the two nations are not identical—the Russians have more land-based missiles and fewer at sea, their bombers have far less range, and their missiles tend to have more explosive power but less accuracy than those of the United States—it is difficult to define precisely what equivalence means. For example, even with the recent expansion in Soviet strength, the United States has far more warheads than the Soviet Union, while the Russians have more missiles.

When pressed, Defense officials have admitted that the purpose of maintaining equivalence with the Soviet Union in terms of nuclear arsenals is largely symbolic; if the United States does not modernize its force as an answer to recent Soviet moves, we will be perceived by the world as weak, giving the Russians political and diplomatic leverage in the world's trouble spots. Since the MX will cost tens of billions of dollars and dig up huge tracts of Nevada and Utah, this seems like an excessively expensive exercise in symbolism. Even without MX, the United States has 9,000 nuclear weapons capable of hitting targets in the Soviet Union, all of them many times more powerful than the bomb that devastated Hiroshima. And there are additions and improvements to the nuclear arsenal already underway with cruise missiles, Trident missiles and submarines, Europe-based Pershing II missiles, new warheads on the Minuteman III, and improved guidance with NAVSTAR satellites. With such a mass of firepower, no one can consider the United States to be weak.

(4) A fourth argument in favor of the MX is that a new, highly accurate, and secure missile is needed in order to increase the options available to the United States and its allies in the event of a crisis involving Soviet bloc nations. Deploying the MX will add 2,000 warheads to the force, with the most sophisticated guidance systems available. Increased accuracy, in principle, increases the probability of destroying smaller and better

protected targets, such as command posts and missile silos. With present forces, a conflict with the Soviet Union that escalated beyond the confrontation of conventional forces would then involve nuclear weapons aimed at cities, industrial facilities and some military installations. With more accurate warheads, the United States could threaten those Soviet targets that can survive all but a new or direct hit, largely because they have been structurally strengthened to withstand much of the force of nuclear explosion. MX would give the United States the option of threatening the Soviet command structure and its nuclear retaliatory force without having to escalate to an all-out nuclear war.

The MX is a crucial element in a policy of being able to fight limited nuclear wars, the policy that was leaked to the press in 1980 and contained in the unreleased Presidential Directives 58 and 59. For years, U.S. nuclear weapons policy has had two faces. The public face claims that the purpose of the U.S. arsenal is to deter the Soviet Union from launching an attack on the United States. As long as America has a force of nuclear weapons that would survive a first strike and be able to retaliate against Soviet cities and industries, the Russians would never launch an attack. And since the Soviet Union also has a retaliatory force, a condition of mutual deterrence is in force. Only when one country is capable of disabling the other's retaliatory force would a first strike be feasible, and the condition is nowhere close to being a reality.

The more private face of U.S. policy has incorporated a wide range of options and goals for the nuclear arsenal, with deterrence of a first strike only one of them. When the United States had a virtual monopoly of nuclear weapons in the 1950s, the Eisenhower-Dulles doctrine of "massive retaliation" threatened the use of such weapons in a variety of situations. Since then, while the United States has had to accept the development of a significant Soviet nuclear force, U.S. actions, as opposed to stated doctrine, have continued to emphasize the maintenance of superiority over Soviet forces. This is to deter not just an attack on the United States but *any* military move by the Russians and their allies on the United States, its allies, and its interests. As a result, the concept of deterrence has been extended far beyond what has been commonly understood and the number of instances in which nuclear weapons might, in principle, be used has been expanded. The purpose of the MX is to create a weapon that is secure from Soviet attack and, most important, has the power and accuracy to enable the United States to threaten its use in a wide variety of situations.

The problems with an extended deterrence function for the MX are legion. The technical difficulties in achieving the advertised levels of accuracy are immense, and a number of prominent scientists feel that they are, at present, insurmountable. The idea of being able to fight a nuclear war that is limited, both in terms of targets and in terms of size, is an illusion. Nuclear explosions cannot be limited to precise targets because of the extent of the initial blast and resulting firestorms and radioactive clouds. Moreover, the first use of nuclear weapons in a conflict would undoubtedly lead to escalation and there is no guarantee where such escalation would stop. If the purpose of the nuclear arsenal is to deter war, the deployment of the MX as part of a strategy of being able to threaten limited nuclear war is likely to lead to exactly what it is supposed to prevent: nuclear war.

No matter how it is based, the MX is not needed for the deterrence of nuclear war. There is no rationale for the MX missile.

PART II.
Economic Impacts of MX Spending.

10.
Introduction

The decision whether or not to produce the MX should be based upon the legitimate defense needs of the United States. In Part I, CEP concluded that the MX cannot be justified for purposes of national defense. Having said that, it is important to evaluate the economic impact of such a system, its effect on industrial production, on employment and on inflation—in short, on the economy of the country as a whole. The MX is going to cost tens of billions, if not hundreds of billions, of dollars, and that amount of money injected into the economy cannot help but have substantial impacts.

The impact of MX expenditures can be enumerated in a number of ways. One is budgetary cost. CEP analyzed Air Force estimates of MX system costs and found them to be far too low. Whereas the Air Force continues to claim that the MX will cost $34 billion, CEP concludes, based on studies by other government agencies and our own analysis, that the MX system will cost at least $52 billion, and perhaps as much as $116 billion, without taking account of inflation. With inflation included, the MX could cost over $200 billion.

A second measure of impact is to ask what will be the effects on the economy of spending for the MX. The Air Force, as part of its Milestone II Environmental Impact Statement, predicted beneficial effects on employment and income from the $5 to $7 billion planned for Full Scale Engineering Development of the MX. In evaluating the Air Force's research

CEP found flaws which bias their results upwards and lead to estimates of employment that are too high. Also, the Air Force refused to analyze the possible inflationary consequence of MX spending.

The Air Force only analyzed MX expenditures; they did not analyze the effect of spending the same money in some alternative fashion. An important method of assessing the impact of an activity is to compare it with alternatives. Even if the MX were to generate jobs and income, alternative uses of the same money could provide even greater benefits — the jobs and income foregone are a measure of the costs of MX.

Even a brief review of available evidence on the economic impacts of military spending suggests that the Air Force's analysis was both incomplete and much too optimistic. Economists who have studied military spending tend to feel that military outlays are inflationary, occur at the expense of investment and therefore retard economic growth, and generate fewer jobs than alternative uses of the same money. If the Air Force had begun their analysis with a review of available evidence, it would have been hard to justify the narrowness of their work.

CEP undertook economic analysis with the objective of evaluating the impact of MX spending on key economic indicators—output, capital formation, employment and inflation — and comparing the impact with a number of alternatives. Using available input-output data, we calculated the likely impact of increased guided missile expenditures on output, manufacturing industries and other indicators of industrial impact, employment, and prices. We also calculated the likely impacts of spending on a series of alternatives: residential construction, urban rail transit, inter-city rail transit, public utility construction, and solar heating equipment. The results, presented below, are striking: by every criterion and in every comparison, guided missile expenditures have the least beneficial impact on the economy as a whole.

To carry the comparative analysis a step further, CEP posed another question: What would be the effect of shifting MX expenditures to a ten-year program of residential and commercial conservation of fuel oil? This question was originally posed early in 1980, in the context of the emerging crisis in the Persian Gulf, and our concern was with the implications for national security of building the MX on the one hand, or using the money to conserve fuel and reduce oil imports from the Persian Gulf. We found that the MX money could be used to cut oil imports by as much as 75% by 1990.

CEP also investigated how money is being distributed among companies building the MX and its components. Unlike many weapon projects, there is no single prime contracting company for MX; instead, there are several dozen associate contractors, and numerous subcontractors. In a series of tables, we present data on contracting companies, including the amount of money they are receiving and the work they are performing.

11.
What Will the MX Cost?

Addressing the Question

Just how much will the MX cost? Although the Department of Defense has consistently claimed that the system will cost $33 to $34 billion, there is substantial disagreement as to what this figure includes and what the final cost will be.

One source of confusion is inflation. The widely quoted DoD cost estimate is in constant dollars while others, including the General Accounting Office, have used price indexes to project future inflation rates and estimate MX costs in current dollars.* The Air Force recently issued its own current dollar estimate, although that service still emphasizes the figure that excludes inflation.

A second problem lies in determining what actually is included in the various estimates. Some figures measure the cost of acquiring the system, including research, engineering, testing, production of the missiles, and construction of the basing mode, while other figures add in the expense of maintaining the system once it is in place. Acquisition estimates are lower than life-cycle estimates.

---

*"Current" dollars include the effects of inflation while "constant" dollars remove inflation.

Third, no one has paid much attention to the likelihood of cost growth during the life of the system. It is possible the system will be expanded beyond the presently planned array of 200 missiles in 4,600 shelters; it is also possible that a ballistic missile defense system may be added. Moreover, the history of weapons procurement strongly suggests that costs will rise substantially, through contractor problems, engineering changes, slowdowns resulting from the political process, or any one of a number of other reasons. Yet, the Air Force has failed to include a contingency reserve in its budget estimates, or even to admit to the possibility that their estimates might prove to be too low.

Fourth, there are some expenses that do not even appear in DoD budget estimates. For example, the Department of Energy pays for the production of the missile warheads and this item has not been included in any estimate of MX outlays.

Air Force Estimates

In 1979, the Air Force estimated MX system costs, for the life of the system to the year 2000, to be $33.2 billion in 1978 dollars. (See Table 1) This estimate was for the horizontal shelters, race-track-basing mode, and a force of 200 missiles.[1]

In 1980, the Air Force estimated the bill to be $33.5 billion in 1980 dollars: it adjusted the previous estimate by inflation indexes for FY1979 and FY1980. (Table 1) Each agency of government is required to use Office of Management and Budget (OMB) inflation indexes in making budget projections; for the two-year period the DoD inflation indexes came to 17 per cent for development expenditures, 18 per cent for procurement, and 19.7 per cent for military construction.[2]

The shift in base year from 1978 to 1980 should have resulted in a proportionate increase in the estimate of MX system costs; but the estimate rose only 0.9 per cent. How could the Air Force have kept its estimate of system costs essentially constant in the face of an inflation approaching 10 per cent per year? It did it by omitting charges for operations and maintenance in the 1980 figure that were included in the earlier estimate. The figure of $33.5 billion (1980 dollars) should be compared with only $28.3 billion (1978 dollars), a growth of $5.2 billion (18.4 per cent) in only two years. By dropping operations and maintenance charges the Air Force converted the estimate of total system costs to one of acquisition costs only, not to a full estimate of life-cycle costs.

In Congressional testimony, the Air Force has admitted that its current estimates omit operations and maintenance,[3] but this distinction has not been made to or picked up by the press. Newspaper accounts continually refer to the Air Force's cost of the MX as $33 billion or $34 billion without mentioning the substantial increase that has occurred.

In May 1980 the Department of Defense announced several changes in the basing mode that were expected to save as much as $2 billion. The missiles would be shuttled along straight roadways instead of the original oval racetracks. Each missile, too, would be launched from a shelter, rather than from the transporting vehicles, which would permit the construction of a smaller vehicle. The DoD has also claimed that the use of straight roadways would reduce the amount of land needed.[4]

These changes were greeted in the media with accounts emphasizing how much money would be saved.[5] But, according to subsequent testimony by the former Undersecretary of the Air Force, Antonia Chayes, there might be no overall savings since other modifications would add to costs.[6] The redesigned system requires 4,400 simulators, or dummy missiles, in addition to the 200 real missiles. Costs of the simulators have not been included in the estimates. Former Undersecretary of Defense William Perry has stated that these costs would be $1.4 billion for procurement and $10 million annually for operations and support.[7]

In February 1980, the General Accounting Office identified an additional $700 million in cost growth, attributed to new requirements for the warhead fuze and for construction at one of the military bases in the Nevada-Utah basin. The DoD, however, has not included these new expenses in its estimates, as it is continuing to explore ways to reduce spending in other areas of the program.[8]

Accounting for Inflation

The most widely quoted financial figures for the MX system are in constant dollars; they have already been adjusted to allow for inflation in the 1980s and 1990s. Deflating yearly dollar estimates to obtain "real" costs is a valid procedure for many purposes, but not for all. Taxes are collected and tax money appropriated in current, not constant, dollars. Each year, Congress will be asked to appropriate an amount of money for the MX that reflects inflation. As Rep. John Murtha (D-PA) has stated, "Bills must be paid when expenses are incurred."[9]

The General Accounting Office, in early 1980, estimated current dollar costs of the MX to be $50.7 billion for development, acquisition, and construction; $55.6 billion including operations and maintenance until the year 2000.[10] At the time, according to an industry source, there was annoyance within the MX program and a feeling that "the GAO figure adds an unnecessary complication to the MX debate."[11] More recently, the Air Force has released its own estimate of current dollar costs, which the GAO reports to be $70 billion for the entire life cycle of the project while other sources indicate an estimate of either $78 billion (for 20 years of operations and maintenance) or $108 billion (for 30 years).[12]

OMB inflation indexes have been used to shift the estimate of constant dollar costs of the MX from 1978 as a base year to 1980, and also to estimate current dollar costs for the life of the system, which involves projecting rates of inflation far into the future.

The OMB indexes may be seriously understating inflation rates. The General Accounting Office feels that, "on the basis of past experience . . . these rates are probably understated. DoD officials have acknowledged that projections of inflation rates have historically been low."[13] Inflation rates for development, procurement, military construction and operations and maintenance are projected to be 10.6 per cent and below for FY 1981 and FY 1982, and to fall to between 6.2 and 6.7 per cent by the middle of the 1980s.[14] Actual inflation in military industries appears to be substantially higher. In the summer of 1980, the Defense Science Board reported that "increasing parts, materials, and labor costs and long lead times are increasing weapon system costs at a current annual rate of at least 20 per cent far in excess of the inflation factors used in DoD planning. . . ." Aircraft engine costs, for example, were up 28 per cent over a year earlier, while production lead times for engines had reached three years (168 weeks).[15]

While OMB insists that the actual inflation in the aerospace industry remains in the 10-to-15 per cent range, shortages of materials and labor, tight capacity among key sub-systems manufacturers, and long lead times exist throughout the industry.[16] Commercial aerospace business boomed in the late 1970s, and while it slowed during 1980 and 1981, there are good prospects of further expansion starting about 1982 or 1983, which make it unlikely that there will be a significant shift toward defense production. Projected large increases in defense spending, continued pressure for military pay raises, and rising fuel and construction costs suggest that inflation will affect all areas of defense outlays. Thus, OMB inflation indexes may be far too optimistic.

The understating of future rates of inflation where the MX is concerned may be even greater than that of most other military programs. This is due to a number of factors: the project will call on a particularly intense labor market; there will probably be delays in the withdrawal of land from the public domain; the resolution of energy and political problems will also delay the finishing date; and construction costs — a major portion of the system's overall budget — will be extremely high in an area of the country where materials are scarce and competition from other projects is strong.[17]

Areas of Possible Cost Increases

Costs of the MX system are most likely to increase in three areas: (1) testing and procurement of the missile, (2) construction of the basing mode, and (3) changes in the size of the system.

1. Testing and procurement of the missile.

The entire system's budget was based on an engineering cost model developed and run for the Air Force by TRW Corporation; neither the

Air Force nor TRW has released detailed information. The original estimates used 1978 as the base year; the shift to 1980 as the base year meant that OMB-mandated inflation rates were applied to the 1978 estimate.

There are a number of problems that could contribute to an escalation in cost. The GAO has highlighted some of the technical difficulties, such as the use of new materials and uncertainties involving liquid fuel tanks and the arming and fuzing systems of the warheads. By February 1981, new requirements for the warhead fuze and base construction had added $700 million to system costs. Delays, too, are likely to become increasingly critical. The test facilities at Vandenburg Air Force base were originally projected to cost $56.3 million in current dollars for the period from 1980 through 1983. In February 1980, the GAO reported a cost growth of 83 per cent, to $103.2 million. The reasons given included "preliminary estimates being too low," "more precisely defined design requirements," "a shift from two operationally configured vertical shelters" to "four operationally configured horizontal shelters," and the need to construct "two non-operationally configured interim facilities" due to delays in choosing a basing mode.[18] The delays have forced some of the funding to be shifted to later years and therefore have increased the cumulative impact of inflation. It is important to note that these delays are based on actual changes in design even though they will show up as inflation-induced cost increases.

Management problems have slowed the program, which led the House Appropriations Committee to delete $120 million from the FY 1981 funding request on the grounds that, since the Air Force was behind schedule, it could not possibly spend all it had requested within the fiscal year. According to the committee, this situation had existed for over a year, and would continue; it predicted even greater delays in the future.[19]

Slipping behind schedule adds to costs for several reasons. Many resources, such as labor, equipment, land, factory, warehouse and office space, and borrowed funds must be committed to a specified project, no matter how long that project takes. If it takes too much time, the government or contractor must continue to pay wages and salaries, rental payments, interest, and so on. Even the fact that the resources cannot be used on other projects is another form of cost, as is the forced inactivity of further resources, kept waiting while earlier stages of the system are completed.

As a result, delays in the schedule impose real costs. When more time is needed than was planned for, inflation also increases the final figure. The Air Force has claimed that a year's delay in achieving operation of the MX system would add $4 billion to the missile's costs, measured in current dollars.[20]

There are also cost overruns among contractors to be taken into account, and the MX will require a large number of such firms. Several companies that have received contracts have been involved in large cost overruns with other weapon systems. Rockwell, the most prominent, was the prime contractor on the B-1 bomber whose costs grew dramatically as the project continued. Earlier, the Autonetics division of Rockwell built guidance and control apparatus for the Minuteman II. Costs rose $150 million or 90 per cent in 12 months due to increased overheads, inefficiencies in production and poor quality control. The resulting system had a predicted life span one-third the length specified by the contract.[21]

Rockwell Autonetics is constructing guidance and control systems for MX. Past cost overruns are not proof of similar experiences in the future, but they indicate areas for concern.

2. Construction of the basing mode.

The cost of construction in this area of the country is likely to be far greater than the Air Force anticipated. The MX will require huge amounts of labor and materials, most of which must be imported. It is almost impossible to come up with a rigid budget or schedule in any project of this size, since it will take so much time and involve so many logistical problems. In addition, there are eight other large construction projects that will be underway at the same time as the basing-mode construction. These will place even more pressure on already scarce resources.[23]

Political actions will probably also delay the schedule as local officials try to reduce the negative impact of the system, local residents seek a more thorough environmental review and challenge the system in the courts, national groups debate the military and arms control aspects, and Congressional critics question the appropriations.

A significant proportion of the basing-mode costs will be borne by agencies other than the Department of Defense and the Department of Energy (for warhead development). While the missile's budget does not now include them as costs of the system, they nevertheless represent outlays of government funds arising from construction of the MX. Town, county, state, and federal agencies in areas such as education, housing, health, law enforcement, highway construction and maintenance, agriculture, land and water use, mining, small business, and overall government administration may incur expenses due to changes brought about by the MX. There will, of course, be added tax revenues as incomes, property values, and economic activity increase, but it is unlikely that such revenues will compensate for all the extra governmental costs.[23]

The costs of the basing mode could jump if the project were split between two areas. If the Nevada-Utah Basin is limited to 100 missiles and 2,300 shelters, and the remainder of the system is housed elsewhere, support services will have to be duplicated. Of greater importance, a second basing area would require the Air Force to purchase land rather than simply shifting it from the Bureau of Land Management. The Air Force has claimed that split-basing would add $3.5 billion to system costs.[24]

3. **The size of the system.**

The Administration asserts that the MX system is designed to protect the U.S. land-based ICBM force from a Soviet first strike. The size and configuration of the system are intended to assure that 1,000 warheads will survive a Soviet strike. This assumes that the Soviet modernization and expansion program stays below ceilings established by the still unratified SALT II. If the Russians build up to and beyond SALT II ceilings, they will have more warheads and could attack the MX in greater force, destroying a large portion of the system. To protect against such an event, the United States would have to expand the presently projected force of 200 missiles or add a ballistic missile defense system, or some combination of the two, to preserve the system's integrity.

The Congressional Budget Office has estimated the cost of responding to various Soviet changes. The CBO estimates were based upon a slightly different MX configuration from the present one; the dollar costs may not be strictly comparable, but the percentage increases are likely to be similar. The CBO estimated that if the U.S.S.R. moves from present force levels to the maximum number of MIRVed ICBMs permitted under SALT II, a 15 per cent increase in MX costs—building more missiles and shelters—would be required to ensure the survival of 1,000 warheads. Other Soviet options would increase MX system costs by between 46 and 158 per cent.[25] The Los Alamos Scientific Laboratory has claimed that if the Russians expand from their present total of 5,000 re-entry vehicles to 10,000, the cost of the MX would need to rise $23 billion, or 70 per cent over the baseline estimate of $33 billion, bringing the costs to $56 billion (1978 dollars).[26]

More recently, the General Accounting Office, in testimony before the Public Lands Subcommittee of the House Interior Committee, stated that the Air Force was now projecting an expansion of the system even if the Soviet Union remains within SALT II ceilings. The GAO estimated the current dollar cost of a 360-missile, 7,600 shelter system at $100 to $130 billion, not including warhead costs or the costs of adding a ballistic missile defense system.[27]

A second option is to counter Soviet warhead expansion with a ballistic missile defense (BMD) system tied to the MX, abrogating the Anti-Ballistic Missile treaty in the process. The Army is currently conducting development work on several BMD systems, one of which, the Low Altitude Defense (LoAD) system, is being designed for compatibility with MX. The decision to proceed with engineering development of MX is cited by Major General Grayson Tate, manager of the BMD program, as a major motivation for current work in ballistic missile defense research and testing. The missiles that comprise the LoAD system would be housed in one of the empty 22 shelters in each MX roadway; there would be one LoAD unit for each MX missile. The Ballistic Missile Defense Program will "be working very closely with the MX program manager, making certain that the C³ [Command, Control, Communications] system that is actually built and made a part of these shelters is adequate for the needs of this Low Altitude Defense system." While LoAd could be designed to protect Minuteman or other hardened targets, it is seen as "a particularly attractive option to extend the survivability of MX should there be unconstrained growth in the Soviet threat."[28]

A LoAD system tied to the MX is expected to cost between $6 and $9 billion with up to $1.4 billion budgeted for research and development.[29] If the MX is expanded beyond 200 missiles in 4,600 shelters, and then a BMD system is added, it would cost even more. The estimated cost of LoAD is also subject to increase, both from inflation and real sources.

Estimating System Costs

It is clear that the MX will cost far more than the $34 billion which the Pentagon is currently claiming as the system's acquisition cost. One need only look at the recent cost growth of major weapon systems to be reasonably certain that the MX budget will prove to be too low. In 1979, major systems then being acquired by the DoD had experienced an average cost growth of 70 per cent over their baseline estimates.[30] Since then, weapons costs have grown at an even faster rate, especially in such major systems as the M-1 tank (Chrysler/Avco), up 220 percent in eight years, the F-18 plane (McDonnell Douglas/Northrop/General Electric), up 140 per cent in five years, and the Trident ballistic missile submarine (General Dynamics), with the cost growth of 95 per cent in six years.[31]

A more realistic assessment of MX costs is possible, but it would require that the Air Force stop defending a figure that is far too low and begin admitting that a higher one is likely. The more realistic estimate would include the following:

1. Life cycle rather than acquisition costs should be used throughout. No one expects the cost of a weapon to end when the last one rolls off the assembly line. Adding operations and maintenance costs for a 20-year lifespan of the system would bring life-cycle costs to $39.4 billion (1980 dollars), based on the DoD estimate of $33.5 billion to acquire the system.

2. Budgetary costs that are not borne by the Department of Defense, including costs of warheads and of local economic adjustment, should be included since they are legitimate costs of building and using the system.

3. The MX was designed as a 200-missile system under the assumption that the SALT II agreement would restrict Russian warhead growth and limit the threat to MX. Current U.S. policy is that the MX will proceed in the absence of SALT II and before additional arms limitation negotiations are begun with the U.S.S.R. Without a SALT limit, the Soviet Union can build more warheads, theoretically threaten the MX, and force the United States to expand the system or build a ballistic missile defense

system to protect the MX. Since the likelihood of such a set of events has increased over the last year, the Pentagon should prepare and make public cost estimates for expanding the MX.

4. Costs will grow due to production problems, design changes, and contractor mismanagement. The General Accounting Office identified $750 million in such increases. The May 1980 changes in basing design, which supposedly found $2 billion in cost savings, also show that the inclusion of simulators would increase the budget by more than $1.4 billion. None of these changes have been incorporated in official budgets. Problems with contractors have to be considered as very likely, since they occur on most large weapons projects and several of the major MX contractors have a poor record in this respect. Delays often lead to cost growth that is attributed to inflation: in reality, however, the source is found in production or management.

5. All of the above are changes in the constant dollar cost of the MX. The Air Force should, in addition, present estimates of the current dollar costs. Both constant and current dollar estimates are needed since they measure different things; constant dollars estimates are a measure of real resource use while current dollar estimates measure the tax revenues that will be needed to finance the system. In preparing current dollar estimates, the Air Force should use realistic projections of price changes and should continually revise the projections to make use of the most recent information as well as to account for schedule changes and other events that, by altering the timing of production, also alter the effect of future price changes. At present, current dollar estimates are roughly twice the size of constant dollar estimates for an assumed 20-year life of the system.

Based on Air Force and GAO estimates, MX will cost over $40 billion in constant (1980) dollars to acquire and maintain to the year 2000. Allowing a 10 per cent reserve for cost growth due to contractor problems and design changes brings the estimate to about $45 billion. This figure increases by an additional but unknown amount by adding items from other budgets, such as Department of Energy costs for warhead development. Expanding the system to meet a large Soviet threat increases costs by between 15 per cent and 185 per cent according to the Congressional Budget Office — not counting the possible addition of a Ballistic Missile Defense system. The MX costs rise to between $52 and $116 billion (1980) dollars), after adding in the CBO estimate and still excluding warhead and BMD costs.

Shifting to current dollars, OMB inflation indexes yield a current dollar figure for system life-cycle costs that is approximately twice as large as the constant dollar figure. Since OMB indexes have consistently underestimated actual inflation, and since inflation in defense industries is likely to be higher than national inflation rates for the foreseeable future, including the period of heavy expenditures for production of the MX system, the current dollar estimates are probably understated. The current dollar cost of the MX, treated as being twice the size of constant dollar estimates again excluding warhead and BMD costs, come to between $104 and $232 billion, depending upon the eventual size of the system.

Occasionally, Pentagon officials have acknowledged the complexities and uncertainties of the MX program. Shortly before leaving office, Undersecretary of Defense William Perry described the "enormous difficulty" involved in achieving "a reconciliation between what can technically be done and what the requirements were [for the MX]." The task "was about as complicated as any program I've ever been involved in."[32] Earlier, in testimony before the Senate Armed Services Committee in May 1979, Dr. Perry admitted there was substantial uncertainty regarding program costs:

Senator Culver. What are the differences between vertical shelter MPS and the horizontal MPS? Are they both still viable now, and what are the differences other than verification and relocation speed?

Dr. Perry. I think those are the fundamental differences. There are some technical differences between the two and some differences in cost which are probably on the order of 10 percent or more. *Really, it is not within our ability to estimate cost on a program this large over this period of time.* (emphasis added)

A short time later, the DoD apparently discovered it could, after all, make such long-term cost projections. President Carter announced his approval of the MX system in June and his choice of the horizontal multiple protective structure basing mode in September. The system as a whole was advertised as costing $33 billion, a figure the Pentagon tried firmly to implant in the public mind as precise. Only in rare moments of candor do they admit that they just do not know.

Footnotes

1. Comptroller General of the United States, "The MX Weapon System—A Program With Cost and Schedule Uncertainties," *Report* to the Congress, U.S. General Accounting Office, February 29, 1980, p. 20.
2. Air Force Systems Command informed CEP, in June 1980, that the acquisition cost of MX in 1980 dollars was $33.5 billion. Press accounts generally use $33 or $34 billion, without reference to a base year.
3. e.g., Testimony of Maj. Gen. John W. Hepfer, Director, Ballistic Missile Office, Air Force Systems Command, Subcommittee on the Department of Defense, Committee on Appropriations, U.S. House of Representatives, *Hearings* on Department of Defense Appropriations for 1981, Part 7, pp. 339–340, Washington, USGPO, 1980. General Hepfer attributes the lifecycle estimate of $33.8 billion (1978 dollars) to the GAO. The GAO, however, gives the Air Force as its source. GAO *Report*, February 29, 1980, p. 19.
4. Testimony of Secretary of Defense Harold Brown and Undersecretary of Defense for Research and Engineering William J. Perry before the Subcommittee on Military Construction of the Committee on Appropriations of the United States Senate, May 6, 1980 (copies of prepared testimony obtained from the Department of Defense).
5. e.g., "Pentagon Seeks $2 Billion Savings in Simplifying MX Missile Program," *New York Times,* April 30, 1980, and "MX Deployment Changes Would Reduce Cost, Topographical Impact," *Aerospace Daily,* May 1, 1980.
6. Undersecretary Chayes told the House Defense Appropriations Subcommittee: "There are the cost decreases which may be offset by cost increases. . . . So we have now come to a hard number that the system design that has emerged thus far is on the whole substantially cheaper. It will not in my view, be $2 billion cheaper, because of the addition of some other things like the simulators." *Hearings,* op. cit., p. 336. A year later, the Air Force has still not changed their cost estimate to reflect either the $2 billion savings or the increased costs of other items.
7. William J. Perry, "The Department of Defense Statement on MX and Strategic Force Modernization," Testimony Before the Committee on Foreign Relations of the U.S. Senate, September 12, 1979.
8. GAO *Report,* February 17, 1981, pp. 4–5.
9. House Defense Appropriations Subcommittee *Hearings,* op. cit., p. 339.
10. GAO *Report,* February 29, 1980, p. 20.
11. *Aerospace Daily,* October 20, 1980, p. 266.
12. GAO *Report,* February 17, 1981, p. 5.
13. GAO *Report,* February 17, 1981, pp. 5–6. Jerome Stolarow, at the time Director of the GAO's Procurement and Systems Acquisition Division, told the House Committee on Government Operations in 1979 that there was a pattern of weapon system program managers underestimating system costs, including projections of inflation, partly to convince the Pentagon and Congress to proceed with the program. Subcommittee on Legislation and National Security of the Committee on Government Operations, U.S. House of Representatives, *Hearings,* Inaccuracy of Department of Defense Weapons Acquisition Cost Estimates, June 25–26, 1979, pp. 5–8, USGPO, 1979.
14. GAO *Report,* February 17, 1981, p. 43.
15. Defense Science Board, 1980 Summer Study, Task Force on Industrial Responsiveness, Summer Briefing, August 15, 1980, p. 7.

16. *Aerospace Daily*, October 23, 1980, quotes an OMB official that aerospace industry inflation "might be 10–15 percent." Numerous witnesses testified before the House Armed Services Committee, in Fall 1980, on deteriorating conditions in the defense industrial base. See "The Ailing Defense Industrial Base: Unready for Crisis." *Report* of the Defense Industrial Base Panel of the Committee on Armed Services, House of Representatives, December 31, 1980, Washington, USGPO, 1980.
17. Telephone interview, U.S. Air Force Cost Analysis office, September 19, 1980.
18. GAO *Report*, February 29, 1980; GAO *Report*, February 17, 1981.
19. Committee on Appropriations, U.S. House of Representatives, Department of Defense Appropriation Bill, 1981, *Report*, September 11, 1980, Washington, USGPO, 1980, pp. 319–320.
20. Testimony of Maj. Gen. John W. Hepfer, op. cit., pp. 337, 340.
21. For cost growth on the B-1 see Gordon Adams, *The B-1 Bomber: An Analysis of Its Strategic Utility, Cost, Constituency, and Economic Impact*, New York, Council on Economic Priorities, 1976. On Minuteman see A. Ernest Fitzgerald, *The Priests of Waste*, New York, W.W. Norton & Company, 1972.
22. Amy K. Glasmeier, *A Socio-Economic Impact Study of the Proposed MX Missile Project*, Department of City and Regional Planning, University of California, Berkeley, June 1980.
23. The Air Force has agreed to provide $4 million in impact planning aid to Nevada and Utah, President's Economic Adjustment Committee, EAC Newsletter, III, 2 (February 21, 1981)
24. David R. Griffiths, "MX Split Basing Study Reveals Benefits, Higher Costs," *Aviation Week and Space Technology*, February 2, 1981, pp. 20–1. An earlier *New York Times* story (Richard Burt, "Pentagon Favors Curb on Missiles in Utah, Nevada," May 24, 1980) reported "preliminary studies" indicating that split basing could cost up to $7 billion.
25. Congressional Budget Office, Congress of the United States, Resources for Defense: *A Review of Key Issues for Fiscal Years 1982-1986*, January 1981, pp. 24–27.
26. *Aerospace Daily*, June 11, 1980, p. 226.
27. *Defense Daily*, March 16, 1981, pp. 88, 94, reporting on testimony of Hugh H. Wessinger, associate director of the GAO's Community and Economic Development Division.
28. Testimony of Maj. Gen. Grayson D. Tate, Jr., Program Manager, Ballistic Missile Defense Program, Subcommittee on the Department of Defense, Committee on Appropriations, U.S. House of Representatives, *Hearings*, Department of Defense Appropriations for 1981, Part 9, June 11, 1980, pp. 513, 499, Washington, USGPO, 1980.
29. *Aerospace Daily*, February 26, 1980, puts LoAD at $6 billion; Gen. Tate, op. cit., p. 519, stated that LoAD development costs would be $1.1 billion (references to total system costs in Gen. Tate's testimony were deleted from the published version); The Los Alamos Scientific Laboratory stated LoAD costs at $7 billion (*Aerospace Daily*, June 11, 1980, p. 226). More recently, *Aerospace Daily* (March 9, 1981) reported on some system modifications and put LoAD costs at $1.4 billion for development and $8–9 billion for a ten-year life-cycle cost, in 1980 dollars.
30. Jerome Stolarow, testimony, op. cit., calculated from data on p. 4.
31. Calculated from Department of Defense, Office of the Secretary of Defense (Comptroller), *Selected Acquisition Reports*, as of December 31, 1980.
32. *Aerospace Daily*, Jan. 13, 1981, p. 50.
33. Armed Service Committee, U.S. Senate, Department of Defense Authorization for Appropriations, 1980, *Hearings*, Part 3, p. 1433, Washington, USGPO, 1979.

TABLE 1
AIR FORCE ESTIMATES OF MX SYSTEM COSTS

Life-Cycle Cost of MX System
(billions of 1978 dollars)

Development		$ 6.5
Acquisition:		
Aircraft procurement	$ .3	
Missile procurement	10.7	
Facility design and construction	10.8	21.8
Subtotal of development and acquisition		28.3
Operations and maintenance		4.9
Total life-cycle cost		$ 33.2

ACQUISITION COST OF MX SYSTEM
(billions of 1980 dollars)

Development		$ 7.65
Procurement:		
Aircraft	$ .35	
Missile	12.6	12.95
Construction		12.94
Total acquisition costs		$ 33.54

SOURCE: General Accounting Office, "The MX Weapons System—A Program with Cost and Schedule Uncertainties"

SOURCE: Air Force Systems Command

12.
The Air Force's Analysis of the Economic Impact of MX Spending*

When President Carter announced his decision, in June 1979, to proceed with the engineering development of the MX, there were widespread press reports of the economic benefits that would accrue to the nation in general and to key states and regions in particular.[1] The source of these optimistic estimates was the Air Force's Environmental Impact Statement (EIS) for Full-Scale Engineering Development (FSED) of the MX.[2] According to the Air Force, FSED expenditures of approximately $1 billion per year for five years would generate 130,000 new jobs nationally, and up to 46,000 jobs in California. (These estimates are for FSED on the missile alone, and do not include the basing mode.)

The Air Force derived its estimates from statistical analysis performed as part of its environmental impact analysis.[3] On the basis of a thorough evaluation of this work, as presented in the EIS, CEP has concluded that the Air Force substantially overstated the gains from the project and understated or even ignored significant costs. The Air Force's conclusions and, since those conclusions have been widely disseminated through uncritical press accounts, the perceptions of the general public are far too optimistic about the economic impact of money spent on the MX.

---

*For a more complete rendering of the material in this chapter, and in chapter 14, see Gail Shields, "Multipliers, Models, Missiles" Council on Economic Priorities, 1980 (unpublished).

Two methods were used to estimate the effect on the national economy. One was an input-output model,** modified to include Keynesian demand effects. In order to use this model, a number of assumptions had to be made which, according to the Air Force, "result in estimates that are at the upper end of the range of all results that might be expected. There are, in fact, conditions under which these results would obtain, but the probability of these conditions prevailing throughout the period of FSED is small."[4] Despite this small probability, the Air Force released the model's estimate that 130,000 jobs would be created by the billion dollars per year of FSED expenditures.

A second set of estimates came from the quarterly econometric model developed by the Bureau of Economic Analysis of the U.S. Department of Commerce.[5] The Air Force obtained employment results for three different estimated unemployment levels for the five years of FSED expenditures. Each result is given as a range, because data limitations force analysts to recognize that the upper limit of the range is likely to be too high, and the lower limit too low, and there is no way for the analysis to yield a good estimate of the most likely point in between.

If the national unemployment rate is assumed to be 8 per cent during the period, the Air Force predicts that FSED expenditures would add between 88,000 and 126,000 jobs to the economy for the period as a whole. If the national unemployment rate were 4 per cent, the prediction is that there would be between 15,000 and 22,000 new jobs.[6] The wide range of results implies that the effects of FSED expenditures depend heavily on the state of the economy, a conclusion that is hardly surprising. However, it is a conclusion that should have precluded the Air Force from releasing an estimate of job creation — 130,000 — that is outside of the upper bound of the highest range of their own estimates.

Moreover, the Air Force did not use this model correctly. They describe their method as follows:

Published results from the BEA model (Hirch, June 1977) provide Gross National Product (GNP) multipliers for each of five policy simulations. Of these, two are appropriate to required FSED analysis:

a) An increase of $5 billion in government purchases from the private sector, expended at the rate of $1 billion per year over a 5 year period. This will be used to represent the expenditure of MX FSED.

b) An increase of $5 billion in personal taxes collected by the government, at the rate of $1 billion per year for 5 years, This will be used to represent an opportunity cost of MX FSED in terms of consumption and investment in the private sector which be [sic] foregone.

---

*Input-output models are described in chapter 14.

The net effect of MX on the national economy will be represented by the difference between the effects. . . .[7]

The Air Force did not use the BEA quarterly econometric model; they simply used multipliers* derived by Albert Hirch in 1977 from simulations of the model. Use of multipliers to predict MX effects is considered by Hirch himself to be inappropriate.[8] The BEA model is useful over short prediction periods (two years) to assess what government spending and investment patterns on alternative projects would do to the economy as a whole. The model is not capable of analyzing industries or of isolating a "missile sector," let alone the impact of increasing demand in that sector.

Moreover, the Air Force did not investigate expenditures on guided missiles, or even on military procurement. In using the model the Air Force was forced to substitute "government purchases" for missiles as the key variable whose impact is predicted. In addition, since the model does not deal with sectors of the economy but with the economy as a whole, the national unemployment rate was used as a measure of supply conditions in the missile industry and in the sectors which feed into missile production.

The use of a tax increase was supposed to provide a measure of what MX would cost. The reality, however, is that MX and other military programs will be financed by cuts in social service and other civilian government outlays, a form of funding that produces a totally different effect than that produced by a tax increase. This curtailment will include mass-transit funding, solar energy development, housing, funding for urban capital infrastructure and the like.

These points are not minor considerations. The specific intent of the Air Force was to assess MX and not "government purchases" and the highly aggregative nature of the model precludes any assessment of the effect of capacity and labor pressures on the missile and other defense industries. The use of several levels of a national unemployment rate does not in any way convey supply conditions prevailing in the missile industry.

Since the Air Force analysis ignored both the impact on specific industries and the industrial and occupational composition of the employment that would be generated, a great deal of the detailed economic impact was eliminated from the start in favor of concentrating on a single variable—employment. The resulting figure, 130,000 jobs per $1 billion increase in final demand, would be difficult to justify had it even been correctly calculated.

The narrowness of the Air Force's focus is further illustrated by their comments on the possible inflationary impact of MX expenditures. The

---

*A multiplier is the effect on output (GNP) of a change in some item of expenditure, in this case government purchases and personal taxes. The impact on GNP will be some multiple of the initial change in expenditure.

Air Force has been excessively sanguine about the effects of inflation on MX system costs, and essentially has ignored the possibility that the MX will cause higher inflation. Yet their own analysis indicates the opposite is true. The econometric tests referred to above compared the job-generating capabilities of MX expenditures at different levels of national unemployment. Under conditions of low unemployment, the Air Force concluded that "positive net effects would persist for only a short time; the high level of employment and capacity utilization in the economy result in the positive impacts of MX FSED being transformed into price-level changes."[9] In other words, if national unemployment is low, MX expenditures will tend to generate substantial inflationary pressures.

As late as 1981, the Air Force had ignored its own conclusion. In response to a question submitted by Nebraskans for Peace commenting on the draft Milestone II EIS, the Air Force stated that "The national inflationary impact of the MX system is beyond the scope of this EIS. Such impacts are considered in the overall Federal funding allocation process, and thus are more properly within the purview of the Office of Management and Budget and the Congress."[10]

As far as CEP could determine, the Air Force had not sought the advice of other Federal agencies concerned with economic impacts, for example, the Department of Commerce, where the economic models are developed.

It appears that the Air Force has been willing to conduct analysis, and widely publicize the results, of economic impacts that they see as supportive of the MX system, but they are unwilling to analyze negative ones.

The Air Force was not required to present socioeconomic analysis in the EIS. The agency chose to do so, and the results from the economic analysis formed the basis of press accounts as to how MX expenditures would affect the economy. It is quite striking, then, for the Air Force to claim that certain economic impacts were beyond the scope of their analysis.

Footnotes

1. For example, Pamela G. Hollie, "MX Missile: New Source for Jobs, Revenue," *The New York Times,* June 12, 1979.
2. Department of the Air Force, *Environmental Impact Analysis Process,* MX: Milestone II, Final Environment Impact Statement, Six volumes, no date (issued 1978) Hereafter referred to as Milestone II EIS.
3. The actual work was performed by HDR Associates, Santa Barbara, California.
4. Milestone II EIS, vol. II, p. 125.
5. Albert A. Hirch, "Policy Multipliers in the BEA Quarterly Econometric Model," *Survey of Current Business,* 57, p. 6.
6. Milestone II EIS, vol. II, p. 127.
7. Ibid., p. 126.
8. Telephone conversation with Albert Hirch, Bureau of Economic Analysis, U.S. Department of Commerce, July 2, 1980.
9. Milestone II EIS, vol. II p. 128.
10. Ibid., vol. VI, Part 4, p. 19.

13.
Economic Impact of Military Spending

The Air Force has presented a rosy picture of the economic effects of MX expenditure for the period of full-scale engineering development. The optimism that pervades the Air Force analysis is consistent with the tendency, over the past three decades, to regard military outlays as beneficial to the overall economic health of the country. In contrast, there is a growing body of economic research on the impact of military spending, the results of which imply that money spent by the military imposes substantial burdens on the economy.[1]

This is hardly a new conclusion, even if the research on which it is based is recent. Economists since Adam Smith — and even earlier — thought that military spending, while necessary, burdened a national economy and should be kept within bounds.[2] Military spending has always been thought to reduce standards of living and economic growth by cutting into consumption and investment, and by creating inflation. As recently as the late 1940s, prominent economists and U.S. government officials argued that an expansion of military spending would undermine the private economy since it would cause "ruinous inflation, economic dislocation, or both."[3]

Until 1950, it was thought unnecessary to keep a large peacetime military. Large-scale mobilization took place when war was imminent, and de-mobilization when it was over. Now the existence of a large, peacetime military force means large, ongoing military expenditures with further increases in times of war, like the Korean and Vietnam wars.

Also since about 1950, the emphasis upon government expenditures as a means of stimulating the economy and preventing depressions helped create an environment for the growth of military outlays. Military spending met a variety of needs — national security, jobs, revenues and profits for companies, income and facilities for communities — and soon the presumed economic benefits of military expenditures came to be used to justify expanded military programs, while their costs were largely ignored. The Air Force's analysis of the impact of MX spending is an example of this type of reasoning.

The notion of the military as an economic burden began to recede, perhaps, as Ron Huisken of the U.N. Centre for Disarmament has noted, as a logical consequence of the prominence given to national security.

> For all nations the security of territory and population ranks as the first responsibility of Government and has first claim on the national product. The cost of providing for the national security, while not unimportant, is a very secondary consideration. If, to the first approximation, the requirements of national security must be met regardless of cost, it follows that there is no great incentive to determine the true extent and character of these costs. . . .
>
> There are several grounds on which one can question the wisdom of this attitude. First of all, it is widely acknowledged that the true foundation of national security is a strong healthy economy. . . . It is very much within the interests of states to know whether the defense effort is positive, neutral or negative in its effects on the basic vitality of the economy over the longer term.
>
> Secondly, . . . the relative importance of cost rises significantly if it is the case that maintaining or expanding the defense effort is accompanied by a growing sense of national insecurity. . . .
>
> [Thirdly,] over the postwar period, for all practical purposes, the objective of national security has been pursued as though it were synonymous with military security. But, properly conceived, security is a much broader notion.[4]

Military budgets, and the awarding of military contracts and the opening or closing of military bases, are frequently discussed in terms of the effects of the action on employment. Military spending is correctly seen as a source of jobs, and military contracts as creators of employment for regions and communities. This claim has been widely trumpeted in the case of the MX. The Air Force's Milestone II EIS projected substantial job gains from FSED spending; as contracts are awarded, the press details how many jobs the local community will gain, and when President Carter approved the advancement of the MX project into FSED, the national press reported on the jobs to be created and the income to be earned.[5]

There can be no doubt that military spending generates employment. U.S. military outlays are approaching $200 billion for FY 1982, and that amount of spending can create large numbers of jobs. However, according to Ron Huisken, "this occurs because it is expenditure, not because it is *military* expenditure. Indeed, from the standpoint of creating jobs, military expenditure is relatively inefficient."[6]

A growing body of evidence supports the notion that miltary spending is an inefficient job generator. An increase in military expenditure stimulates employment and a decrease destroys existing jobs. But when explicitly compared with an alternative, such as a change in taxes or a change in some other government program, money spent on the military shows up poorly. Military spending creates fewer jobs than alternative forms of government expenditures. An increase in military outlays that is compensated for by an increase in taxes or a cut in other forms of government spending will tend to result in fewer, not more, jobs in the economy as a whole. A cut in military spending that is compensated for by a tax cut or a rise in alternative government programs will tend to result in a net gain in employment.[7]

Similar results have been found with respect to investment and economic growth. A rise in military outlays induces slower rates of growth of output and slower growth, or even a decline, in investment spending. A trade-off between military spending and investment—that has been discovered in several studies—occurs for two reasons. One is that military spending and investment spending frequently compete for the same resources, such as technical, managerial, and other highly skilled labor, productive capacity in capital goods industries, raw materials, and finance. Second, higher military outlays result in higher taxes or, more likely, larger government borrowing requirements and higher interest rates. Both higher taxes and higher interest rates are disincentives to new investments.[8]

There is widespread agreement that military spending is inflationary. Data Resources, Inc., a prestigious private research and forecasting firm, introduced a study of the Carter Administration's five-year defense spending program for FY1981-85 by stating that "Military spending is typically thought to be more inflationary than most other forms of federal spending because it adds to aggregate demand without increasing the supply of privately consumable goods."[9]

Economic conditions are crucial in assessing the inflation caused by military outlays. Higher defense expenditures tend to be more inflationary if the economy as a whole, and those industries that produce for the Defense Department, are operating at high levels of output. Thus, the military build-up for the Vietnam War was inflationary because of the strong state of the economy as a whole, while the military expansion of the early 1980s is likely to worsen existing inflationary conditions within military industries, already plagued by shortages of materials, production bottlenecks, and substantial cost growth.

The inflationary effects of higher military spending can, however, be offset by monetary and fiscal policies. If these expenditures are not accompanied by tax increases or cuts in non-military programs, and if money and credit are allowed to grow with the rising budget deficit, inflation will be higher and result in lower real levels of consumption and investment, as well as a riskier climate for new private investment projects. If planned growth in defense budgets is defined in real terms, as at present, then the military will be insulated from the effects of inflation, even as the higher military outlays are a prime cause of inflation.

The effects of rising military outlays can be illustrated by a recent set of studies commissioned by the Department of Defense. In the fall of 1980, the DoD asked five of the nation's leading private economic research and forecasting firms to assess the impacts of an annual real growth in the defense budget of 4 per cent, and one of 10 per cent, both for the period from 1982 to 1986. Each firm was given identical assumptions and asked to assess the impacts. The basic results, as summarized by a senior DoD economist, are as follows:

> First, . . . the 10% increase must be compensated [for] by reductions in non-defense spending or by higher taxes.
>
> Second, the real danger from uncompensated increases in defense spending is not inflation, per se, but rather the reaction of the capital markets to the possible enlarged federal government deficits. Higher levels of defense spending if they come at the expense of new private capital investments designed to increase productivity will be inflationary in the long run. Fiscal and monetary policies must be pursued so increases in defense spending do not reduce private sector spending on much needed new equipment and facilities.
>
> Third, . . . the 10% growth target is probably the maximum that could be adopted under current economic conditions without imposing allocation procedures to channel supply to government. . . . Bottlenecks will develop in key industries at budget growth rates in excess of 10%, and, in fact, bottlenecks may even inhibit completion of planned defense programs on schedule and at programmed cost at growth rates significantly below . . . 10%. . . . The available measures of industry capacity utilization and for the entire economy are not accurate indicators of real potential excess capacity in sectors affected by defense production. . . . There is a significant amount of available excess uncompetitive U.S. industrial capacity and only a limited amount of excess competitive capacity.*

---

*Competitive industries are those able to maintain or expand their U.S. market share, at the same time marketing their goods internationally; uncompetitive industries are those facing declining domestic markets, shrinking U.S. market shares, and inability to sell their output internationally.

Fourth, the increase in real output cannot be totally met through domestic production. . . . one likely outcome of any increase in U.S. expenditures is that a large part of the increase in demand could only be met easily by purchases of foreign-made products. . . .[10]

The analysis presented at the symposium is consistent with evidence, summarized above, on the economic impact of military spending. The Reagan Administration, however, has embarked on a long-term program of rapidly rising military outlays, including the MX, reductions in non-military spending, and substantial tax reductions. Thus, the chances that rising defense outlays will be compensated for by tax increases is slight. And since cuts in non-military outlays are balanced by expected tax cuts, the immediate result will be a widening of the budget gap and a likely increase in pressures for both inflation and interest rates to rise.

In this context, the assumption the Air Force employed in its analysis of the MX, that MX expenditures would be paid for by higher tax revenues, is highly unrealistic.

Footnotes

1. Some of this research is summarized in Michael Edelstein, *The Economic Impact of Military Spending,* New York, Council on Economic Priorities, 1977. See also, David Gold, "MX and the American Economy," *Arms Control Today,* February 1980.
2. Adam Smith, *The Wealth of Nations,* any edition, especially Book V, Chapter 1.
3. Edward Flash, Jr., *Economic Advice and Presidential Leadership,* New York, Columbia University Press, 1965, p. 37. See, also, Fred L. Block, *The Origins of International Economic Disorder,* Berkeley and Los Angeles, University of California Press, 1977, pp. 102-108, and Daniel Yergin, *Shattered Peace: The Origins of the Cold War and the National Security State,* Boston, Houghton Mifflin Company, 1977, pp. 398-404.

4. Ron Huisken, "Economic and Social Consequences of the Arms Race," Address to the NGO Conference on the Arms Race and the Human Race, United Nations, NY, June 12, 1980, pp. 1-2.
5. Department of the Air Force, Environmental Impact Analysis Process, Final Environmental Impact Statement, MX: Milestone II, undated (issued 1978); Pamela G. Hollie, "MX Missile: New Source for Jobs, Revenue," *New York Times*, June 12, 1979; Larry Levy, "Rockwell Will Construct MX Parts in Tulsa, *Tulsa Tribune*, September 14, 1979.
6. Huisken, op cit., p. 6.
7. Roger Bezdek, "The 1980 Economic Impact — Regional and Occupational — of Compensated Shifts in Defense Spending," *Journal of Regional Science*, 15, 2 (1975), pp. 183-198; summarized in Edelstein, op. cit.
8. R.P. Smith, "Military Expenditure and Capitalism," *Cambridge Journal of Economics*, 1 (1977), pp. 61-76.
9. Dr. Robert A. Gough, Jr. Dr. Paul H. Earl, and Stephen H. Brooks (all of Data Resources, Inc.), "More for Defense?" *Hearings* before the Committee on the Budget, United States Senate, March 3, 1980, Washington, USGPO, 1980, p. 283.
10. Dr. David L. Blond, "Symposium on the Impact of Higher Levels of Defense Expenditures on the United States Economy in the 1980's," U.S. Department of Defense, photocopy, 1980; sections quoted are from the forward and summary. See, also, David Gold and Robert DeGrasse, Jr., "Economic Recovery Vs. Defense Spending," *New York Times*, February 20, 1981, and Robert DeGrasse, Jr. and Paul Murphy, "The Impact of Reagan's Military Budget," *Newsletter*, Council on Economic Priorities, May 1981.

14.
Input-Output Analysis of Guided Missile Production

To provide a structure for analyzing how money spent on a new ICBM would affect the economy, CEP undertook an examination of the most recent Input-Output (I-O) table of the U.S. Department of Commerce.* Our objective was to assess the effects of MX expenditures on output, employment, inflation, and the industrial base. In order to provide a comparative perspective, CEP also analyzed five examples of alternative expenditure patterns. The five were chosen to reflect non-defense public policy options, each of which had two additional characteristics: they could be represented by final demand categories in the I-O tables and they were basic expenditures with well-known technologies and significant but not extremely high capital utilization. We had no prior knowledge of their economic impact except at the most general level; we avoided choosing projects needing a very high level of technology, such as space research, or employing unusually large numbers of people, such as education.

One of the industries whose activity is measured in the I-O table is "complete guided missiles;" it was selected to represent the MX. This meant that we could only investigate expenditures on the missile and not on the extensive basing system since there is no I-O category to correspond to missile basing. However, since the design of the basing system was subject to extensive revision, and remains so at the time of this writing, we felt that analyzing the missile would be significant.

Other industries we examined included: "residential construction," to represent new housing; "public utilities construction," to represent the building of solid waste treatment facilities; "railroad equipment manufacturing," for inter-city rolling stock; "mass-transit equipment manufacturing" to represent rail vehicles for urban transportation; and "solar energy equipment," representing the manufacture of solar collectors for housing and business. The last-named category is not itself represented in the I-O tables but was derived from other I-O categories by Professor Craig Peterson of the University of Utah.

Any economic activity, whether it be the construction of weapons, railroad cars, or houses, requires the use of materials and labor both at the point of production and elsewhere in the economy. A demand for a product, whether generated by households buying consumer goods, businesses engaged in new investment, or government purchasing goods and services, will stimulate demand for a variety of inputs. It is possible to trace the effects, throughout the economy, of an increase in the demand for a particular product, in this case guided missiles. Input-Output analysis is a widely used analytical method for tracing such effects and deriving a variety of measures of how the manufacture of a single product affects the economy as a whole.

I-O analysis uses a transactions table which is based on relationships among industries and consumers (including government), in the economy as a whole. The transactions table is derived from the fact that what is produced by an industry either meets final demand or is used in further production. The table is arranged in columns and rows. One side represents demand, both transactions between industries and final demand by households, investors, government, and the international sphere. The other side of the table represents the supply of inputs, entering into production.

The entries across a row of an input-output table are the sales of a specific industry's output to every industry that uses that output in production, including itself. There are also entries across a row that measure an industry's contribution to final demand, say of households. Adding along the row gives the value of gross output.

The entries in the columns of an input-output table are inputs used by a given producing industry, including those drawn from itself. Adding all inputs gives the value of total inputs for that industry.

The table is usually divided into segments, representing the principal classes of transactions that occur in the economy: intermediate transactions, which occur among industries in order to create final output; and final-demand transactions, which are purchases for final use by households, business, government, and foreign purchasers of U.S.-produced output.

The totals obtained by adding columns and rows include both final and intermediate transactions. Gross output is equivalent to sales. Since it includes both final and intermediate sales, it is not the same as the more familiar gross national product (GNP): to obtain GNP, intermediate transactions are deleted. GNP is equivalent to final demand. Thus, gross output is equal to intermediate output plus GNP.

Most I-O analysis focuses on the intermediate-demand section of the transactions table. The amounts of purchases and sales depicted in this segment outline the structural relations in the production economy as a whole. It is possible to obtain, from a transactions table, a coefficient measuring the percentage of final output of any industry that is represented by the inputs obtained from any other industry. This is a measure of the on-site use of inputs. However, each input used in the production of an output is itself produced using a variety of inputs. Each final output will have an array of inputs, and each intermediate input will also have an array of inputs. To analyze this process fully, the transactions table must be manipulated, to obtain what is known as the "Leontief Inverse," named for Nobel Laureate Professor Wassily Leontief, the creator of I-O analysis. With the Leontief Inverse, a numerical measure of the entire array of direct and indirect inputs can be otained.

There are two additional features of I-O transactions tables that bear mention. The tables are designed to facilitate analysis of the input structure of final demand. The most common use is to postulate a change in final demand, in one or a collection of industries, and then to trace the effects throughout the entire economy. In the table produced by the Bureau of Economic Analysis (BEA) of the U.S. Department of Commerce, complete guided missile production is one of the sectors of final demand. Thus, we were able to use the transactions table directly to analyze the effect on inputs of increasing the demand for guided missiles. The alternatives we chose were also amenable to analysis through the transactions table.

I-O transactions are measured in constant prices, which is equivalent to assuming that, in the language of economic theory, all supply curves are perfectly elastic. Thus, I-O analysis by itself has nothing to say about inflation. In order to address this issue, I-O analysis must be supplemented by analysis and information from other sources. This we have done, and our approach will be described in a separate section below.

The Impact on Industrial Production of an Increase in Guided Missile Spending

Guided missiles, like other sophisticated modern weapon systems, are thought to embody high levels of technology, sophisticated labor and technical skills, and substantial inputs from metals and manufacturing industries. Expenditures on sophisticated, or "state-of-the-art," weapon systems are frequently justified on more than military grounds; they are considered to have beneficial impacts on technological developments for the economy as a whole. Testifying before the Senate Budget Committee in February 1980, Defense Secretary Harold Brown argued that military outlays "are beneficial in the longer term to the civilian economy, since much of the additional spending promotes domestic production in our most capital- and technology-intensive sectors."[1]

CEP investigated the effect of increases in the final demand for guided missiles and compared it with the effects for five alternatives. Initially, we focused on the amount and distribution of inputs for the six categories of demand. We used the inverse matrix of output coefficients calculated from the 1972 Department of Commerce I-O tables, aggregated for 157 industries. Using the inverse for guided missiles we can show the distribution of inputs required to produce guided missiles. The entries are in the form of multipliers, telling how much is required of each input to produce a unit ($1, $1 million, $1 billion, etc.) of guided missiles for final demand. Adding the entries in the column gives the gross output multiplier; subtracting final output—a multiplier of 1 since final demand can only equal itself—gives the secondary output multiplier, a measure of the effect of the increase in final demand on input demands. The total and secondary output multipliers for guided missiles and five alternatives are presented in Table 2.

Solar energy equipment manufacturing has almost twice the secondary impact of guided missiles, with the other alternatives arrayed in between. Even residential construction, with well-known and relatively straightforward technologies, has a larger secondary multiplier than guided missiles. In I-O analysis, the magnitude of the secondary output multiplier is considered to be related to the production requirements of the commodity being produced. In general, the more complicated, sophisticated, and demanding the technology of production, the larger the indirect, or secondary, effects. A higher level of technology tends to draw more resources from other sectors, and to draw from a greater number of sectors. Yet, according to the secondary output multipliers presented above, guided missiles, generally considered to be a technologically sophisticated product, has a smaller impact on the structure of production than any of the alternatives tested.

Table 3 shows how the secondary output multiplier is distributed among industries that provide inputs. Each element of the missile column of the inverse matrix was divided by the secondary output multiplier for guided missiles (.937) to obtain a percentage distribution of input requirements. The importance of each industry in the total requirements for guided missiles varies considerably. For example, Industry 1, dairy and poultry products, contributes 0.1 per cent of inputs for each unit increase in the demand for guided missiles, whereas Industry 156, gifts, entertainment, and travel, contributes 5.0 per cent of the inputs. This means that an increase in the demand for guided missiles will boost sales of gifts, entertainment, and travel substantially more than it will increase dairy and poultry sales. The industries that receive the most stimulation from the increase in final demand will then command the labor and materials they need. The distribution of input requirements is, in effect, a portrait of how resources can be expected to move as final demand is increased.

Using data from Table 3, we calculated the impact on input industries divided into the traditional broad industry categories of services, manufacturing, construction, and agriculture and mining. All six of the final-demand categories draw almost all of their inputs from services and manufacturing. Comparing the distribution of inputs for the six alternatives, we found that guided missiles has the highest service content of its inputs, and the lowest manufacturing content, while solar energy has the highest manufacturing and lowest service content.

Guided missiles draws 36 per cent of its inputs from service industries, and 60 per cent from manufacturing. Every one of the five industries used for comparison draws a smaller proportion of its inputs from services, and a larger portion from manufacturing. Housing has a 32.5 per cent service content, and has 61 per cent of its inputs from manufacturing; railroad manufacturing draws 22.1 per cent from services and 74 per cent from manufacturing; and solar equipment has a service content of 11 per cent and a manufacturing content of 85.3 per cent. Guided missile production does draw input from manufacturing. But, when compared with the five alternatives, it is clear that guided missile expenditure is a weak stimulator of manufacturing.

For guided missiles, the high service content is largely attributable to business services and gifts, entertainment and travel (G.E.T.). These inputs probably reflect the high administrative costs associated with major military production activities and the extensive travel and lobbying expenditures characteristic of military industries.[2] The 7 per cent business services content of guided missile production reflects the importance of highly-paid professional and consulting services to military production. Defense production requires considerable technical expertise, often provided through consulting firms and think tanks as well as the staffs of large weapons manufacturers.[3]

Marketing in the defense sector requires services to coordinate initial contracts between the Department of Defense and contracting companies and also throughout the extensive subcontract work. There were more than 12 million separate procurement orders in FY 1980 involving 32,472 firms; an additional large number of firms were involved in subcontracting, which on a major weapons project can be immense.[4] On the B-1 project, for example, Rockwell International Corporation had lined up 5,000 separate firms to do subcontract work,[5] while Boeing, for the Minuteman missile, had 40,000 suppliers.[6] In addition, someone must constantly evaluate contract performance, maintain product quality, and supervise cost accounting. For the MX, one company, TRW Inc., has been awarded sizeable contracts solely to perform this coordinating function.[7]

Lobbying is an integral part of the defense industry and accounts for some part of the gift, entertainment, and travel expense. Many defense contractors need a steady stream of prime contracts for survival, and spend heavily for lobbying and campaign donations. They use the most costly forms of travel and entertainment, such as corporate aircraft, first-class tickets, and luxury hotels and restaurants.

CEP also calculated the relative distribution of the impact within manufacturing, distinguishing between "key" capital goods industries (those industries that primarily produce plant and equipment for others) and "other" manufacturing industries, which produce final demands. Key manufacturing industries include basic metals (steel, copper, aluminum), forging and foundries, machine-tool production, and so forth. "Other" manufacturing industries include apparel, glass, cement, aircraft, and solar collectors. These latter industries do make intermediate products, but they are primarily producing for final demand.

Table 4 presents the distribution of manufacturing inputs between the two classifications, for guided missiles and the five alternatives. Guided-missile production is the smallest of the six alternatives in its impact on key industries, with only 14.4 per cent of the input for guided-missile production drawn from the capital-goods sector. Any of the alternatives would stimulate more activity in these industries. Almost half of the secondary demand stimulated by an increase in railroad-equipment manufacturing would be concentrated in the capital-goods industries.

Despite Harold Brown's argument that defense spending stimulates production in high-technology industries, it appears to be just the opposite with guided missiles. Guided missile expenditure:

- has a smaller effect on output than any of the alternatives studied, and a smaller total level of stimulation;
- has the smallest relative impact on manufacturing, and low degree of stimulation of manufacturing output;
- has the smallest relative impact on capital-goods manufacturing industries; and
- has the largest relative impact on service industries.

The Impact on Employment of an Increase in Guided Missile Spending

Whenever a large amount of money is poured into the economy, it stimulates employment. Defense spending is no exception, and the money allocated to the MX would create a number of jobs, especially in those states that have a high concentration of contractors, such as California, Utah, and Massachusetts.

Jobs are generated in two ways. Prime contractors hire more people in order to undertake the contracts; subcontractors add employees when they begin work on particular sub-systems. Prime and subcontract employment is measured by I-O tables, prime contractors corresponding to the direct component of production and subcontractors to the indirect component. As individuals begin receiving and spending their income from the project, there is more ready money available in the community. This in turn stimulates demand, sales, and production, resulting in the creation of yet more jobs. The establishment of new jobs because of increased purchasing power is known as the "induced effect." I-O analysis measures the direct and indirect effects.*

Using I-O tables, it is possible to calculate, for each category of final demand, employment coefficients to measure the number of jobs that would be generated for each billion-dollar addition to final demand. The employment per billion dollars of final demand for guided missiles and alternatives is presented in Table 6. For this comparison, we supplemented our work with employment data from other studies. Each of the alternatives would generate more employment than guided missiles.**

The relatively low employment derived from the direct and indirect output for guided missiles has two causes. One is the high service component, which means low secondary output multiplier effects. Since secondary output is low, not many people will be needed to produce this output. In addition, military industries tend to employ a high proportion of skilled labor, including scientists, engineers, managers, finance and lobbying specialists, as well as skilled machinists and other production workers. These workers receive wages and salaries far above the average for the labor force as a whole, which means that a given value of output will generate a smaller number of jobs than most alternatives. Industries providing materials for guided missile production also employ highly skilled labor.

A billion extra dollars spent on guided missiles will create fewer jobs than the same amount added to any of the alternatives listed in Table 5. Furthermore, a comparatively small increase in jobs caused by the in-

---

*I-O analysis does not measure all employment gains that follow an increase in final demand. With induced effects excluded, there may be some variation among the six alternatives we cite that is not measured by I-O analysis. However, the multiplier effects for induced expenditures will tend to be lower the larger the portion of the injection of final demand that is saved. Since military expenditures tend to go to those at higher ends of the income distribution, where savings rates are higher, the employment multiplier for induced expenditures on military procurement projects will probably be lower than the employment multipliers for alternatives where savings rates are lower. The exclusion of induced employment may bias the employment comparison in favor of guided missile expenditures.

**These calculations are for the missile alone, and exclude employment generated by the construction of the basing mode. However, each of the alternatives also excludes some complementary activity. For example, housing construction does not include the building of roads, sewers, schools, shopping centers, and so on.

crease in expenditure for guided missiles will actually turn into a loss if those funds are taken from one of the alternatives, for example, by cutting federal aid for mass transit. In such a situation, extra money for the MX could, in the short run, make the overall employment situation worse for the nation as a whole.

Perhaps even more important are the long-term effects on the economy. The manufacture and increased use of transit equipment, solar collectors, and waste-disposal facilities would tend to reduce costs and improve prospects for economic growth throughout the economy. The use of solar collectors, for example, can reduce demand for fossil fuels and mitigate the rise in their costs. Improved transportation facilities can make it cheaper and quicker to transport people and goods, and, as a result, can stimulate trade and factory and housing construction. Thus, the employment-generating effects extend outward, both in time and across economic activities.

With missiles, there are no such beneficial effects. A guided missile in its silo or its submarine does not make it more economical to produce other products, nor does it reduce costs or stimulate output in other sectors of the economy. What missiles are intended to purchase is national security. We contend, however, that building and deploying the MX is likely to make the United States less, not more, secure in at least one respect: it would undoubtedly weaken the economic component of our national security when considered as an alternative to other, more productive, expenditures.

The Inflationary Potential of an Increase in Guided Missile Spending

CEP also explored the possible inflationary consequences of MX expenditures. As we noted above, the Air Force did not analyze inflationary effects of MX outlays, arguing that such analysis was the responsibility of other government agencies. There are a number of reasons, however, why CEP became convinced that inflation would be one like consequence of proceeding with the MX.

Input-output analysis assumed that all inputs are freely available and that final demand can bet met. In fact, production is frequently hampered by bottlenecks in production of parts, shortages of key materials, and rising prices. Various simplifying assumptions are needed to make mathematical and statistical manipulations manageable, but the results must be modified to take account of actual conditions. The main simplifying assumption in I-O analysis is that all materials are freely available at constant prices. However, if some items have limited availability, the impact of the output multipliers can be reduced or significantly offset through price increases or shifts of resources among sectors.

Rising costs, shortages of capacity and inputs, and increased imports would all contribute to reducing the stimulation of the U.S. economy that might occur from an increase in military industry output, including guided missiles. Even without the MX, the industries that produce for the Department of Defense are having a hard time keeping up with the major expansion in the 1980s of military spending, with its emphasis on research and development and the procurement of new weapons; they are experiencing severe shortages of capacity, labor, and materials, and rapidly rising costs.

The 1980 Summer Study of the Defense Science Board reported extensive cost growth in important components and materials, lead times of up to two and three years, and extreme shortages of engineers, technicians, and skilled laborers leading to large increases in labor costs. In addition, the study considered that a widespread undercapitalization in defense industries contributed to insufficient production capacity, and it raised doubts about the ability of the industry to expand capacity in the near future. There have been similar reports from other observers, and from researchers who have studied defense production over a long time. [8]

These problems have led to an increase of imports by defense industries. The cost of imported machine tools, aircraft parts, electronic components and telecommunications equipment have doubled and in some cases tripled between 1977 and 1980. [9]

Table 6 lists the major production requirements for guided missiles, along with the estimated rate of capacity utilization, as of 1980, for industries where that information is available. The capacity utilization rates for guided missile production are all very high, in many cases at or approaching 100 per cent. The industries contributing to the five alternatives have lower rates. This discrepancy reflects conditions in the defense industrial base, as against the greater use of more traditional and presently underutilized, industries, such as basic metals, in the alternative production patterns.

With the four largest supplying industries operating at 100 per cent of capacity, they will obviously find it difficult to avoid severe problems with production resulting in using costs delays. An increase in the final demand for complete guided missiles will face quite inelastic supply curves for inputs. The output multiplier will be smaller than was predicated from the I-O analysis. The price rises resulting from these difficulties will reduce the ability to use all the available inputs efficiently. There may also be costly and time-consuming shifts in technology, production methods, and searches for new inputs.

All of the five alternatives investigated have considerable available capacity for expansion, so that their full multiplier effects are more likely to be realized. Capacity utilization tends to be highly cyclical, with excess capacity occurring in recessions and shortages appearing during boom periods. Thus, the sluggish economy forecast for 1981 will mean the continuation of spare capacity in many basic industries. However, the continuing demand for military equipment means that the problems plaguing the defense industrial base will continue, unaffected by normal business cycle movements. Thus an expansion of guided missile production will be more costly and less stimulating to the economy as a whole, and more likely to generate further inflationary pressures, than any of the alternatives we studied.[10]

Labor constraints are more difficult to measure, since there is no periodic index of occupational unemployment. A review of trade literature and Labor Department data on employment can give some idea of the employment picture in specific industries. The recent and continuing increase in military spending has occurred at a time of severe aerospace labor shortages, due to the boom in civilian aircraft production in the late 1970s. In many companies, the major bottleneck preventing expanded production was not the availability of manufacturing capacity, but the unavailability of appropriately trained engineers and technical specialists. Many companies, seeing labor shortages looming, tried to stockpile experienced workers through excess hiring in the late 1970s, but even such foresight proved insufficient. A study by the Machine Tool Builders Association found that 70 per cent of its member firms reported significant labor shortages. The lack of skilled labor is so acute that several of the missile production input industries had to cancel plans to initiate second shifts.[11]

There are very few problems of labor supply in the industries representing the alternative spending patterns. Unemployment in basic production industries, such as automobiles, lumber and wood, and metal production, is high. This is only partly due to the 1980 recession, for many of these industries have high long-term unemployment rates. In general, operatives and non-farm laborers have higher unemployment rates than professional, technical, and managerial workers. Since missile production employs a much higher ratio of professional to production workers than the alternative industries, labor shortages will be more prevalent in the production of guided missiles than in any of the alternatives, whatever the ups and downs of the business cycle.[12]

Footnotes

1. Secretary of Defense Harold Brown, Prepared Statement, *Hearings* before the Committee on the Budget, U.S. Senate, February 27, 1980, Washington, USGPO, 1980, p. 82.
2. Seymour Melman, *The Permanent War Economy*, New York, Simon and Schuster, 1974, Ch. 2; Gordon Adams, *The Iron Triangle*, New York, Council on Economic Priorities, 1981.
3. According to Labor Department figures, about 30% of employees in firms producing guided missiles and space vehicles are production or nonsupervisory workers, the remaining 70% presumably being managers, salespeople, scientists and so forth. For durable goods manufacturing as a whole, the proportions are reversed. U.S. Department of Labor, Bureau of Labor Statistics, *Employment and Earnings*, monthly.

    See also, Jacques Gansler, *The Defense Industry*, MIT Press, Cambridge, Mass., 1980, pp. 51, 53. Of the seven defense industries Gansler lists, five have less than 70% of their employees in production, with guided missiles having a percentage of 27.8, based on 1972 data.
4. Data on orders and prime contractors from Directorate for Information, Operations, and Reports, Washington Headquarters, Services, Department of Defense. There are no official estimates of the number of companies engaged in subcontracting.
5. Gordon Adams, *The B-1 Bomber: An Analysis of Its Strategic Utility, Cost, Constituency, and Economic Impact*, New York, Council on Economic Priorities, 1976, p. 13.
6. Gansler, op. cit. p. 43.
7. The MX uses an associate prime contractor system, in which companies receive direct contracts from the DoD to produce components of the overall system, and the Air Force's Ballistic Missile Office at Norton Air Force Base in California acts as coordinator of the project. The Air Force has contracted with TRW to perform much of this coordination work.
8. For example, *Business Week*, "Why the US Can't Rearm Fast," February 4, 1980; Jacques Gansler, op. cit.; "The Ailing Defense Industrial Base: Unready for Crisis," *Report* of the Defense Industrial Base Panel of the Committee on Armed Services, U.S. House of Representatives, December 31, 1980, Washington, USGPO, 1980.
9. Derived from data in Department of Commerce, Bureau of the Census, *U.S. General Imports*, No. FT135, 1977, 1978, 1979, first quarter 1980.
10. In February 1980, the DoD applied its highest priority rating, DX, to MX contracting. Under the Defense Production Act, a DX rating allows the DoD to instruct companies to perform MX work first, in effect leapfrogging other projects. While use of DX priority will benefit MX, it will not change the cost picture. *Armed Forces Journal International*, May 1980, p. 17.
11. Telephone conversation with Tom Jackson, Bureau of Industrial Economics, U.S. Department of Commerce, June 1980. See also *Christian Science Monitor*, February 8, 1980, p. 1; *Wall Street Journal*, April 2, 1980, p. 1.
12. Data in U.S. Department of Labor, Bureau of Labor Statistics, *Employment and Earnings*, monthly.

TABLE 2
COMPARISON OF THE SECONDARY EFFECTS OF GUIDED MISSILE PRODUCTION AND SELECTED ALTERNATIVES

Final Demand Categories	Gross Output Multiplier	Secondary Output Multiplier
Guided Missiles	1.937	.937
Residential Construction	2.250	1.250
Public Utilities Construction	2.261	1.261
Railroad Equipment	2.528	1.528
Mass Transit	2.629	1.629
Solar Energy Equipment	2.781	1.781

SOURCE: Bureau of Labor Statistics, Office of Economic Growth, U.S. Department of Labor, 1972 Input-Output Study, INVC1973, for guided missiles, residential construction, public utilities construction, railroad equipment, and mass transit. For solar energy equipment, source is Craig Peterson, Sector-Specific Output and Employment Impacts of a Solar Space and Water Heating Industry, prepared for the National Science Foundation, Research Applied to National Needs (RANN), December, 1977.

TABLE 3
TOTAL INTERMEDIATE GOODS REQUIREMENTS PER ONE BILLION DOLLAR INCREASE IN FINAL DEMAND FOR GUIDED MISSILES
(In Billions of 1973 dollars)

Industry		Requirements	Percent of Total
Aircraft	(104)	.192,715	20.0%
Miscellaneous Business Services	(139)	.66,990	7.0
Business Travel, Entertainment & Gifts	(156)	.046,088	5.0
Electronic Components	(101)	.035,256	3.8
Real Estate	(135)	.033,101	3.5
Communication (except radio & tv)	(124)	.031,435	3.4
Retail Trade	(130)	.027,674	2.9
Wholesale Trade	(129)	.023,267	2.5
Machine Shop Products	(90)	.020,438	2.2
Primary Aluminum & Aluminum Products	(74)	.019,532	2.1
Plastic Products	(63)	.019,332	2.1
Blast Furnace & Basic Steel Products	(71)	.019,179	2.0
Air Transportation	(121)	.017,562	1.9
Miscellaneous Professional Services	(141)	.016,251	1.3
Scientific & Controlling Instruments	(109)	.012,357	1.3
Other Primary Non-ferrous Products	(75)	.012,169	1.3
Electric Utilities	(126)	.011,456	1.2
Maintenance & Repair Construction	(21)	.011,430	1.2
Radio & Communication Equipment	(100)	.011,292	1.2
Truck Transportation	(119)	.010,814	1.2
Metalworking Machines	(87)	.010,012	1.1
Other Fabricated Metal Products	(82)	.009,490	1.0
Industrial Inorganic & Organic Chemicals	(52)	.008,883	.9
Petroleum Refining & Related Products	(60)	.008,564	.9
Primary Copper & Copper Products	(73)	.008,179	.9
			72.3%
Other Requirements		.259,678	27.7
Total Indirect Requirements per $1 Billion Increase in Final Demand for Guided Missiles		.937,468	100.0%

SOURCE: Bureau of Labor Statistics, Office of Economic Growth, U.S. Department of Labor. "Values for Matrix INVC73", Charles Bowman, Washington, D.C., February, 1980. The values are calculated from the Matrix INVC73, or $(I-A)^{-1}$ matrix of total industrial requirement coefficients necessary to a one billion dollar (1973 dollars) increase in final demand for guided missiles, BLS Code 23. This industrial requirement distribution is the most recent available information regarding the direct and indirect input structure of the guided missile industry. The table consists of 157 industries. The above level of disaggregation was taken directly from the BLS table.

TABLE 4
MANUFACTURING IMPACT OF MX AND ALTERNATIVES
DISTRIBUTION OF 'SECONDARY IMPACT' AMONG "KEY" MANUFACTURING INDUSTRIES AND "OTHER MANUFACTURING" IN PERCENTAGE FORM

	Guided Missile	Mass Transit	Solar[1] Energy	Rail Roads	Public Utility	Housing
"Key"[2] Manufacturing Industry Impact	14.4%	30.0%	33.9%	46.2%	40.0%	18.0%
Other Manufacturing Impact[3]	45.6%	47.0%	51.1%	27.8%	26.0%	43.0%
Total Manufacturing Impact	60 %	77 %	85 %	74 %	66 %	61 %

SOURCE: Bureau of Labor Statistics, Office of Economic Growth, Department of Labor, U.S. Government, Washington, D.C. "Leontieff Inverse" (I-A)$^{-1}$ INV73, in 1973 dollars, based on 1972 Input-Output Table, published by Bureau of Economic Analysis, Department of Commerce. Survey of Current Business. February 1979.

1. Peterson, Craig, *"The Solar Energy Industry, An Input-Output Analysis"*, Utah University, 1975. This study consisted of creating a column within the 1967 Input Output table (A Matrix) and finding the inverse multipliers for the solar industry (the solar 'column' with the A Matrix) by inversing the 1967 table after including the new or added column for solar. We have used these inverse multipliers despite the fact that they embody the 1972 structure rather than the 1972 structure as used for all other alternatives.
2. "KEY" MANUFACTURING loosely refers to those industries within the manufacturing sector which produce plant and equipment (capital goods) for other industries rather than an 'end product' for final demand (other than for investment final demand). An example would be the metal working equipment industry which produces metal working machines needed by the aircraft and solar development industries, respectively, for jet fighter planes and solar heating collectors.
3. "OTHER" MANUFACTURING would include, for example, the aircraft and solar industries which produce predominantly for final demand rather than for other industries. Their products are 'end products', such as jet fighter planes or solar collectors. Other examples would be apparel, glass, and cement. While many of these products are produced for industry as well as for final demand, their character is not as directly 'capitalized' as is plant and equipment.

TABLE 5
EMPLOYMENT IMPACT OF ALTERNATIVE USES OF ONE BILLION DOLLARS OF NEW FINAL DEMAND
Numbers of Jobs per One Billion 1972 Dollars

Alternatives	Direct Plus Indirect Employment	Direct Employment	Indirect Employment
Missile	53,248	25,055	28,193
Mass Transit	77,356	32,889	44,467
Public Utility	65,859	32,173	33,686
Railroads	54,220	20,260	33,960
Housing	68,657	31,016	37,641
Solar Energy/Energy Conservation	65,079	+	+
Solar Energy Equipment	57,235	+	+

Sources of Data:

Bureau of Labor Statistics, Office of Economic Growth, U.S. Department of Labor. Charles Bowman, Supervisory Economist. Data taken from the Employment Requirements Table 1977 (Employment Inverse), which gives labor requirements for each industry in 1972 dollars. Direct requirements per industry cited are given in that industry's row and column number (i=j). Total requirements are listed in row 158. Industries cited above are given under the following BLS number system: Guided Missiles 23, New Public Utilities Construction 17, Other Transportation Equipment 108, Railroad Equipment 106, Residential Construction 15.

Buchsbaum, Steven et al., *Jobs and Energy: The Employment and Economic Impacts of Nuclear Power, Conservation and Other Energy Options* (Council on Economic Priorities, New York, 1979). See Table 2-2 "Conservation Scenario Net National Employment." This figure (48.8) was converted from 1976 dollars to 1972 dollars using an implicit GNP deflator (1.334) from the Economic Report of the President, January 1977, p. 192.

Peterson, Craig, *Sector-Specific Output and Employment Impacts of a Solar Space and Water Heating Industry* Prepared for the National Science Foundation, Research Applied to National Needs (RANN), December 1977. See especially, Table VI, Page 37, for the breakout of percentage requirements of industrial sectors of BLS categories (1963) for a solar industry. The percentages given in Table IV were applied by industry to the appropriate employment requirements given in the BLS Employment Table (op. cit.) to arrive at the total requirements listed in (3) above, under 'Solar Energy.'

TABLE 6
MAJOR INDUSTRIAL REQUIREMENTS FOR GUIDED MISSILES AND ALTERNATIVE EXPENDITURES COMPARED TO CURRENT INDUSTRIAL CAPACITY UTILIZATION

GUIDED MISSILES

INDUSTRY	TOTAL REQ.%**	C.U.* RATE 1979***
Aircraft	20.0	100%
Business Services	7.0	—
Travel, Entertainment, Gifts	5.0	—
Electronic Components	3.8	100%
Real Estate	3.5	—
Communications	3.4	100%
Retail Trade	2.9	—
Wholesale Trade	2.5	—
Machine Shop Products	2.2	100%
Primary Aluminum & Alum. Products	2.1	85%
Plastics	2.1	99%
Blast Furnace Basic Steel	2.0	77%
Air Transport	1.9	—
Professional Services	1.3	—
	59.7%	

SOLAR ENERGY

INDUSTRY	TOTAL C.U.* REQ.%**	RATE 1979***
Solar	17.7	—
Steel	11.1	77%
Copper	10.5	62%
Plastics	6.3	99%
Aluminum	5.4	85%
General Industrial Machinery	3.4	98%
Scientific & Control Instruments	2.8	94%
Millwork & Plywood	2.6	94%
Primary Non-Ferrous Metals	2.2	93%
Chemicals	2.1	98%
Plastic & Rubber	2.1	87%
Cement	2.1	90%
Wholesale Trade	2.0	—
Truck Transportation	1.6	—
Glass	1.6	92%
	73.0%	

Table 6 (Continued)

RAILROAD MANUFACTURING

INDUSTRY	TOTAL C.U.* RATE REQ.%**	1979***
Steel	17.8	77%
Railroad Equipment	13.0	100%
Iron & Steel Foundries & Forgings	8.3	94%
Enginers—Turbine	4.8	90%
Machine Shop Products	4.5	100%
Aluminum	3.8	85%
Retail Trade	3.8	—
Real Estate	3.1	—
Business Services	2.6	—
Fabricated Metal	2.5	95%
Truck Transportation	2.2	—
Copper	2.1	62%
Railroad Trans.	1.6	—
Other Primary Non-Ferrous Metals	1.6	93%
Metal Working Machines	1.4	100%
	76.0%	

Table 6 (Continued)

RESIDENTIAL CONSTRUCTION

INDUSTRY	TOTAL C.U.* REQ.%**	RATE 1979***
Millwork & Plywood	8.0	96.2%
Sawmills & Planing Mills	6.5	91.1%
Cement, Concrete	5.2	90.5%
Professional Services	4.4	—
Wholesale Trade	3.9	—
Fabricated Metal Products	3.7	97.2%
Retail Trade	3.6	—
Blast Furnace & Basic Steel	3.2	76.8% 81.4%
Business Service	2.9	—
Real Estate	2.9	—
Logging	2.9	91.1%
Copper	2.7	62.4%
Truck Transport	2.3	—
RR Transport	1.6	—
Travel, Entertainment, Gifts	1.6	—
Other Metal Products	1.6	98.7%
Heating & Plumbing	1.6	98.4%
Petroleum Refining	1.6	94.1%
	60.3%	

Table 6 (Continued)

MASS TRANSIT

INDUSTRY	TOTAL C.U.* REQ.%**	RATE 1979***
Motor Vehicles	23.9	—
Blast Furnaces & Basic Steel	7.5	76.8% 81.4%
Metal Stampings	3.9	—
Iron & Steel Foundries	3.8	74.0%
Wholesale Trade	3.2	—
Business Services	2.0	—
Real Estate	2.0	—
Other Fabricated Metal Products	1.9	98.7%
Truck Transport	1.9	—
Misc. Electrical Products	1.7	—
Auto Repair	1.7	—
Primary Copper & Copper Products	1.5	62.0%
Service Industry Machinery	1.5	—

Table 6 (Continued)

PUBLIC UTILITIES

INDUSTRY	TOTAL C.U.* REQ.%**	RATE 1979***
Cement Concrete Products	23.9	90 %
Primary Copper & Copper Products	10.1	62 %
Blast Furnace & Basic Steel	8.8	76.8% 81.4%
Fabricated Structural Metal	8.3	95 %
Wholesale Trade	3.3	—
Business Services	3.2	—
Other Fabricated Metal Products	3.1	98.7%
Real Estate	2.7	—
Millwork, Plywood & other Wood	2.5	96.2%
Professional Services	2.5	96.2%
Truck Transport	2.4	—
Iron & Steel Foundries & Forgings	2.3	74 %
Electrical Lighting & Wiring	2.2	—

* Capacity Utilization
** Requirements
***U.S. Department of Labor, 1972 Input-Output Study.
  Wharton Econometric Forecasting Associates: Capacity
  Utilization Rates are as of the last quarter of 1979.

Table 6 (Continued)

15.
Shifting MX Expenditures to Energy Conservation

As part of our analysis of the economic impact of MX expenditures, CEP investigated what would happen if the money proposed for MX were shifted to a long-term program of energy conservation.* Dependence on costly foreign sources of energy is one of the main reasons for the weak economic performance of the Untied States; it is also a factor influencing stepped-up military appropriations.

In 1980, the U.S. imported about 39 per cent of all petroleum products consumed domestically; 31 per cent — almost one-third — of those imports came from the Persian Gulf. America's total oil import bill in 1980 cost about $79 billion, about $55 billion *more* than the entire balance of trade deficit that year.[1]

The MX missile cannot add to energy supplies. On the contrary, it would consume substantial amounts of energy during its construction and operation. Moreover, the MX will require substantial capital resources that, if used for energy efficiency, could significantly contribute to

---

*This analysis was initiated in response to a question Representative John Seiberling (D-OH), Chairman of the Public Lands Subcommittee of the House Interior Committee, asked CEP's Director of Military Research David Gold, about the implications of using the proposed MX expenditures in alternative ways. The alternative we chose to examine was the long-discussed goal of U.S. energy self-sufficiency. The analsis was originally published as a CEP Occasional Paper by Robert DeGrasse Jr., "Shifting MX Expenditures to Energy Efficiency: Memo on the National Security Implications of Alternative Energy Development." May 5, 1980.

U.S. energy supplies and the overall economic health of the country.

By transferring the proposed $52 billion expenditure (in 1980 dollars)[2] for MX to funding a ten-year program subsidizing investments in energy-saving measures, we estimate that the United States could cut oil imports by between 44 and 75 per cent and provide over 178,000 jobs. Such a program would also create a substantial balance of trade surplus, stabilizing the U.S. dollar in foreign currency markets.[3] Results are expressed in a range to include a broad variety of efficiency measures and to reflect the uncertainty of conservation pricing projections (see footnotes 5 and 6).

United States Energy Demand

During 1980, the United States consumed just over 76 "quads" (quadrillion British Thermal Units) of energy. There are 172 million barrels of oil in a quad. Energy production and use is displayed by sector in Table 7.

In 1980, the United States imported 13.3 quads of crude oil refined petroleum products accounting for about 39 percent of total petroleum consumption and 17 per cent of total energy use.[4]

If the U.S. government were to pay for energy efficiency measures in oil-using homes and factories instead of building the MX, we could save enough oil by 1990 to offset between 44 and 75 per cent of U.S. petroleum imports (see Table 8). This energy efficiency would offset more than the 31 per cent of our imports derived from the Persian Gulf.

Program Assumptions

CEP assumed that one quad of energy saved by conservation measures would require between $5 and $10 billion of investment by residential users and between $3 and $8 billion by industrial users. These ranges capture the majority of energy-efficiency measures according to researchers familiar with energy pricing.[5] Residential measures falling within this range include: insulating walls and ceilings, adding storm windows, caulking window frames, installing automatic thermostats and buying more efficient appliances. Industry could become more energy efficient using co-generation, improving the efficiencies of furnaces, air-conditioning, and machinery, and by insulating facilities. For both residential and industrial conservers, the cost of saving energy will vary based on the state of existing equipment and facilities. For example, if a home is already heavily insulated, each additional dollar spent on insulation will yield less energy savings.

For the purposes of this analysis, CEP assumed that the federal government would directly purchase any investment in energy efficiency that saved oil within the $5 to $10 billion per quad price range. This would be analogous to present targeted federal subsidy programs designed to induce utilities to shift from petroleum to coal. $5.2 billion would be spent each year for ten years, equalling the MX's $52 billion. For the purposes of comparing this investment with the MX, we did not assume that subsidies could stimulate private funding, even though most federal programs are based on the assumption that tax credits or grants will induce the private sector to invest a greater amount than the original subsidy. Also, we simplified this analysis by *not* discussing a broader energy conservation program that would save natural gas and electricity in addition to petroleum. On average, if one quad of energy is saved in the residential/commercial or industrial sector, only about 30 per cent of the savings will be petroleum unless the program is specifically targeted to do so.[6] A more inclusive energy-efficiency program would have the same impact if it were coupled with a program allowing easier trade-offs between natural gas or electricity and petroleum. We did assume that for each quad of petroleum saved, a quad of imports would not be imported because of market pressures and public policy.

Jobs and Balance of Trade

Roughly 179,000 to 207,000 jobs could be provided for ten years in the energy-efficiency industry (direct employment) and its suppliers (indirect) by this $52 billion program (1980 dollars). Additional jobs would be created by the multiplier effect of employees spending their wages within the economy. This estimate is based on Bureau of Labor Statistics figures for gross product and employment in the durable goods manufacturing and residential construction sectors.[7] This compares favorably with the approximately 161,000 to 176,000 direct and indirect jobs that could be created by the MX missile for the life of that project.[8]

Our balance of trade deficit in 1980 was $24.4 billion. If this conservation program had been in place in 1980, it would have trimmed $34.8 to $59.3 billion from U.S. net imports, creating a $10.4 to $34.9 billion trade surplus. We assume that these savings would be used to help pay off the initial investment in conservation and create jobs in the United States rather than exporting more dollars abroad and weakening our currency in the international market place. The percentage of the trade deficit that would be offset by such a program will at least remain constant since the cost of imported crude oil is higher than the $33.9 average price per barrel in 1980. As the cost of oil goes up, the value of oil not used will increase correspondingly.

Conclusion

The most effective solution to the security crisis posed by U.S. dependence on oil from the Persian Gulf is the often discussed goal of energy self-sufficiency. Steps toward this objective would begin to defuse the possible superpower confrontation in the area. Such actions would also decrease the concern among oil-producing nations like Saudi Arabia that the West is pressuring them to keep oil production high, depleting their most valuable resource faster than may be economically optimal for them.

The results presented above indicate the magnitude of the potential benefits of such a program. The health of the economy and our relations with other nations would be greatly enhanced if, instead of using our dollars inefficiently to develop the MX missile, we redirect our resources to improving the energy efficiency of the American economy.

Footnotes

1. Department of Energy, *Monthly Energy Review,* April 1981, p. 13.
2. $52 billion is the low end of CEP's estimate of MX system costs. See chapter 11.
3. Our analysis is based on the projection of 1979 figures for oil imports and balance of trade deficit to 1990. Deputy Secretary of Energy John Sawhill stated in his testimony to the Senate Foreign Relations Committee on February 20, 1980 that imports will, at best, remain stable through 1985. Inflation in oil prices will bias our numbers downward, making them understate the positive impact of such a program. As oil prices go up, conservation investments are more economical and the negative contribution of oil imports to the balance of trade increases.
4. *Monthly Energy Review,* April 1981, p. 10.

5. The price ranges for conservation energy were chosen to reflect the uncertainty about how much each dollar of investment could save in such an ambitious program. Alan Meier of Lawrence Berkeley Laborabory estimates that, at $5 billion a quad, about 28 percent of residential natural gas could be saved by currently cost-effective conservation measures in California. Our program, which seeks to offset a more expensive fuel, petroleum, is projected to save between 44 and 75 per cent of residential/commercial and industrial oil use. The government could fully pay for these investments by reallocating the funds earmarked for the MX. Our price ranges for each quad of energy saved are high, underestimating the total import savings, considering the estimates Dr. Leonard Rodberg made in his study *Employment Impact of the Solar Transition* for the Congressional Joint Economic Committee (Washington, 1979). He found that it would cost about $3.8 billion per quad to save 34.7 quads of energy. We would expect that the marginal cost of saving a quad would increase as more conservation measures are employed. Rodberg's program also requires a correspondingly larger investment. Industrial efficiency was priced more cheaply, based on industry's better record in identifying possible savings (see *Energy Future,* Robert Stobaugh and Daniel Yergin, eds., Random House: New York, 1979, Chapter 7, "Conservation: The Key Energy Source," by Daniel Yergin).
6. Derived from *Monthly Energy Review* (March 1980) statistics on energy consumption by sector. Petroleum used for electricity production is factored in.
7. U.S. Department of Labor, Bureau of Labor Statistics, "BLS 1977 Employment Requirements Table," Office of Economic Growth, December 1979. BLS figures indicate that 34,400 employees are required to produce a billion dollars of output (adjusted for 1980 dollars) in household appliance manufacturing. The figure is 39,900 jobs per billion for new residential construction. These sectors provide a range that simulates the energy efficiency industry. We assume that $5.2 billion output is produced every year during this ten year program.
8. Ibid. BLS projections for complete guided-missile production indicate that 31,000 workers are required for a billion dollars of output (adjusted for 1980 dollars). In new highway construction, the figure is 33,800 employees per billion. These industries should approximate the range of employment to develop the MX missile and its basing mode.

TABLE 7
1980 U.S. DOMESTIC ENERGY PRODUCTION AND CONSUMPTION (QUADS)

Sector	Source Petroleum	Natural Gas	Coal	Hydroelectric	Nuclear	Electricity Distributed & Lost	Total
Residential Commercial & Industrial	4.4	7.6	.2	—	—	15.1	27.3
	8.9	8.4	3.4 (incl. coke)	*	—	9.7	30.4
Transportation	18.0	.6	—	—	—	*	18.6
Electrical Energy Produced	3.0	3.8	12.1	3.2	2.7	Total Electricity + 24.8	
Total	34.3	20.9	15.7	3.2	2.7		76.3

* Less than 0.1 quad. Energy produced by wood, geothermal, and waste was also less than 0.1 quad.
+ Electrical energy is tracked by how it is produced and where it is used. Figures for electricity distribution include over two-thirds portion lost through entropy.
Source: Department of Energy. *Monthly Energy Review*. April 1981. pp. 25-27.

TABLE 8
MX FUNDED
ENERGY EFFICIENCY PROGRAM

Sector	Investment (billions of 1980 $)	Investment Required Per Quad Saved (billions of 1980 $)	Total Quads Saved	Per cent of Imports Offset
Residential & Commercial	$26	$5–10	2.6–3.3*	19%–25%
Industrial	$26	$3–8	3.3–6.7*	25%–50%
TOTAL	$52	—	5.9–10.0	44%–75%

* CEP assumed that no more than 75 per cent of oil consumption can be saved in any sector.

16.
The MX Contracting Network

As part of its analysis of the economic impacts of MX expenditures, CEP collected data on the companies and government agencies that are involved in testing and building the MX system.

The MX is currently in Full Scale Engineerng Development (FSED), having been moved beyond the Research and Development stage by President Carter in 1979. According to the present schedule the project will move into production in 1983 with the first missiles in place by 1986. FSED involves the construction and testing of prototypes of the missile, shelters, transporters, launchers, and other equipment. Preliminary site selection studies for shelters and base facilities are underway in the Great Basin area of Nevada and Utah.

A large contracting network is now in place. The MX project is structured under an associate contractor system. Many weapon systems have a single prime contracting company. for example, the F-15 fighter aircraft (McDonnell Douglas), the B-1 bomber (Rockwell), or the Trident missiles (Lockheed). For the MX, a series of associate prime contractors are assigned different components of the system with a separate contract issued for each task. As of February 1981, thirty seven companies had contracts from the Department of Defense (Table A). In a number of cases (e.g., Rockwell, Northrop, Martin Marietta, Boeing, TRW, Draper Labs) a company received more than one contract.

The Air Force's Ballistic Missile Office (BMO) at Norton Air Force

Base, San Bernardino, California, acts as the coordinating agency for the project. The BMO has contracted with TRW to perform management and coordination functions. Martin Marietta will handle the final assembly of the missile and the basing system. Thus BMO, TRW, and Martin are sharing the functions usually performed by a prime contractor. Each of the associate contractors is listed along with the component of the system that they are responsible for, in Table B.

The associate contractors subcontract a substantial portion of their work to other companies. On most weapons projects, fifty to sixty per cent of the value of the prime contract is subcontracted.[1] A portion of the subcontracts are then further subcontracted, and so on down the line. Many subcontractors supply highly specific components for the MX; others, usually called vendors, supply general off-the-shelf items. Table C lists subcontractors for each of the associate prime contractors while Table D lists subcontractors alphabetically. As we discuss below, the coverage of this aspect of MX contracting is much less complete than for prime contractors.

In addition to the companies that have received prime and subcontracts for MX, there are companies that have received contracts for work closely related to the MX project. These companies are listed in Table E. Some of these contracts were awarded by agencies other than BMO for work directly relevant to MX. The Army Corps of Engineers, for example, is the contracting agency for the construction of MX test facilities. Some contracts are for work where the MX is one component; the Olin Corporation received a contract for propellants for MX and other applications. Still other contracts are for work where the possible application to MX is one of the stated goals. Ballistic missile defense is one example. The Army is testing several BMD systems and one, the Low Altitude Defense system (LoAD), is being designed to be compatible with MX.[2]

A variety of government agencies, in addition to the Ballistic Missile Office, have been involved in work for the MX program. Some of these are civilian agencies, such as the Bureau of Land Management of the Department of the Interior, which has been involved because of the planned use of public lands for the basing mode in Nevada and Utah. Others, such as the General Accounting Office and the Office of Technology Assessment, have performed studies of the massive project. Warhead development is under the Department of Energy.[3] Government agencies involved in the MX program are listed in Table F.

Associate Contractors

CEP's primary source of data for associate contractors was the Ballistic Missile Office. The BMO was quite helpful in providing lists of active prime contractors (the most recent as of February 1981) and in responding to various inquiries. BMO data was supplemented by data gathered by NARMIC,[4] by journalistic accounts, especially announcements of contract awards and modifications in *Aerospace Daily* and the *Wall Street Journal*, and by interviews with company representatives. Many of the companies were quite responsive to CEP inquiries about their prime contracts, supplying information about the amount of the award, location of the work, and other data. Others were largely unresponsive, supplying either no information or only confirming what was already published in the press.

CEP has identified 37 associate contractors for FSED of MX. (We also identified 12 contractors with $126 million in contracts involved in work closely related to the MX program.) A number of smaller contractors no longer active on the project were not included. On the other hand, a few contractors who are apparently no longer active, since the closing date on the period of performance of their contract has passed, were included either to identify a crucial function or because the inactive contract appears to be simply a predecessor of the active contract. These 37 companies have 47 contracts, some going to different divisions of the same company.

The value of the 47 contracts is over $3.5 billion. The FSED phase was originally budgeted at $5 to $7 billion and is scheduled to last into FY83. $2.2 billion was authorized by Congress for Fiscal Year 1980 and 1981 and the Reagan Administration has requested $2.9 billion for FY82. Thus, substantial amounts of money beyond the $3.5 billion CEP has identified remain to be contracted. It is most likely that this will be done via modifications to existing contracts.

The largest MX prime contracts are cost-plus-incentive-fee (CPIF) contracts. They establish a target cost, a target profit, and a formula for allocating cost increases between the contractor and the government. The initial contract awards, in the case of the largest contracts, defined the period of performance as being the period of FSED; in practice, many of the contracts began earlier and were simply updated. One of the difficulties in assessing how much money has been contracted is the fairly continual revisions that occur in agreements between the DoD and the contractors. Most changes are described simply as "face value increases" and include both changes in design as well as cost increases and schedule changes. Small changes (under $5 million) are often not reported and are lumped together with larger adjustments. In at least one instance, an alteration in the design of the missile's first stage, the contract modification was not announced until ten months after the design change decision was made.[5] It presumably took that long for the change to work its way through the bureaucracy. As one example of the data problems this creates, a list of contracts that CEP obtained from Air Force Systems Command included the following message: "Dollar amounts are not included because the figures experience frequent revisions."

Contracts have been awarded for MX work since the late 1960s, long before there was an MX program. The main characteristics of the new missile were first defined in 1967 (See Chapter 3). One of the key features was a Self Aligning Boost and Reentry (SABRE) guidance system considered essential for a mobile land-based missile as it permitted the missile to be lowered from the vertical launch position to the horizontal and back again without major adjustment. Development of SABRE began at Charles Stark Draper Laboratory in 1965, and SABRE contractors included Northrop, Honeywell, and the Autonetics Division of Rockwell, all of whom have guidance development contracts for the MX.[6]

Early development of MX occured under budget line items for Minuteman, Advanced ICBM Technology, and Advanced Ballistic Reentry Systems. By 1970 some $250 million had been allocated for MX work, and additional companies receiving contracts included Avco, Martin, TRW, Lockheed, General Electric, and Goodyear, most of whom have large contracts for the current MX program.[7] Contracts specifically for MX were awarded to Aerojet Strategic Propulsion ($19.6 million for design of second-stage propulsion system) and to United Technologies ($4.6 million for development of a nozzle system for the MX booster stage) in 1974, while the initial request for an MX development program was still pending before the House and the Senate Armed Services Committees. The Air Force claimed legitimacy on the basis that the money had been appropriated as part of continuing Minuteman development.[8] In 1975 guidance awards were made to Northrop (some $35 million), Draper ($5 million) and Rockwell Autonetics ($3.3 million).[9] By 1976 the present contracting structure was largely in place with regard to the missile itself—the basing system had not yet been chosen—and the companies that had been involved with early development work had a clear advantage in obtaining further contracts.[10] In making inquiries among companies, CEP found very few instances where a company felt it was in serious competition with another company for a contract; most awards went to the company that already had a contract for early development work.

In addition, most of the companies with major MX contracts had performed similar work on past ICBM programs, especially Minuteman. Fourteen MX associate contractors are performing work that is very similar to the work they performed as Minuteman associate contractors.* One company, Boeing, responsible for missile assembly for Minuteman, has a different task in the new project—constructing the transporter vehicle for MX. Martin Marietta, the test and assembly contractor on MX, did not have a major role in Minuteman but was the assembly contractor on the Titan ICBM program. Northrop's Electronics Division, with a large guidance and control contract for MX and a small

---

* The fourteen companies are Aerojet General, Avco, Draper, General Electric, GTE Sylvania, Hercules, Honeywell, Logicon, Northrop Precision Products Division, Parsons, Rockwell Autonetics Division, Science Applications, Thiokol, and TRW.

role in Minuteman, and Rockwell's Rocketdyne Division, with the Propulsion Stage IV contract for MX, are the only other examples of sizeable MX business for companies not heavily represented in the Minuteman project.

The Minuteman program experienced extensive cost management problems. The entire program, according to Pentagon cost analyst A. Ernest Fitzgerald, was subject to inadequate cost and quality control by both the contractors and the Air Force. The most widely reported example was the performance of the Autonetics division of North American Aviation, now Rockwell, in producing guidance and control equipment. Within a year after the contract had been awarded the cost had risen 90% and the equipment was rated by Air Force engineers as having a life span one-third the length specified by the contract. According to Fitzgerald's account, the Air Force responded by ordering and paying for spare equipment from Autonetics.[11]

Rockwell is the largest single contractor on MX to date in terms of dollar amount of awards with $724 million in prime contracts and several small subcontracts, primarily to its Autonetics and Rocketdyne divisions. They have also been a major contractor on two recent projects where large cost growth has been an issue, the B-1 bomber and the Space Shuttle.[12] Other MX contractors have been involved in cost management or quality control problems on major projects, for example Boeing with the Short Range Attack Missile, General Electric with the Mark 12 warhead, Avco with the engine for the M-1 tank, and McDonnell Douglas, the main contractor for research on LoAD, with the F-18.[13] In recent years, most large military projects have had serious difficulty controlling costs and there have been some major problems of quality control.[14] In many instances the bulk of the problems are outside of the control of any company, in some cases reflecting national economic conditions and in some cases resulting from program changes and management problems within the Department of Defense. Past problems of cost growth are certainly no proof that problems will occur on MX. But a project of this scale is bound to experience some difficulties in the best of circumstances—the GAO has identified significant cost growth in the first year of FSED—and the cost and quality problems should be expected to occur as the project proceeds.

Subcontractors

Subcontract data is very difficult to obtain. The BMO does not systematically track subcontracts. For one year, FY1979, Washington Headquarters Services of the Department of Defense obtained data by asking contractors to poll their subcontractors, with about 20 per cent compliance. CEP obtained this data for the MX, using prime contract numbers, but since the survey has not been continued the information is not up-to-date. The other main sources were NARMIC, press reports, and the prime contracting comapnies. Our survey of the companies yielded uneven results. Some companies were helpful. Avco, for instance, gave CEP a list of its major subcontractors. Other companies were totally unresponsive. Thiokol, to give one example, refused to provide any information. CEP also polled some of the subcontractors to ask for information on the size of their contract, the type of work performed, and the location of the work. The subcontracting companies were even less responsive than the prime contractors often claiming that releasing such data would compromise their relations with the associate contractor.

The data on subcontractors is seriously incomplete and we have little idea of how incomplete it is. The number of subcontracting companies on a major military project can run into the thousands and even tens of thousands.[15] Thus it is clear the CEP was barely able to scratch the surface in obtaining data on subcontracting for MX. This is a general problem in tracing the impact of military contract dollars; the paucity of data on subcontractors is a serious impediment to any attempt to study the distribution and impact of defense expenditures.

CEP has identified 88 companies that have received 101 subcontracts from MX associate prime contractors. (One major subcontract is second-tier, a subcontract from a company that is itself working on a subcontract. In this instance Hercules has a subcontract from Westinghouse which in turn is a subcontractor to Martin Marietta on the MX launcher.) We have identified $124 million in value for subcontracts. In most instances, however, the dollar value of the subcontract is not available. Six of the subcontractors are also associate contractors working on other components of the system. The six are Avco, E-Systems, Hercules, Honeywell, Northrop, and Rockwell. Given the history of past weapon systems, it is certain that the number of subcontractors and the amount of money involved will be substantially larger as the program moves into production.

Footnotes

1. Jacques Gansler, *The Defense Industry*, Cambridge, MIT Press, 1980, p. 43.
2. See Chapter 11 above, for links between LoAD and MX.
3. "The Energy Department plans to start in FY 1981 a three-year, $35 million construction program to equip seven sites for production of the MX warhead, and increasing work on two MX warhead designs is the main reason the department plans to beef up its weapons development workforce by more than 3% during the coming fiscal year." *Aerospace Daily*, April 9, 1980.
4. *MX Missile Contractors*, NARMIC Map Series, National Action/Research on the Military Industrial Complex, December 1980.
5. Telephone conversation, Ballistic Missile Office, Norton Air Force Base.
6. *Aviation Week and Space Technology*, June 22, 1970, p. 222; *Space/Aeronautics*, January 1970, p. 69.
7. *Space/Aeronautics*, January 1968, p. 103; January 1970, p. 69.
8. James W. Canan, *The Superwarriors*, New York, Weybright and Talley, 1975, p. 159.
9. *Aviation Week and Space Technology*, May 6, 195, p. 20.
10. *Business Week*, October 25, 1976.
11. A. Ernest Fitzgerald, *The High Priests of Waste,* New York, W.W. Norton & Company, 1972, pp. 15–18, 122–123. See also Richard Kaufman, *The War Profiteers*, Garden City, New York, Doubleday & Company, 1972, pp. 81–83, and United States Congress, Joint Economic Committee, "Hearings on the Military Budget and National Economic Priorities," Part 2, Washington, D.C., U.S. Government Printing Office, 1969.
12. On the B-1 see Gordon Adams, *The B-1 Bomber: An Analysis of Its Strategic Utility, Cost, Constituency, and Economic Impact,* New York, Council on Economic Priorities, 1976. On the Space Shuttle see *Aerospace Daily*, February 11, 1980, p. 217.
13. On Boeing and General Electric, see Fitzgerald, op. cit., pp. 166–170, 194–198; on Avco and the engine for the M-1 tank see Comptroller General of the United States, "XM-1 Tank's Reliability is still Uncertain," *Report* to the Congress, U.S. General Accounting Office, January 29, 1980; on the F-18 see Comptroller General of the United States, "F/A-18 Naval Strike Fighter: Progress Has Been Made but Problems and Concerns Continue, "*Report* to the Congress, U.S. General Accounting Office, February 18, 1981.
14. As of December 30, 1980, 50 weapons projects currently in procurement had cost growth averaging 114 per cent of their baseline cost estimates. See Department of Defense Comptroller "Selected Acquisition Reports as of December 30, 1980." On other recent problems in procurement see James Fallows, *National Defense*, New York, Random House, 1981.
15. Gansler, op. cit., p. 43, reports that Boeing had 40,000 suppliers in performing final assembly work on Minuteman. Rockwell had 5,000 subcontractors on the B-1 when that project was still in development. See Adams, op. cit., p. 13.

TABLE A
MX ASSOCIATE CONTRACTORS BY COMPANY

Company and Location	System Component	Purpose of Contract	Value ($ millions)	Contract Number	Contract Type	Period of Performance
Aerojet Strategic Propulsion Co.[a] Sacramento, CA	Missile: Propulsion Stage II	Stage II full-scale engineering and development (FSED).	$152.3	78-C-0010	CPIF	5/78-6/84
		face-value increase to contract	7.1[b]			
		face-value increase	83.1[g]			
Avco Corp., Systems Division[c] Wilmington, MA	Missile: Reentry System	Reentry system integration; design and development of ascent shroud. Development of decoy system.	175.4	79-C-0062	CPIF	9/79-6/84
		face-value increase	3.6[g]			
Boeing Aerospace Co. Seattle, WA; Las Vegas, NV	Basing System: Transporter and Shelter Development	Development of support equipment for transporter and shelter components. FSED.	155.8	80-C-0029	CPIF	1/81-7/84
		Redirection to FSED for horizontal basing mode.	97.8	78-C-0035	CPIF[d]	10/78-8/80

Company	Work Area	Description	$ (M)	Contract No.	Type	Period
Boyden, Kennedy & Romney Salt Lake City, UT	Other: Legal Services	MX legal services: Utah.	.05	80-D-0034	FFP/LOE	8/80-7/81
Charles Stark Draper Laboratory, Inc. Cambridge, MA Grand Rapids, MI Dallas, TX San Diego, CA Cambridge, MA	Missile: Reentry, Guidance and Control	Accuracy evaluation, guidance and control technical work.	45.7	80-C-0046	CPFF	9/80-3/82
		Technical support to strategic missile program.	41.7	78-C-0002	NA	2/78-3/81
Economics Technology Associates Los Angeles, CA	Other: Documents	MX ATE acquisition procedures document development.	.3	81-C-0009	NA	11/80-11/81
Edaw, Inc. San Francisco, CA	Basing System: Base Selection and Shelter Development	Comprehensive planning of facilities and functional systems for potential MX operating bases in NV, UT, TX and NM.	11.9	81-C-0016	FFP	2/81-5/82

Company and Location	System Component	Purpose of Contract	Value ($ millions)	Contract Number	Contract Type	Period of Performance
(Continued)						
E-Systems, Inc. Seattle, WA Greenville, TX	Basing System: Security	Develop and operate security system in Sinai Desert toward a network designed to conceal locations of MX missiles. Will lead to development, acquisition and implementation of an MX security system.	.37	80-C-0013	FFP[d]	3/80-9/80
Earth Technology Corp.[e] Long Beach, CA	Basing System: Base Selection and Shelter Development	Geotechnical siting investigations.	35.1	80-C-0006	FFP/LOE	11/79-9/81
General Dynamics Corp. Pomona, CA	Missile: Reentry System	Reentry advance impact fuse[f]	1.8	80-C-0023	CPIF	5/80-3/82
General Electric Co. Philadelphia, PA	Missile: Reentry Vehicle	Adaption of Mark 12A reentry vehicle to MX missile.	69.9	80-C-0016	FPIF	6/80-6/84
Geodynamics Corp. Santa Barbara, CA	Basing System: Base Selection and Shelter Development	Geodetic and geophysical support.	2.4	78-C-0008	CPFF	10/78-9/81

Company	Category	Description	Amount	Contract	Type	Dates
GTE Sylvania, Inc., Strategic Div.; Systems Group. Needham Heights, MA	Command, Control and Communications (C^3)	Development of enduring and survivable C^3 FSED.	325.5	79-C-0070	CPIF	2/80-1/85
		face-value increase: for design of communications system for testing.	3.7[b]			
		face-value increase:	4.5[g]			
Henningson, Durham and Richardson Santa Barbara, CA	Other: Environmental Studies	Environmental baseline studies and statements.	11.8	80-C-0008	FFP/LOE	3/80-9/81
		Environmental studies.	13.0	78-C-0029	CPFF[d]	10/78-6/80
Hercules, Inc., Aerospace Division Magna and Bacchus, UT	Missile: Propulsion Stage III	Stage III FSED.	175.4	78-C-0012	CPIF	5/78-6/84
Honeywell, Inc. St. Petersburg, FL	Missile Reentry: Guidance and Control	Engineering development of guidance and control: specific force integrating receiver (SFIR).	34.0[h]	80-C-0004	CPFF	1/80-2/83
Itek Corp. Lexington, MA	Other: Analysis	MX Strategic Arms Limitation analysis.	.1	80-C-0025	FFP	8/80-9/81

Company and Location	System Component	Purpose of Contract	Value ($ millions)	Contract Number	Contract Type	Period of Performance
(Continued)						
Karagozian & Case Structural Engineers Los Angeles, CA	Basing System: Base Selection and Shelter Development	Nuclear hardness design and fragility analysis.	1.6	79-D-0001	FFP	1/80-9/81
		Nuclear hardness and survivability support.	.8	78-D-0001	FFP[d]	11/77-3/80
Logicon, Inc. San Pedro, CA	Overall Weapon System: Targetting	SAC and MX software analysis.	3.8[i]	81-C-0005	CPFF	10/80-9/81
		Software performance and technical evaluation.	9.1	80-C-0020	CPFF	7/80-9/82
		face-value increase	17.3[g]	(80-C-0020)		
Martin Marietta Corp. Denver, CO; Vandenberg AFB, CA	Overall Weapon System: Assembly, Test and System Support	Assembly, test and system support. FSED. (A,T & SS)	$588.6	78-C-0016	CPIF	4/78-6/84
		face-value increase: A, T & SS conversion of hot gas/sabot generator system to lower temperature steam/gas generator.	5.2[b]			
		face-value increase	4.7[b]			
		face value increase: A,T & SS transportation and handling changes in-	19.3[g]			

Contractor	Work Area	Description	Amount ($M)	Contract Number	Type	Period
		volving revisions to equipment to reflect design changes.				
		face-value increase	3.1[b]			
		face-value increase	5.5[g]			
	Basing System: Launcher	Engineering development of missile launcher canister.	62.3	78-C-0044	CPIF	10/80-9/82
		face-value increase: initiation of FSED.	25.0[b]			
Northrop Corp., Electronics Division[j] Hawthorne, CA	Missile Reentry: Guidance and Control	Engineering development of inertial measuring unit and construction of gyros and accelerometers for guidance platform.	238.0	80-C-0003	CPIF[k]	12/79-11/83
Northrop Corp., Precision Products Division[j] Norwood, MA	Missile Reentry: Guidance and Control	Engineering development of MX third generation gyro.	36.2	80-C-0005	FPIF/ FFP/LOE	1/80-2/83
Questron, Inc. La Jolla, CA	Missile: Stage IV	Hardened electronic analysis for Stages I-III guidance & control.	.5	74-C-0057	NA	3/79-2/81
R.A. Hanson Co. Spokane, WA; Danville, CA	Basing System: Base Selection and Shelter Development	Horizontal shelter test project.	12.9	81-C-0012	FFP	12/80-6/82

(Continued) Company and Location	System Component	Purpose of Contract	Value ($ millions)	Contract Number	Type	Period of Performance
Ralph M. Parsons Co. Pasadena, CA; Luke AFB, CA	Basing System: Base Selection and Shelter Development	Buried trench construction advanced development program.	33.3	77-C-0012	CPFF	3/77-5/81
		MX basing and protective structures.	12.9	81-C-0001	CPIF[l]	11/80-9/81
Rockwell International, Autonetics Div. Anaheim, CA	Missile Reentry: Guidance and Control	Design, develop and integrate guidance & control system and associated support environment.	389.9	78-C-0021	CPIF	5/78-6/84
		face-value increase	6.3[g]			
Rockwell International, Rocketdyne Div. Canoga Park, CA	Missile: Propulsion Stage IV	System definition including flight-proof test and production readiness, review and delivery of 10 models for flight tests. FSED.	328.5	77-C-0028	CPIF	4/78-6/84
Science Applications, Inc. La Jolla, CA	Other: Studies	Deployment planning studies.	$.2	81-C-0004	FFP/LOE	11/80-9/81
Softech, Inc. Waltham, MA	Command, Control & Communications	Development of the MX Jovial Compiler.	2.5	79-C-0058	CPFF	8/79-9/82

Company	Area	Description	Amount	Contract	Type	Period
Systems Planning Corp. Arlington, VA	Basing System: Base Selection and Shelter Development	Position location uncertainty surety program.	.09	80-C-0043	FFP/LOE	10/80-9/81
Systems, Science & Software La Jolla, CA	Basing System: Base Selection and Shelter Development	Nuclear hardness and survival studies.	1.5	80-C-0001	FFP	11/79-9/81
Systems Technology Laboratories Arlington, VA	Basing System	Basing studies.	.2	80-C-0015	FFP	4/80-7/80[m]
TRW, Inc. Norton AFB, CA Vandenberg AFB, CA Redondo Beach, CA	Overall Weapon System: Integration	Systems engineering and technical support.	64.0	80-C-0018	FFP	10/80-9/81
Redondo Beach, CA	Overall Weapon System: Targetting	Engineering support for MX targetting and analysis program.	9.9	80-C-0024	FFP	10/80-9/81
Thiokol Corp. Wasatch & Elkton Divisions Brigham City, UT Elkton, MD	Missile: Propulsion Stage I	Development, ordnance and integration for all four stages. Production of 21 development motors, Stage I motor. Ordnance, initiation and flight termination systems for first 10 missile flights FSED.	162.5[n]	78-C-0009	CPIF	5/78-6/84

(Continued) Company and Location	System Component	Purpose of Contract	Value ($ millions)	Contract Number	Contract Type	Period of Performance
		face-value increase: switch from mechanical to hydraulic actuation for the thrust vector control system on Stage I.	15.8[b]			
		face-value increase	77.5[g]			
		face-value increase	4.0[g]			
Ultrasystems, Inc. Norton AFB, CA Irvine, CA	Other: Logistics	MX integrated logistics support.	.8	80-C-0032	FFP	1/81-12/81
University of Houston Houston, TX	Other: Studies	Maintenance management studies.	.2	80-C-0038	Cost	10/80-9/81
Van Cott, Bagley, Cornwall & McCarthy Salt Lake City, UT	Other: Legal Services	MX legal services in Utah.	.05	80-D-0033	FFP/LOE	8/80-7/81
Weidlinger Associates New York, NY	Basing System: Base Selection and Shelter Construction	Nuclear hardness and survivability studies.	.1[o]	80-C-0007	FFP/LOE	1/80-9/81

Woodburn, Wedge, Blakey & Jeppson Reno, NV	Other: Legal Services	MX legal services in Nevada.	.05 80-D-0035 FFP/LOE 8/80-7/81

Explanations and Footnotes

OTHER TERMS:

Face-Value Increase—within the US Air Force procurement process, this term indicates that the total value of the contract has been modified. This is not a new contract, but simply an award increasing the dollar value of the previously awarded contract.

Full Scale Engineering and Development (FSED)—the second phase for the MX system, following Research & Development (R&D). All active contracts are for this phase.

COLUMN TITLES:

System Component—Component of the MX system on which the contractor is to perform work.

Purpose of Contract—specific description of the work to be performed by the contractor.

Value—total dollar value of the contract awarded for the entire period of performance. This dollar amount is not usually obligated all at once, but disbursed throughout the period of performance. Total value of contracts can be modified, regardless of the type of contract.

Contract Number — US Air Force/Ballistic Missile Office contracts (the contracting agency for the MX) are prefixed with the following code: F04704; for example, Boeing's contract would read: FO4704-80-C-0029. This prefix has been deleted from all entries in this table. All MX contracts, without exception, have this prefix.

Contract Type—The following types are listed: *CPIF* = Cost Plus Incentive ; *FFP/LOE* = Firm Fixed Price/Level of Effort; *CPFF* = Cost Plus Fixed Fee; *FPIF* = Fixed Price Incentive Fee; *FFP* = Firm Fixed Price.

Period of Performance—indicates the span of time within which the work contracted for is to be performed. This, as with the value, is subject to modification.

FOOTNOTES:
a. A subsidiary of the General Tire & Rubber Company.
b. Recent face-value increase: may not be accounted for in the total value of the contract (recorded as of February 1981).
c. A division of Avco Corp.
d. Contract is now inactive (terminated).
e. Formerly Fugro National, Inc. Earth Technology bought this company from its Dutch parent, ownership was transferred on March 25, 1981. The MX contract is retained by the new owner.
f. Contract may be for work related to the ABRES (Advanced Ballistic Reentry System) program which may be integrated into the MX program.
g. Face-value increase is in addition to the total contract value recorded.
h. Honeywell received two previous contracts (now inactive) for research and development work on guidance and control including work on the SFIR, general power program, and accelerometers (the latter work performed at Horsham, PA) with total combined value of $8.2 million.
i. Logicon received a previous contract (now inactive) for research and development performed for the same purpose as the current award with a value of $8.1 million.
j. A division of Northrop.
k. Northrop previously received 2 contracts (now inactive) for research and development work on reentry guidance and control with a combined value of $8.2 million.
l. Parsons previously received a contract (now inactive) for vertical basing shelter investigations with a value of $1 million.
m. Systems Technology's contract may be inactive as of July 1980.
n. According to sources outside the USAF/BMO, the total value of Thiokol's contract is $178.2 million as of January 1981. The value listed is quoted from USAF/BMO sources. Thiokol refused to cooperate in verifying this or any other data.
o. Weidlinger Associates previously received a contract (now inactive) with the same description of purpose with a value of $0.17 million, work performed at Menlo Park, CA.

Table B

TABLE B
ASSOCIATE CONTRACTORS BY SYSTEM COMPONENT

System Component	Associate Contractors	Contract Value ($ millions)
OVERALL WEAPON SYSTEM:		
System Integration	TRW, Inc.	$64.0
Assembly, Test and System Support	Martin Marietta Corp	588.6 + 19.3[a] + 55[a]
Targetting	Logicon, Inc.	9.1[b] + 17.2[a]
		3.8
	TRW, Inc.	9.9
MISSILE PROPULSION:		
Stage I	Thiokol Corp.	162.5 + 77.5[a] + 4.0[a]
Stage II	Aerojet Strategic Propulsion Co.[c]	152.3 + 83.1[a]
Stage III	Hercules, Inc.	175.4
Stage IV	Rockwell International, Rocketdyne Div.	328.2
	Questron, Inc.	.5
REENTRY:		
Reentry System	Avco Corp., Systems Division	175.4 + 3.6[a]
	General Dynamics Corp.[d]	1.8

Reentry Vehicle	General Electric Co.	69.9
Guidance & Control	Charles Stark Draper Laboratory, Inc.	45.7
		41.7[e]
	Honeywell, Inc.	34.0
	Northrop Corp., Electronics Div.	238.0
	Northrop Corp., Precision Products Div.	36.2
	Rockwell International Autonetics Div.	389.9 + 6.3[a]

BASING SYSTEM:

Base Selection and Shelter Development	Boeing Aerospace Co.	*
	Edaw, Inc.	11.9
	Earth Technology Corp.[f]	35.1
	Geodynamics Corp.	2.4
	Karagozian & Case Structural Engineers	1.6
	R.A. Hanson Co.	12.9
	Ralph M. Parsons Co.	33.3
		12.9[g]
	Systems, Planning Corp.	.09
	Systems, Science & Software	1.5
	Weidlinger Associates	.1
Transporter	Boeing Aerospace Co.	155.8*
Launcher	Martin Marietta Corp.	62.3
Security	E-Systems, Inc.	.37
Studies	Systems Technology Laboratories	.22

(Continued) System Component	Associate Contractors	Contract Value ($ millions)
COMMAND, CONTROL & COMMUNICATIONS:		
	GTE Sylvania, Inc., Strategic Div.	325.5 + 4.5[a]
	Softech, Inc.	2.5
OTHER:		
Environmental Impact Statements	Henningson, Durham & Richardson	11.8
		13.0[h]
Legal Services	Boyden, Kennedy & Romney	.05
	Van Cott, Bagley, Cornwall & McCarthy	.05
	Woodburn, Wedge, Blakey & Jeppson	.05
Studies/Analysis/Documents[i]	Economics Technology Associates	.3
	Itek Corp.	.1
	Science Applications, Inc.	.2
	University of Houston	.2
Logistics	Ultrasystems, Inc.	.8

FOOTNOTES:

* Boeing's major involvement is with the launcher component although part of its contract is related to work on shelter development. Total value of the contract is $155.8 million. See entry in Table A.
a. the additional dollar amount is a face-value increase to the original contract.
b. Logicon was awarded two separate contracts for work on this component of the MX system.
c. a subsidiary of General Tire & Rubber Co.
d. General Dynamic's contract is for work related to the ABRES technology program which may be integrated into the MX system.
e. Draper was awarded two separate contracts for this component.
f. formerly Fugro National— see entry in Table A (and related footnote).
g. Parsons was awarded two separate contracts for this component. See entry in Table A.
h. HDR received two separate contracts for environmental studies. See entry in Table A.
i. other than environmental studies.

TABLE C
SUBCONTRACTORS BY ASSOCIATE CONTRACTOR/SYSTEM COMPONENT

Associate Contractor and System Component	Subcontractor*	Location	Purpose of Contract	Value ($ millions)
Aerojet Strategic Propulsion Co.[1] Missile: Propulsion Stage II	Airesearch Mfg. Co.[2]	Phoenix, AZ	Build TVA actuator	NA
	Avco Corp.	Wilmington, MA	Advanced development	NA
	Brunswick Corp.	Lincoln, NB	"	$.02
	Data Resources, Inc.[3]	Sacramento, CA	"	.03
	Digital Equipment Corp.	Sacramento, CA	"	.05
	Ford Aerospace and Communications Corp.[4]	Newport Beach, CA	Advanced development	.02
	Garret Corp.[2]	Moonachie, NJ	NA	NA
	Hitco	Gardena, CA	NA	NA
	Kaiser Aerotech	San Leandro, CA	NA	NA
	Kirkhill Rubber Co.	Brea, CA	Advanced development	.12
	McDonnell Douglas Corp.	Huntington Beach, CA	NA	NA
	Metal Mart Inc.	Whittier, CA	Advanced development	.02
Avco Corp., Systems Division Missile: Reentry System	Alcoa	Cleveland, OH	Aluminum forgings	NA
	Atlantic Research Corp.	Gainesville, VA	Rocket motor	NA
	Avco Aerostructures Inc.[5]	Nashville, TN	Deployment model structure.	NA

	Grumman Corp.	Bethpage, NY	Titanium welding to fashion ascent shroud.	10.0
	G&H Technology Automation Industries[6]	Santa Monica, CA	Separation connector	NA
	Honeywell Avionics Div.[7]	St. Louis Park, MN	Automatic test equipment	NA
	OEA, Inc.	Denver, CO	Separation nut/gas generator	NA
	Timex	Pittsburgh, PA	Shroud structure material	NA
	Unidynamics, Inc.[8]	Phoenix, AZ	Arm/disarm device	NA
	Abex Corp.[10]	Columbus, OH & Willets, CA	Advanced development	.74[11]
	Cameron Iron Works, Inc.	Houston, TX	"	.43[11]
	Certified Mfg. Co.	Shelton, WA	"	.24[11]
	Ebco Industries	Canada	"	.55[11]
	E-Systems, Inc.	Greenville, TX	"	.20
	GTE Sylvania Inc.	Needham, MA	"	.60
	General Motors Corp., Terex Div.	Hudson, OH	"	7.25[11]
	Georgia Institute of Technology	Atlanta, GA	"	.15
	International Business Machine Co.	Gaithersburg, MD	"	.30
	RCA Corp.	Camden, NJ	"	.20

Boeing Aerospace Co.[9]
Basing System: Transporter and Shelter Development (contract # 78-C-0035—see Table A)

(Continued)

Associate Contractor and System Component	Subcontractor*	Location	Purpose of Contract	Value ($ millions)
	Rockwell International	Anaheim, CA & Richardson, TX	"	.20[11]
	US Steel Corp.	Homestead, PA	"	.23
	Western Gear Corp.	Everett, WA	"	1.95[11]
(contract # 80-C-0029—see Table A)	E-Systems Inc.	TX	NA	NA
	General Motors Corp., Terex Div.	Hudson, OH	NA	NA
	Hughes Aircraft Co.	CA	NA	NA
	Mission Research	CA	NA	NA
	New Mexico Inst. of Mining & Technology	NM	NA	NA
Edaw, Inc. Basing System: Base Selection and Shelter Development	Bingham Engineering	Salt Lake City, UT	NA	NA
	Brown & Caldwell	Walnut Creek, CA	NA	NA
	CRS Group, Inc.	Houston, TX	NA	NA
	Ehrenkrantz Group	New York, NY	NA	NA
	Flack & Kirtz	Denver, CO	NA	NA
	Gustavson Group	Salt Lake City, UT	NA	NA
	John A. Martin & Associates	Las Vegas, NV	NA	NA
	Stern Telecommunications	New York, NY	NA	NA

General Dynamics Corp. Missile: Reentry System	Summit Engineering[12]	Reno, NV	NA	NA
	Camond Labs	NM	NA	NA
GTE Sylvania, Inc. Command, Control & Communications	Computer Sciences Corp.	Falls Church, VA	Supply analytical & systems engineering services	NA
	Hayes International[13]	Birmingham, AL	integrate air-borne launch control center	NA
	Norden Systems[14]	Norwalk, CT	Produce hardened version of Digital Equipment Corp's PDP-11	$60.0
Hercules, Inc. Missile: Propulsion Stage III	Airesearch Mfg. Co.[2]	Phoenix, AZ	NA	.08
	Hydraulic Research[15]	Valencia, CA	Thrust vector actuation	.44
	Ingersoll Rand Co.	Salt Lake City, UT	NA	.03
	Rockwell International	NA	NA	NA
Honeywell, Inc. Missile: Reentry Guidance & Control	NH Research Inc.[16]	Santa Ana, CA	NA	.08
Martin Marietta Corp. Overall Weapon System:	BDM Corp.	Albuquerque, NM	Assistance on missile system nuclear survivability.	NA

(Continued)

Associate Contractor and System Component	Subcontractor*	Location	Purpose of Contract	Value ($ millions)
Assembly, Test and System Support	Cincinnati Electronics	Cincinnati, OH	Range and Safety receivers	.94
	Endevco[17]	San Juan Capistrano, CA	Dynamic data measurement system of 750 channels for MX testing	NA
	Goodyear Aerospace[18]	Litchfield Park, AZ	Design, fabrication of transportation and handling equipment	NA
	Ralph M. Parsons	Pasadena, CA	Assistance in development of specifications for flight test facilities	NA
	Reynold Electric & Engineering Co.[19]	Las Vegas, NV	Construction support for Nevada system	6.5
	SCI Systems Inc.	Huntsville, AL	Provide portion of missile instrumentation system	NA
	Systems Engineering Labs	Ft. Lauderdale, FL	Computers for MX program	NA
Basing System: Launcher	Bell Aerospace[15]	Buffalo, NY	Basing system	NA
	Hamilton Standard[20]	Windsor Locks, CT	Truck assemblies	(multi-million)
	Westinghouse Corp.	Sunnyvale, CA	Canister	6.0[21]
	Hercules, Inc.[22]	Bacchus, UT	Graphite composite launch tube for missile canister	

Northrop Corp., Electronics Div. Missile Reentry: Guidance & Control	American Beryllium Co.[23]	Sarasota, FL	Beryllium spheres for guidance system.	$2.0
	Systems Engineering Labs.	Ft. Lauderdale, FL	Computers for MX program.	NA
	Northrop Precision[24] Products Div.	Anaheim, CA	Advanced development, manufacture of gyro.	4-5.0
Ralph M. Parsons Co. Basing System: Base Selection and Shelter Development	Ameron	Monterey Park, CA	Protective shelters.	NA
	Dallas-Jetco	Grand Prairie, TX	"	NA
	M I Jack	Hazelcrest, IL	"	NA
Rockwell International, Autonetics Div. Missile Reentry: Guidance & Control	Bunker Ramo Corp.	Chatsworth, CA	Guidance & control	.02
	G&H Technology[6]	Santa Monica, CA	"	NA
	Hamilton Standard[20]	Windsor Locks, CT	Flight control systems	4.5
	Honeywell, Inc.	St. Petersburg, FL	Test hardware changes for guidance & control computer housing system.	12.4
	Mission Research Corp	Santa Barbara, CA	NA	.09
	Stanford Telecommunications	Sunnyvale, CA	NA	.02
	Systems Engineering Labs.	Ft. Lauderdale, FL	Computer systems	3.0
	Yardney Electric Co.[25]	Denver, CO	Guidance & control batteries	1.0
Rockwell International.	ARDE, Inc.	Mahwah, NJ	Stage IV	NA

(Continued)

Associate Contractor and System Component	Subcontractor*	Location	Purpose of Contract	Value ($ millions)
Rocketdyne Div. Missile: Propulsion Stage IV	Aerojet Mfg. Co.[1]	Fullerton, CA	"	NA
	Bell Aerospace[15]	Burbank, CA	"	NA
	Carlton Controls Corp.	East Aurora, NY	"	NA
	Fairchild Stratos[26]	Manhattan, CA	"	NA
	Gulton, SCD	Costa Mesa, CA	"	NA
	Moog, Inc.	East Aurora, NY	"	NA
	Parker Hannifin Corp.	Irvine, CA	"	NA
	Physics International[27]	San Leandro, CA	"	.40
	Pyronetics Devices, Inc.[28]	Denver, CO	"	NA
	Rockwell Intl. Missile Systems Div.	Columbus, OH	Stage IV support.	NA
	Space Ordnance Systems	Canyon Country, CA	"	NA
	Tiline, Inc.	Albany, OR	"	.05
TRW, Inc.[29] Overall Weapon System: Integration	HRS	Los Angeles, CA	Economic analysis	NA
Thiokol Corp. Missile: Propulsion Stage I	Airesearch Mfg. Co.[2]	Phoenix, AZ	NA	.18[11]
	Heesacker, Edward J.	Brigham City, UT	NA	.01
	Lockheed Missile[30] Systems Co.	Sunnyvale, CA	Ordnance initiations sets/ flight termination ordnance sets.	NA

Moog, Inc.   East Aurora, NY   Thrust vector actuation control system.   NA

Explanations and Footnotes

Information on subcontractors is not readily available. The Department of Defense and the associate contractors will not provide complete information on the MX subcontracting network. Most of the subcontractors listed are considered "major" subcontractors. This list is by no means complete. In addition, it has not proved possible to identify which subcontractors are still active and which have now terminated their contracts.

FOOTNOTES:
1. Subsidiary of General Tire & Rubber Co.
2. Subsidiary of The Signal Companies, Inc.
3. Subsidiary of McGraw-Hill, Inc.
4. Subsidiary of Ford Motor Co.
5. A division of Avco Corp.
6. Subsidiary of GK Technologies, Inc.
7. A division of Honeywell, Inc.
8. Subsidiary of UMC Industries.
9. Boeing reported to CEP that a set of subcontracts from its current prime (# 80-C-0029) will be awarded shortly. Subcontracts listed under contract # 78-C-0035 are inactive, but many many of the subcontractors may be retained under the new contract.
10. Subsidiary of IC Industries, Inc.
11. The total dollar value is composed of a sum of several subcontracts awarded from the same prime contract.
12. A division of the Dana Industrial Group of Dana Corporation.
13. Subsidiary of City Investing Co.
14. Subsidiary of United Technologies Corp.
15. A division of Textron, Inc.
16. This subcontract is now part of an inactive prime contract. Honeywell has a current contract which continues the type of work initiated on its earlier contract; it is quite possible that it has retained this subcontractor.

17. A division of Becton-Dickinson & Co.
18. Subsidiary of the Goodyear Tire & Rubber Co.
19. Subsidiary of EG & G, Inc.
20. A division of United Technologies Corp.
21. This dollar amount remains unverified by the contractor despite repeated inquiries by CEP.
22. Hercules is a second-tier subcontractor (a subcontractor to a subcontractor) to Westinghouse.
23. Subsidiary to Loral Corp.
24. Precision Products, a division of Northrop Corp., is currently an associate contractor working on the MX gyro (see Table A). It remains unclear when this subcontract was active and whether it was subsequently terminated and awarded as a prime contract. Northrop would not respond to CEP inquiries.
25. Subsidiary of Whittaker Corp.
26. A division of Fairchild Industries, Inc.
27. Subsidiary of Rockcor, Inc.
28. Subsidiary of OEA, Inc.
29. TRW reported to CEP that it will have very few subcontracts due to the nature of its work on the MX.
30. A Lockheed Corp. company.

Table D

TABLE D
SUBCONTRACTORS BY COMPANY

Subcontractor	Associate Contractors	Value ($ millions)
Abex Corp.	Boeing Aerospace Co.	.74[11]
Aerojet Mfg. Co.[1]	Rockwell International, Rocketdyne Div.	NA
Airesearch Mfg. Co.[2]	Aerojet Strategic Propulsion Co.	NA
	Hercules, Inc.	.08
	Thiokol Corp.	.18[11]
Alcoa	Avco Corp., Systems Division	NA
American Beryllium Co.[23]	Northrop Corp., Electronics Div.	2.0
Ameron	Ralph M. Parsons Co.	NA
ARDE, Inc.	Rockwell International, Rocketdyne Div.	NA
Atlantic Research, Corp.	Avco Corp., Systems Division	NA
Avco Aerostructures[5]	Avco Corp., Systems Division	NA
Avco Corp.	Aerojet Strategic Propulsion Co.	NA
BDM Corp.	Martin Marietta Corp.	NA
Bell Aerospace[15]	Martin Marietta Corp.	NA
Bingham Engineering	Edaw, Inc.	NA
Brown & Caldwell	Edaw, Inc.	NA
Brunswick Corp.	Aerojet Co.	.02

Bunker Ramo Corp.	Rockwell International, Autonetics Div.	.02
CRS Group, Inc.	Edaw, Inc.	NA
Cameron Iron Works, Inc.	Boeing Aerospace Co.	.43[11]
Camond Labs	General Dynamics Corp.	NA
Carlton Controls Corp.	Rockwell International, Rocketdyne Div.	NA
Certified Mfg. Co.	Boeing Aerospace Co.	.24[11]
Cincinnati Electronics	Martin Marietta Corp.	.94
Computer Sciences Corp.	GTE Sylvania, Inc.	NA
Dallas-Jetco	Ralph M. Parsons, Co.	NA
Data Resources, Inc.[3]	Aerojet Co.	.03
Digital Equipment Corp.	Aerojet Co.	.05
Ebco Industries	Boeing Aerospace Co.	.55[1]
Ehrenkrantz Group	Edaw, Inc.	NA
Endevco[17]	Martin Marietta Corp.	NA
E-Systems	Boeing Aerospace Co.	.20
Fairchild Stratos[26]	Rockwell International, Rocketdyne Div.	NA
Flack & Kirtz	Edaw, Inc.	NA
Ford Aerospace & Communications	Aerojet Co.,	.02
G&H Technology Automation Industries[6]	Avco Corp., Systems Division Rockwell International, Autonetics Div	NA NA
Garret Corp.[2]	Aerojet Co.	NA
General Motors	Boeing Aerospace Co. (2 subcontracts)	(1) 7.25[11] (2) NA

(Continued)

Subcontractor	Associate Contractors	Value ($ millions)
Georgia Institute of Technology	Boeing Aerospace Co.	.15
Goodyear Aerospace[18]	Martin Marietta Corp.	NA
Grumman Corp.	Avco System Div.	1.0
Gulton, SCD	Rockwell International, Rocketdyne Div.	NA
Gustavson Group	Edaw, Inc.	NA
Hamilton Standard[20]	Martin Marietta Corp.	(multi-million)
	Rockwell International, Autonetics Div.	4.5
Hayes International[13]	GTE Sylvania, Inc.	NA
Heesacker, Edward J.	Thiokol Corp.	.01
Hercules, Inc.[22]	Martin Marietta Corp.	NA
Hitco	Aerojet Co.	NA
Honeywell Avionics Div.[7]	Avco Corp. Systems Division	NA
Honeywell Inc.	Rockwell International, Autonetics Div.	12.4
HRS	TRW, Inc.	NA
Hughes Aircraft Co.	Boeing Aerospace Co.	NA
Hydraulic Research[15]	Hercules, Inc.	.44
Ingersoll Rand Co.	Hercules, Inc.	NA
International Business Machines Co.	Boeing Aerospace Co.	.30
John A. Martin & Associates	Edaw, Inc.	NA
Kaiser Aerotech	Aerojet Co.	NA

Kirkhill Rubber Co.	Aerojet Co.	.12
Lockheed Missile Systems Co.[30]	Thiokol Corp.	NA
Metal Mart Inc.	Aerojet Co.	.02
McDonnell Douglas	Aerojet Co.	NA
M I Jack	Ralph M. Parsons, Co.	NA
Mission Research	Boeing Aerospace Co.	NA
	Rockwell International, Autonetics Div.	.09
Moog, Inc.	Rockwell International, Rocketdyne Div.	NA
	Thiokol Corp.	NA
New Mexico Inst. of Mining and Tech.	Boeing Aerospace Co.	NA
NH Research Inc.[16]	Honeywell, Inc.	.08
Norden Systems[14]	GTE Sylvania, Inc.	60.0
Northrop Precision[24]	Northrop Corp., Electronics Div.	4-5.0
OEA, Inc.	Avco Corp., Systems Division	NA
Parker Hannifin Corp.	Rockwell International, Rocketdyne Div.	NA
Physics International[27]	Rockwell International, Rocketdyne Div.	NA
Pyronetics Devices, Inc.[28]	Rockwell International, Rocketdyne Div.	NA
Ralph M. Parsons	Martin Marietta Corp.	NA
RCA Corp.	Boeing Aerospace Co.	.20
Royhold Electric & Engineering Co.	Martin Marietta Corp.	6.5
Rockwell International	Boeing Aerospace Co.	.20[1]
	Hercules, Inc.	.03

(Continued)

Subcontractor	Associate Contractors	Value ($ millions)
Rockwell Intl., Missile Syst. Div.	Rockwell Intl., Rocketdyne Div.	NA
SCI Systems, Inc.	Martin Marietta Corp.	NA
Space Ordnance Systems	Rockwell Intl., Rocketdyne Div.	NA
Stanford Telecommunications	Rockwell Intl., Autonetics Div.	.02
Stern Telecommunications Corp.	Edaw, Inc.	NA
Summit Engineering[12]	Edaw, Inc.	NA
Systems Engineering Labs	Martin Marietta Corp.	NA
	Northrop Corp., Electronics Div.	NA
	Rockwell International, Autonetics Div.	3.0
Tiline, Inc.	Rockwell Intl., Rocketdyne Div.	.05
Timex	Avco Systems Div.	NA
Unidynamics, Inc.[8]	Avco Systems Div.	NA
US Steel Corp.	Boeing Aerospace Co.	.23
Western Gear Corp.	Boeing Aerospace Co.	1.95[11]
Westinghouse Corp.	Martin Marietta Corp.	6.0[21]
Yardney Electric Co.[25]	Rockwell International, Autonetics Div.	1.0

Footnotes see TABLE C.

Table E

TABLE E
CONTRACTORS INVOLVED IN WORK RELATED TO MX PROGRAM
(NON-MX ASSOCIATE CONTRACTORS)

Company and Location	Description of Involvement	Value ($ millions)	Contract Data*
BDM Corp. Albuquerque, NM	Test preservation of location uncertainty concepts.	7.4	Awarded 5/13/80 Contracting activity: AFTEC at Kirkland AFB, NM.
Cardan Co. Los Angeles, CA	Construction of MX maintenance facility at Vandenberg AFB.	5.0	Awarded: 5/80. Army Corp of Engineers contract.
Fred Arnold Construction Co.	Integrated test facility.	10.5	Army Corp of Engineers—LA District Officer
Horizons Technology Inc. San Diego, CA	MX command, communications & control and basing mode assessment study.	.05	OTA contract.
Industrial Contractors, Inc. Idaho Falls, ID	Modifications to MX rocket motor test facilities at Arnold Engineering Development Center, TN.	5.9	Awarded: 4/25/80: FFP.
J. Watson Noah Inc. Falls Church, VA.	MX basing cost analysis.	.06	OTA contract.

Company	Description	Value	Notes
Martin Marietta Corp.	Development of BMD missile	NA	NA
McDonnell Douglas Aerospace Co. Huntington Beach, CA	Advanced Ballistic Re-entry System Program (ABRES) which may be integrated into the MX system.*	NA	U.S. Army Ballistic Missile Defense Systems is contracting activity.
	Ballistic missile defense system** analysis, experiment design and testing.	41.6	Total value the company has received as of 7/80. This work is part of effort for the ballistic missile defense system (BMD)
St. Louis, MO	Low Altitude Defense (LoAD) pre-** prototype demonstration program.		
Olin Corp. Stamford, CT	Propellants used to support MX, Space Shuttle, Titan missiles and the F-16	40.1	Awarded: 5/14/80. San Antonio Air Logistics Ctr., at Kelly AFB is contracting activity.
Riha Construction Co. La Mesa, CA	Construction of missile assembly building at Vandenberg AFB.	15.4	Awarded: 5/12/80. Army Corp of Engineers contract.
Sperry Univac Defense Systems Div. St. Paul, MN	Computer management for Minuteman program. ABRES* involvement.	NA	NA
The Analytical Sciences Corp. Reading, MA	Work on the ABRES* program.	NA	NA

Explanations

This table is by no means complete. The number of companies involved in work related to the MX (both potential and actual) is difficult to determine as they are not classified as "MX Associate Contractors" by the Department of Defense. Most of these contracts are not awarded by the BMO, but through other government agencies involved in MX work (see Table F).

*The ABRES program is an alternative technology development project for potential application to the MX program. It involves work on the development of greater accuracy potential for ICBM's.

**The ballistic missile defense system is a continuation of the Anti-Ballistic Missile Defense program (ABM; this system was proposed for deployment 10 years ago, but was cancelled by the implementation of a treaty with the U.S.S.R.). The plan would be to deploy this resurrected system around the MX. LoAD is the acronym for a version of a BMD system.

Table F

TABLE F
GOVERNMENT AGENCIES INVOLVED IN THE MX PROGRAM

Agency & Location	Description of Involvement	Contractors and Location (millions)	Purpose of Contract and Contract Data*
Ballistic Missile Office/ Air Force Systems Command Norton Air Force Base, CA	System acquisition and management for MX program.	All MX associate contracts are awarded through BMO	
Air Force Regional Civil Engineer – MX Norton Air Force Base, CA	Civil Engineering technology.		
Air Force Test and Evaluation Center (AFTEC) Edwards Air Force Base, CA	Support for advanced development programs.		
	Test and evaluation studies.	BDM Corp. Albuquerque, NM	Test preservation of location-uncertainty concepts for MX. Value: $7.4 m. Awarded 5/13/80.
Kirtland Air Force Base, NM			
Air Force Contracts Management Div. Kirtland Air Force Base, NM	Research on weapons effects.		

Armament Div. Eglin Air Force Base, NM		RDT&E systems procurement.
Arnold Engineering Development Center Arnold Air Force Station, TN		Laboratory for testing ballistic conditions
Strategic Air Command/USAF		
Air Force Systems Command Headquarters		
Army Corp of Engineers Div. San Francisco & Los Angeles, CA		Construction of all roads, shelters and buildings for complete deployment of MX. Construction of MX test facilities at Vandenberg Air Force Base, CA
	Cardan Co. Los Angeles, CA	Construction of MX maintenance facility at Vandenberg AFB. Value: $5.0 million. Awarded 5/80.
	Riha Construction Co. La Mesa, CA	Construction of missile assembly building at Vandenberg AFB. Awarded: 5/12/81. Value: $15.4 million.
Mobile Engineering District, US Army, TN		Test facility construction
	Industrial Contractors, Inc. Idaho Falls, ID	Modifications to MX rocket motor test facility at Arnold Engineering Dev. Center, TN. Value: $5.9m. FFP Awarded: 4/25/80.

(Continued) Agency & Location	Description of Involvement	Contractors and Location (millions)	Purpose of Contract and Contract Data*
US Navy (various offices)			
Defense Mapping Agency (DMA) F.E. Warren Air Force Base, WY	Complete MX geographical aerial surveys.		
Defense Nuclear Agency, Department of Defense	Nuclear defense program administration.		
Office of Economic Adjustment, Department of Defense	Economic impact analysis.		
Defense Communications Agency Department of Defense			
Department of Energy	Production facilities for nuclear warheads.		
Bureau of Land Management, Department of Interior	Land use administration.		
Bureau of Standards Department of Commerce			

National Security Agency

Arms Control & Disarmament Agency,
Department of State

Arms control analysis & evaluation

US Congress (especially the following committees:)

Armed Services

Appropriations

Interior
and the following offices:

General Accounting Office Studies/Analysis.

Office of Technology Assessment Economic and technical analysis/studies.

Horizons Technology Inc. San Diego, CA	MX C³ and basing mode assessment study. Value: $.05 m.
J. Watson Noah Inc. Falls Church, VA	MX basing cost analysis. Value: $.06m.

ORDER FORM

☐ Please enroll me as a **SUSTAINING MEMBER** of the Council on Economic Priorities, and send me a copy of CEP **REPORTS** and **NEWSLETTERS** as they are released. (Tax-deductible annual dues are $35/year.)

☐ Please enroll me as a **REGULAR MEMBER** of the Council on Economic Priorities, and send me a copy of all CEP **NEWSLETTERS**. (Tax-deductible annual dues are $15/year; unemployed, students and retired persons may join at $7.50.)

All new CEP Members will receive a complimentary copy of *CEP's First Decade*, a 60-page report on our origins and future, with a summary of the major research from our first 10 year's work.

☐ Please send me the following titles: No. s _____

☐ Please send me a publications list.
☐ Please send Corporate/Governmental/Institutional subscription information.
☐ Please send Library subscription information.
☐ Please bill me. _____ My check for $ _____ is enclosed.

Name: _____

Address: _____

City/State: _____ Zip _____

Council on Economic Priorities, 84 Fifth Avenue, New York, New York 10011
(212) 691-8550

FT136   19